At The Heart of Education

School Chaplaincy & Pastoral Care

Edited by James Norman

VERITAS

Published 2004 by
Veritas Publications
7/8 Lower Abbey Street
Dublin 1
Email publications@veritas.ie
Website www.veritas.ie

ISBN 1 85390 752 9

10 9 8 7 6 5 4 3 2 1

A catalogue record for this book is available from the British Library.

Cover design by Paula Ryan
Printed in the Republic of Ireland by Betaprint Ltd, Dublin

Veritas books are printed on paper made from the wood pulp of managed forests.
For every tree felled, at least one tree is planted, thereby renewing natural resources.

Dedicated to the late David Boylan,
teacher, chaplain and an inspiration to me and others

Contents

Programmatic Pastoral Care

Spiritual Pastoral Care

Contributors

P.J. Boyle CNS MA works as part of the community nursing team in north inner-city Dublin as a clinical nurse specialist for asylum seekers. Following on from his overseas development experience he has conducted research into cultural competence and has studied at the Institute for Cultural Competence in Healthcare in Seattle, Washington, USA. P.J. lectures on interculturalism and healthcare in the School of Nursing, Dublin City University.

Evelyn Breen MA is a teacher at Athlone Community College in County Westmeath where she also worked as chaplain for several years. She has a masters degree in school chaplaincy and pastoral care and is a trained facilitator and co-ordinator with the Rainbows organisation of which she is a registered director. Evelyn is a former Education Officer with the School Chaplains' Association.

Dr Gareth Byrne lectures in religious education at the Mater Dei Institute of Education, Dublin City University, where he has been central to the development of the masters degree programmes in religion, education and culture and the masters degree in religious education for primary teachers which is jointly offered with St Patrick's College, Drumcondra. Gareth has also worked on the preparation of guidelines for the new State religious education programme.

Dr Jennie Clifford is a lecturer in chaplaincy studies at the Mater Dei Institute of Education, Dublin City University. She is also the local co-ordinator for the Mater Dei Institute's outreach centres in Cork and Tralee. Formerly, she was a secondary school teacher, school principal and chaplain at University College Cork.

Dr Finola Cunnane is Director of Religious Education in the Diocese of Ferns, Wexford. She has completed post-graduate studies at Fordham University and lectures with the Mater Dei Institute of Education, Dublin City University, at their Kilkenny outreach centre. She is the author of *New Directions in Religious Education* (Dublin: Veritas, 2004).

Dr Marian de Souza is a lecturer in religious education at the Ballarat Campus of the Australian Catholic University. She has completed and published several research projects on the spirituality of young people and on the strategies used by the Copts and other ethnic communities to hand on their spiritual and cultural heritage to their young people in the secular context of contemporary Australia. She has presented conference papers on related topics in Australia and the UK.

Marjorie Doyle MA is a teacher and works as part of the chaplaincy team at Holy Family Community School in Rathcoole, Co. Dublin. She holds a masters degree in school chaplaincy and pastoral care and has also been a member of the board of management in a large Catholic voluntary secondary school and is a founding member of the Parents Association in the same school.

Edel Greene M. Ed. is a teacher of religion, history, CSPE (Civil, Social and Political Education), RSE (Relationships and Sexuality), and substance abuse prevention in Loreto Secondary School Balbriggan, Co. Dublin. She obtained her masters degree from the National University of Ireland, Maynooth, and is a tutor at the Mater Dei Institute of Education, Dublin City University.

Dr Edward J. Hall is a member of the Passionist Community and presently resides at the Calvary Centre for Spirituality in Shrewsbury, Massachusetts, USA. He is a former Director of Religious Education at St Thomas Aquinas Parish in the University of Connecticut and has lectured at the Mater Dei Institute of Education, Dublin City University. He has also worked in counselling and pastoral education with the Government Commission on Mental Health Services at St Elizabeth's Hospital, Washington D.C.

Paul King MA is a teacher of religious education and geography at Castlecomer Community School, Co. Kilkenny, and lectures in chaplaincy studies for the Mater Dei Institute of Education, Dublin City University, at its Kilkenny outreach centre. He has a masters degree in school chaplaincy and pastoral care and has also worked as a teacher and a school chaplain in the North of Ireland.

Dr Ian Leask lectures in philosophy at the Mater Dei Institute of Education, Dublin City University. His publications include *Questions of Platonism* (London, 2000) and numerous articles on ancient philosophy, German Idealism, and phenomenology.

Dr Maeve Martin is a senior lecturer in psychology in the Education Department at the National University of Ireland, Maynooth (NUIM). She is the author of a government report entitled *Discipline in Schools* (1997) and a 2001 Fulbright Scholar. Maeve is the joint co ordinator for the Higher Diploma in Guidance and Counselling at NUIM.

Eilis Monaghan MA is a former teacher of religious education and is currently chaplain at Collinstown Park Community College in Clondalkin, Dublin. She has a masters degree in school chaplaincy and pastoral care. She is a former development officer with parish development and renewal in the Archdiocese of Dublin.

Siobhán Murphy MA is a graduate of the Mater Dei Institute of Education, Dublin City University, and a teacher in religious education at St Peter's Community School, Passage West, Cork. She has a masters degree in school chaplaincy and pastoral care and has been a class tutor and pastoral care co-ordinator in her school.

John Murray M.Rel.Sc. lectures in moral theology at the Mater Dei Institute of Education, Dublin City University. He was a teacher of religious education and English for seventeen years, first in Presentation Secondary School, Carlow and then St David's Holy Faith Secondary School, Greystones, Co. Wicklow.

James Norman M.Ed. is a lecturer in education and pastoral care at the Mater Dei Institute of Education, Dublin City University, where he has been central to the development of masters degree programmes in pastoral care. He is the author of *Ethos and Education in Ireland* (New York: Peter Lang, 2003) and several research reports on pastoral care in second-level schools. He has presented conference papers on related topics and contributed to several journals including *Oideas* and *Irish Educational Studies*. James is also a member of the NCCA Sub-Committee on Interculturalism in Education and a Ministerial Advisory Group on Gender in Primary Education. He is the Chairperson of the board of management at Jobstown Community College, in Tallaght, Dublin.

Terry O'Brien, MA, Grad. Dip. LIS. is Head of Readers' Services and an Assistant Librarian at the Luke Wadding Library, Waterford Institute of Technology. He is a former Research Officer with the South-East Regional Authority and is currently engaged in research on learning support for library users. Terry is part of the User Education/Learning Support team at WIT Libraries and teaches students and staff of all competencies, research skills and strategies, as well as effective use of online and electronic resources. Terry has been involved in a number of transnational EU programmes and has particular interest in eWork concepts.

Seán O'Driscoll MA is Chaplain at Glanmire Community College, Co. Cork, and lectures for Mater Dei Institute of Education, Dublin City University, at its Cork outreach centre. He holds an MA in Chaplaincy from the University of Leeds and has trained in Critical Incident Management.

Noreen Sweeney M.Sc., MIACP, IGC is an accredited counsellor and supervisor working in private practice in Dublin. She also works as a trainer of counsellors and lectures in counselling at the Mater Dei Institute of Education,

Dublin City University. She also worked in second-level education before taking up her present career.

Dr Kevin Williams is a senior lecturer in education at Mater Dei Institute of Education, Dublin City University, and a past-president of the Educational Studies Association of Ireland. He is author/editor of several books and has published many articles on philosophical and educational issues in Irish and international journals. Most recent books include the jointly edited collection, *Words Alone: The Teaching and Usage of English in Contemporary Ireland* (University College Dublin Press, 2000) and *Why Teach Foreign Languages in Schools: A Philosophical Response to Curriculum Policy* (London, Philosophy of Education Society of Great Britain, 2000). His current research interest is on the notions of identity and allegiance in civic life and he is writing a book on religion and civil society.

Foreword

At the Heart of Education: School Chaplaincy & Pastoral Care is a welcome resource for teachers, school chaplains, student teachers and post-graduate students in education, and adds a further increment to the growing body of literature on pastoral care. Fluctuating standards and values at a global level, and the openness of Irish society to outside influences, together with the changing structure of family life, have reflected themselves in an increasing set of educational and pastoral issues which confront all involved in the task of educating our young people.

Recent legislation, together with the introduction of new syllabi, oblige schools to pay significant attention to the pastoral dimension of education, and to provide a balance to the hitherto prevailing emphasis on the promotion of an academic ethos. This rebalancing of educational objectives, and the extent to which our teachers have integrated a pastoral dimension to their teaching, places our education system very much to the fore. I am aware that the Irish teacher's sense of his/her duty of care is far more embracing than that of colleagues in many other countries.

This book is an inexhaustible source of wisdom and practicality, and opens out possibilities for further study and contemplation. The increasingly onerous role of the school chaplain is clearly delineated, while the pastoral responsibilities of all engaged in the education of the young is prominently addressed.

The pages which follow address a vast range of educational and pastoral issues: from drug abuse, alcoholism and indiscipline to asylum-seeking, the information age and the spirituality of the educator.

I wish every success to this publication, and I recommend it unreservedly to everyone involved in the task of education today.

Noel Dempsey TD
Minister for Education and Science

Introduction

Although it is true that Irish second-level schools have always had a holistic understanding of education, it is also true that the implications of this understanding have not always been fully appreciated. The enormous amount of energy, time and resources that are required to provide a holistic education is only fully impacting on our minds since the decline in the number of religious in our schools and the transfer of the full burden of pastoral care to lay teachers has occurred. That is not to say that lay teachers are new to pastoral care but rather that in the past much of the extra time and services required to support pupils came from the religious personnel who often lived and worked on the school premises. The extent to which pastoral care was a taken-for-granted part of Irish schooling is manifest in the fact that pastoral care was almost absent from policy documents until the *Report of the National Education Convention* in 1995 and the *White Paper on Education* of the same year. Since then, through the Education Act 1998 and the Education (Welfare) Act 2000, schools have been given a strong legal framework in which to address the provision of pastoral care to pupils.

Every school in Ireland claims to offer pastoral care, but on many visits to schools around the country I have observed that schools realise their pastoral obligations in different ways. In some schools pastoral care is identified with activities such as breakfast clubs, in other schools it is identified with the activities of the guidance counsellor, tutor or chaplain, while in others again pastoral care is seen as the delivery of a particular syllabus. Defining pastoral care can be difficult because fundamentally it is the response of the school, through its teachers, chaplains, counsellors and parents to the emerging personal needs of the pupils. However, it is possible to categorise pastoral care into three stages or dimensions, *humanistic, programmatic* and *spiritual*.

I call stage one *humanistic* as it refers to the way in which the school seeks to meet the basic bodily or physical needs of its pupils. This stage of pastoral care relates to the basic security (safety, food, shelter) and social needs (finding love, belonging, self-help) identified by Maslow.[1] The school addresses these needs through the provision of breakfast clubs and by liaising with local community care professionals as well as through the development of positive teacher-pupil relationships within the classroom. Apart from a basic concern for the well-being of the pupil, this stage of pastoral care does not require specific training or skills and can be offered by most teachers with some support from the Home-School-Community Liaison. Stage two, *programmatic*, relates to higher 'ego' needs which have to do with the development of pupils self-esteem, confidence and life-skills through self-actualisation programmes such as *Social, Personal and Health Education* (SPHE), *Civic, Social and Political Education* (CSPE) and *Religious Education* (RE). This stage of pastoral care will require teachers who have been trained in appropriate teaching strategies. Guidance counselling also has a very specific contribution to make at this stage of pastoral care in empowering pupils to make decisions about their future. Stage three, *spiritual*, refers to the young person's need to search for meaning and to be able to deal with the deeper questions of life. The loss of a parent through death or separation, for example, can act as a catalyst in a young person's life, causing them to ask questions which they have not thought about previously. At this stage of pastoral care the young person is helped to reflect on their relationships with self, others, God and the world. The contribution of the school chaplain is obvious hear in that s/he will have been specifically trained in theology and spirituality and will also have the pastoral skills to accompany pupils in their search for meaning and purpose in life.

It can be helpful to identify different stages or dimensions in pastoral care because this allows people to decide where they are best suited to contribute. Yet it would be a mistake to think that any one of the above stages is more important than another or that the mere provision of a breakfast club or SPHE, for example, amounts to the totality of pastoral care. Pupils' needs will dictate what type of pastoral care is required and it is the role of school management to ensure that there are teachers, chaplains and counsellors on the staff with appropriate insight and skills to meet the needs of these pupils. Kevin Williams is correct when he warns that, while 'good teaching involves caring, caring should never replace good teaching'[2] and, later in this book, that fundamentally it is the teacher's task to 'promote learning'. This does not mean, however, that pastoral care should be seen as ancillary to teaching and learning. Through pastoral care pupils are helped to be ready to learn and so it can be justly claimed that pastoral care is central to education. If a pupil's needs become so great to the extent that a teacher has to stop teaching then the teacher should be able to refer the pupil to pastoral care professionals within the school such as the chaplain or counsellor. This book is intended to be a resource for those who study and practice pastoral care in second-level schools. As much of the book is based on the contributors' research the book will contribute to *Praxis* within pastoral care in second-level schools by encouraging reflection on action and action as a result of reflection.

The first nine chapters of this book are rooted in the *humanistic* dimension of pastoral care. Chapter one reports the findings of a survey among teachers on their own perceptions of their pupils' pastoral needs and their own abilities in addressing these needs in the context of the classroom. Kevin Williams' contribution in the second chapter provides a balance to a book that otherwise could be accused of merely 'flag-waving' for pastoral care rather than reflecting on the issues involved in such a vision of education. In chapter three Finola Cunnane connects the experiences of adolescent pupils to a journey of growth that encompasses their emotional and cultural development. In Chapter four Maeve Martin reflects on how an apparent 'clash of cultures' between the pupils' home and school life can impact on the school and its ability to address this through 'positive' codes of discipline. Edward Hall outlines a pastoral approach to young people with emotional disturbance in chapter five. He argues that a full pastoral response to pupils suffering in this way must be underpinned by Christian compassion rather than just psychological theories alone. Noreen Sweeney, who presents a framework from which school chaplains and counsellors can address counselling within the school context, follows this chapter. In chapter seven Seán O'Driscoll provides a template for schools to address pupils' needs when critical incidents such as suicide and death occur within the school community. Much of this book intrinsically calls for co-operation and partnership in schools and Marjorie Doyle reflects on the possible contributions to be made by the chaplain in this area in chapter eight. In recent years the populations of many schools have been enriched by the presence of people of ethnic minority. However, some of these pupils, especially those who have come through the asylum seeking process, will have special needs and P.J. Boyle follows on in chapter nine to reflect on the pastoral needs of asylum seeking pupils.

The second section of this book focuses on the *programmatic* dimension of pastoral care in second-level schools. Chapter ten by Marian de Souza highlights for us the importance of addressing the holistic development of young peoples' development through the various syllabi in the curriculum and in doing so she sets the context for the rest of the chapters in this section. In chapter eleven, Edel Greene presents guidelines for the development of a Relationships and Sexuality programme in second-levels schools. The following chapter by Evelyn Breen provides a review of the Rainbows programme, a commonly used support programme for pupils who have been bereaved through death or separation. In chapter thirteen Paul King explores the implications of the recently introduced State-examined religious education syllabus for the work of the school chaplain and the religious education teacher. Chapter fourteen by Terry O'Brien examines specific barriers to effective learning in second-level schools.

The third section of this book comes at pastoral care from a *spiritual* point of view and the first chapter by Gareth Byrne, picking up from the earlier chapter by Marian de Souza, focuses on the spirituality of the educator (chaplain and teacher) and the implications for his/her relationship with the pupil. In chapter sixteen, Siobhán Murphy probes deeper into the perceptions and experiences of pupils in second-level schools where chaplaincy is concerned and finds that, overall, school chaplains are held in high esteem and are seen as a significant point of reference in the school community. With such a rapid development in recent years of a professional identity for school chaplains, chapter seventeen by John Murray provides a framework from which to reflect on the professional nature of this important and evolving role in second-level education. Chapter eighteen by Jennie Clifford explores the relationship between liturgy and worship with the building of a sense of community in schools. Increasingly teachers and chaplains are having to find creative ways in which they can support pupils who are suffering from a significant loss or bereavement. Chapter nineteen by Ian Leask provides a philosophical reflection on the meaning of death which, with the other chapters on spirituality in this book, will help school staffs to develop an appropriate framework to use in supporting their pupils. In the last chapter Eilis Monaghan considers the chaplain's contribution to the faith development of pupils from a disadvantaged background.

Taken together, all of the chapters in this book provide a vision for schools to develop their approach to pastoral care so as to fully meet the needs of their pupils: body, mind and soul.

James Norman
Mater Dei Institute of Education
Dublin City University

Notes

1   Maslow, A., *Towards A Psychology of Being* (Princeton, New Jersey: Van Nostrand, 1968).
2   Williams, K., 'Understanding Ethos: A Philosophical and Literary Exploration' in C. Furlong and L. Monahan (eds), *School Culture and Ethos: Cracking the Code* (Dublin: Marino, 2000), p. 77.

Acknowledgments

In editing this book I have received tremendous help and support from many people. I want to thank my family and friends for their constant encouragement to me in this project and many others. I also want to thank my colleagues at the Mater Dei Institute of Education, Dublin City University, especially Dr Kevin Williams for all the guidance and support he has offered to me on this project.

I especially want to thank the contributors who have, despite very busy schedules, produced very interesting chapters for us to read and who in doing so have made a very significant contribution to the evolving canon of best practice in pastoral care for second-level schools.

Finally, I want to thank all the post-graduate students I have worked with and whose commitment to pastoral care in schools continues to inspire me.

Pastoral Care in Irish Schools

An International Perspective

James Norman

Introduction

The changing sociology of family life in Ireland, the emergence of new social problems within the school environment and the development of a new multi-cultural climate all pose a new series of pastoral issues in schools that need to be addressed: substance abuse, binge drinking, bullying, teenage pregnancy, suicide, changing sexual mores and racism. The teacher is a significant catalyst among others in enabling the school to address these urgent educational and pastoral challenges.

In recent years the curriculum in Ireland has seen many additions, which have raised our expectations of the goals of education and the role of the teacher. This is reflected in the pastoral goals of recent legislation in Ireland, which obliges schools to promote the 'moral, spiritual and personal' development of the pupil.[1] New syllabi such as *Social Personal and Health Education* (SPHE), *Civic Social and Personal Education* (CSPE) and *Relationships and Sexuality Education* (RSE) have been introduced to promote pupils' social and personal development and to provide a balance to the pervading academic ethos of Irish schools.[2] Despite the fact that these initiatives have been introduced during a relatively short period of time onto an already overloaded curriculum, Irish teachers may be admired for having responded so wholeheartedly to them. Furthermore, the extent to which Irish teachers have embraced the pastoral dimension to education in schools can be admired even further when we compare them with their colleagues in other countries where the teacher's duty of care is not always interpreted so liberally.

Through an initial review of some international literature this chapter will attempt to provide a context in which to consider the commitment of the Irish teaching profession towards pastoral care in schooling. I will then set out the data from a research project undertaken at the Mater Dei Institute of Education, a College of Dublin City University, to assess the pastoral competence of Irish second-level teachers.[3]

International Context of Pastoral Care

The roots of contemporary second-level schooling in Ireland can be traced back to two influential forces. Firstly, in terms of philosophy or ethos, the voluntary secondary schools which were developed in the nineteenth century[4] and were mainly run by religious congregations were very much rooted in a vision of education which encompassed the whole person, body, mind and soul. This philosophy of education remains an influencing force in second-level schools today and despite the increasing alliances between the economy and education,[5] most Irish second-level schools still at least aim to develop the whole pupil.

Secondly, many of the structures that are used to organise learning and promote the holistic development of pupils in Irish schools today have been influenced by the English public school system which was often centred around the maintenance of good discipline and learning. In the public schools of the nineteenth century, which were mainly for boarders, pupils were organised into 'houses' and each house had a 'dean of residence' who was responsible for the discipline and well-being of the pupils in his care.[6] The similarities of this system with the year head and tutor structures in Irish schools today are not hard to see.

Whatever the influences are from the past, in more recent times the development of government policy and legislation[7] has provided schools and teachers with a strong framework in which to address the pastoral needs of their pupils. Furthermore, as the research outlined later in this chapter will show, there is a strong commitment by Irish teachers to realise the pastoral obligations of recent legislation.

In considering the strong commitment on the part of Irish teachers to pastoral care in second-level schools, it should also be noted that this is not something found in every educational system around the world. Though it is not possible to provide a direct comparison between schooling and pastoral care in Ireland with other countries without engaging in a large-scale research project, I will attempt to provide a brief comparison using some international literature.

In Japan, research undertaken into the problem of *ijime* or bullying found that teachers there did not always respond to their pupils' pastoral needs positively. Rios-Ellis et al. explains that:

> Due to the fact that professionals working within a school setting are promoted based on their success at maintaining the standards of the specific school, even a favourable response and resolution of an *ijime* case could be viewed as a demerit based on the fact that it occurred in the first place.[8]

Consequently, it is easy to see why teachers in Japan would not be willing to address bullying as a pastoral issue among their pupils. Anecdotal evidence gathered by myself from a group of Japanese teachers confirmed that they did not see it as part of their job to deal with pupils' personal difficulties; according to these teachers, it was the job of the family or a counsellor to support pupils with their personal difficulties. It is clear from the research by Rios-Ellis et al. that many Japanese teachers either do not see themselves as responsible for the personal well-being of their pupils or are unwilling to address these needs due to the fact that the presence of bullying or some other problem in their classroom could inhibit their careers.

Pastoral care is not as strongly associated with schools in Germany either. Since World War II, somewhat in reaction to the overwhelming presence of the Nazi government in every aspect of German life, the remit of the school decreased in favour of the family's responsibility for personal and social education. In other words, families were suspicious of any attempt to give the State a say in the rearing of their children and this attitude undermined any willingness by schools to develop a pastoral approach to their pupils' education. Even today, Giesecke warns that any attempt in Germany to compensate for the failings of society would put such a strain on the education system that it would fail.[9] Unlike with Ireland, Giesecke interprets the mandate of the school in narrower terms, confining the role of the teacher to cognitive development and leaving the pupils' personal needs to be addressed by the family and other social agencies. While some teachers in Germany will organise school tours and other extra curricular activities, there is not a culture among teachers or in schools there of addressing pupils' personal difficulties in any systematic way.

Elsewhere in this book Kevin Williams highlights the apparently narrow remit of schools in Italy as experienced by Tom Parkes[10] who noted the lack of a 'family' atmosphere and extra-curricular activities in his children's school in Italy. Again, in Italy we find a fundamentally different approach from that of Ireland where pastoral care and schooling are concerned. These three examples are given from Japan, Germany and Italy not as a criticism of teachers in these countries, but rather to highlight the cultural differences between the teaching profession in these countries and Ireland. A more in-depth study may reveal that teachers in these countries have a tremendous concern for their pupils' well-being but that they have not yet been empowered by society to get more involved in pastoral care.

While the above data from Japan, Germany and Italy does reveal that schools and teachers in these other countries may not have as broad an approach to pastoral care in schools as their colleagues in Ireland, it would be a mistake to presume that the pastoral approach to schooling in Ireland is not without its detractors. The recent industrial problems between the teachers' unions and the government did highlight some frustration on the part of teachers in Ireland at the lack of adequate training and clarity of role where pastoral care is concerned. Just because there has been a strong tradition of liberally interpreting the duty of care and teaching, does not mean that we can expect teachers to continue to address pupils' personal difficulties without adequate training and support. There is an urgent need to investigate the pastoral dimension of education in order to assess the needs of teachers in supporting their pupils.

Pastoral Competence of Irish Second-Level Teachers

Consequently, the aim of the Mater Dei Institute research project was to establish the pastoral competence of second-level teachers in Ireland. For the purpose of this research pastoral competence refers to the teachers ability to deal with their pupils' personal needs as they arise within the classroom, in such a way that the pupils' overall well-being is promoted and learning enhanced.

Specifically, the research aims were to find out:

- Do subject teachers perceive pastoral care as a dimension of their professionalism?
- What types of pastoral needs occur among pupils in Irish second-level schools?
- How often do these pastoral needs affect subject teachers' ability to teach?
- What are subject teachers' perceptions of their own pastoral competence?

Those who are involved in teacher training are increasingly aware of the changes in Irish society and the role of the school in addressing the needs of its pupils. Consequently this research will help to inform pre-service teacher training. The colleges of education in Ireland provide academic training in teaching subjects such as mathematics, English and Irish as well as training in teaching methodologies and general pedagogy. However, in the future, student teachers will also require foundation courses that will help them to develop a basic pastoral competence in dealing with pupils and their personal needs. The findings of this research will help to highlight the type of training required to develop teachers who have a basic level of pastoral competence.

Furthermore, as noted above, many teachers in schools today have taken on pastoral responsibilities in the classroom and school generally. While some hold specific pastoral roles (such as chaplains, year heads and tutors) others are involved through special education and through informal contact with pupils. These teachers are at the coal face of schooling and deal with many pastoral problems as they arise in the school. The findings of this research will be of use to government, teachers unions and the colleges of education in that it will help to highlight the type of in-service training required to support teachers already in pastoral care in schools.

Research Aims and Design
The study employed a method that can be categorised as the quantitative survey method. Robson highlights the virtues of this approach because the strength of quantitative research is its ability to gather large amounts of data for a relatively low cost.[11] While the more qualitative form of research can give a deeper and more extended insight into the area being studied it is more time consuming and requires more resources. As the research was privately funded it was important that the researcher was able to access as many teachers as possible using a method that was not overly expensive and that did not require a huge amount of resources. The researcher was also anxious that the findings of this research project would be a good representation of the perceptions and attitudes of most subject teachers in second-level schools. Given the limited funding and resources, and the desire to involve a relatively large sample, it was decided that a self-administered questionnaire was the most effective means of finding the answers to the research questions as set out above.

Sampling
Robson quoting Smith (1975) describes sampling as 'the search for typicality'.[12] In order to make the sample as typical or as representative as possible of teachers and schools in Ireland, the researcher developed a stratified random sample. This is where the researcher divides the population into a number of groups where members of a group share a particular characteristics, i.e. teachers in vocational schools. This type of sampling is the most efficient technique for producing a representative sample.[13]

In the case of the current study the questionnaire was sent to a contact teacher in ten schools, all of whom where graduates of the Mater Dei Institute and therefore accessible through the Institute's alumni mailing list. The teachers were chosen according to the type of school they worked in so as to reflect the overall population of teachers in Irish second-level schools:

- 65% Voluntary Secondary Schools (Single Sex and Co-educational)
- 20% Vocational Schools.
- 15% Community/Comprehensive Schools.

The researcher was anxious to find out how subject teachers perceived their role in the classroom in terms of pupils' personal needs and so school chaplains, guidance counsellors and home-school-liaison teachers were excluded from the sample as they will normally hold specific qualifications or have received extra training in pastoral care beyond that which most subject teachers will have received. Questionnaires were distributed to one hundred teachers, eighty-four of whom responded to the survey.

Self-Administered Questionnaire
The study was aimed at describing to what extent subject teachers perceive pastoral care as part of their duties as a subject teacher and secondly to what extent do they perceive themselves having the competencies to deal adequately with their pupils' pastoral needs as they arise in the classroom. In order to find out this information it is important that the research is carried out in a sensitive manner that will encourage teachers to participate and be open about their perceptions as outlined above. Given the limited resources available to the researcher it was decided that the most efficient method of research would be a self-administered postal questionnaire (see appendix one). As well as allowing for the respondents anonymity, the postal questionnaire can provide data that will give a general picture of a situation. The weakness of such a questionnaire is that it does not allow the researcher to probe into ambiguous or complex issues, however it does allow the researcher to gather a lot more information from a lot of people in more than one place. As a form of quantitative research, surveys are useful when the researcher wants to use the resulting data for descriptive purposes.

General Description of Research Sample

In terms of length of service, the respondents represented a broad range of teaching experience, 49 per cent having over fifteen years experience with a further 32 per cent having between five and fifteen years' experience in teaching. Only 19 per cent had less than five years of experience (see Fig. 1).

Figure 1
Teachers' Years of Service
N = 84

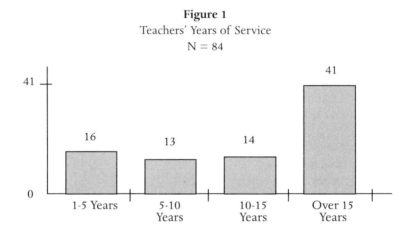

Interestingly, apart from their initial teaching qualification, over half of the teachers had no further post-graduate qualification. Of those who had done further studies, the largest group (18%) had obtained a higher diploma in educational management, which is normally obtained by those who wish to become school principals. Furthermore, half of the participants (50%) held a position of responsibility in their school but only two of these teachers had a post of responsibility that was concerned specifically with pastoral care in their school.

The participants were asked to report the most recent professional development or in-service programme attended. While the majority (75%) had attended some form of in-service programme, only 8 per cent had done an in-service related to pastoral care and none of the respondents had recently attended an in-service specifically concerned with pastoral care such as those organised on a regional basis by the Irish Association of Pastoral Care in Education (IAPCE).

All of the teachers in the study worked in a school with at least one guidance counsellor, while only a third of the respondents (32%) worked in a school with a full-time school chaplain, a further group of respondents (10%) had a part-time chaplain while the majority of the schools (65%) had a home-school-liaison teacher. Of those who responded about half (46%) knew that they worked in a school in a disadvantaged area. In schools without a full-time chaplain, the majority of teachers (96%) believed that it would be beneficial to pupils if there were a full-time chaplain in their school.

Figure 2
Teachers' perception of the need for full-time school chaplains
N = 84

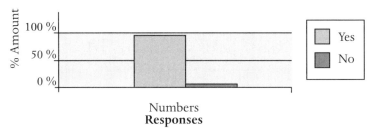

Provisions of School Chaplains

Teachers' Perceptions of Pastoral Care
When asked if they considered pastoral care as one of their duties as a teacher, an overwhelming majority (90%) of teachers in this study said that pastoral care was part of being a teacher. It is also interesting to note that there was absolutely no difference between those who worked in areas of disadvantage and those who worked in schools in non-disadvantaged areas, with the same number (90%) in both types of school considering pastoral care as one of their duties as a teacher.

However, there were a higher number of teachers who had graduated from the traditional universities who did not agree that pastoral care was one of their duties as a teacher (see Table 1). It is not possible to know from the data why there was a higher negative response from these graduates. The fact that the most positive responses came in all but one case from colleges where there is a concurrent model of teacher education as opposed to the consecutive model in use in other colleges may be significant, but this would need further investigation.

Table 1

Do teachers consider pastoral care as one of their duties?

N = 84

Pastoral	Yes	No	Total
Non Response	0.0%	100%	**100%**
UCC	85.7%	14.3%	**100%**
TCD	85.7%	14.3%	**100%**
MI/UL	100%	0.0%	**100%**
UCD	100%	0.0%	**100%**
NUIG	85.7%	14.3%	**100%**
SPD/DCU	0.0%	0.0%	**0.0%**
NUIM	91.7%	8.3%	**100%**
MDI/DCU	100%	0.0%	**100%**
Thomond	100%	0.0%	**100%**
St Angela's	100%	0.0%	**100%**
Other	85.7%	14.3%	**100%**
Total	**90.5%**	**9.5%**	**100%**

Although the majority of teachers did claim that they considered pastoral care as one of their duties as a teacher, the number of teachers who disagreed with this also increased with length of service. In other words, the small number of teachers (10%) who did not agree that pastoral care was part of their job all had ten years service or more (see Fig. 3).

Figure 3

Teachers' perceptions of pastoral care as part of their role

N = 84

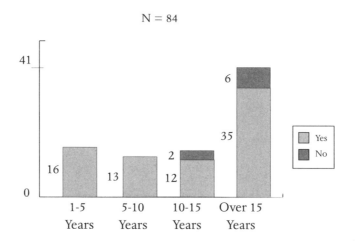

Furthermore, when the teachers are organised into groups according to those with academic training beyond their initial teaching qualification, there was a higher number (14%) of those with the Higher Diploma in Educational Management and an MA by research (17%) who did not agree that pastoral care was part of their role as a teacher while all of those (19%) who had obtained a Masters Degree in Education did belief that pastoral care was one of their duties as a teacher.

However, it is also interesting that the majority of respondents (79%) claimed that the area of pastoral care was not specifically included as part of the curriculum in their teacher training college. Furthermore, the vast majority of the teachers (91%) in the study believed that their teacher training did not adequately prepare them to deal with their pupil's personal issues. This number increases (95%) with those in longer service.

Figure 4
Teacher training in pastoral care
N = 84

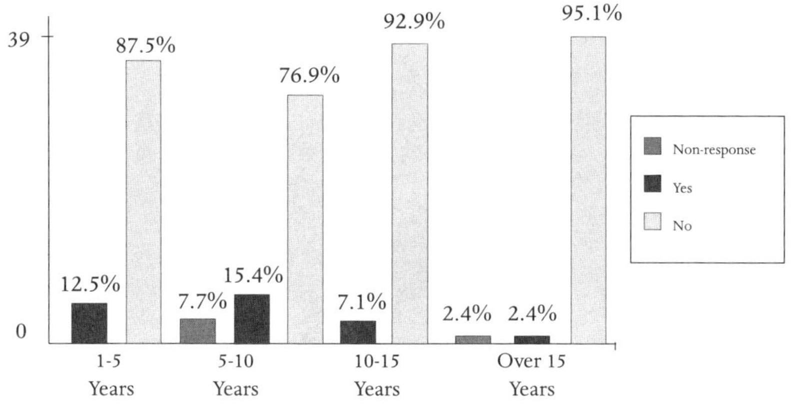

Pastoral Problems Encountered by Teachers

The respondents were asked to rank in order of frequency the various personal problems that they had encountered among their students during the previous twelve months. The parameters of the rank were from 1 (Frequently) to 4 (Never) and in calculating the mean ranking the non-responses were not included. This question was aimed at finding information that would help the researcher to be able to describe the type of problems that classroom teachers deal with in addition to their responsibility to promote pupils' cognitive development.

The teachers who responded to this survey ranked the following problems as the most frequent occurring in the classroom:

1. Illness *(1.51, standard deviation = 0.75)*
2. Chronic Low Self-Esteem *(1.77, standard deviation = 0.75)*
3. Bullying *(1.86, standard deviation = 0.65)*

4. Financial Disadvantage *(1.94, standard deviation = 0.80)*
5. Death, Loss and Change *(2.01, standard deviation = 0.86)*

The respondents also gave a ranking to the other issues listed on the questionnaire. However, for the purposes of this chapter the researcher is only concerned with those given the highest ranking.

Illness
The majority of respondents in this survey gave their highest mean rank (1.51, standard deviation = 0.75) to illness as the most frequently occurring pastoral problem among their pupils (see Fig. 5). This is not surprising when we consider the number of pupils who are either sick themselves or have a member of their family who is ill. Pupil illness can include anything from the common cold, a dental appointment or a more serious problem such as cancer.

Pupils are also affected by illness in the home where parents or siblings can suffer from any number of health problems that in turn can affect their children's well being at school. It is clear from this current research that illness is one of the most frequently occurring pastoral problems among pupils and that teachers are aware of this problem.

Figure 5
Teachers' observation of illness among pupils as a pastoral need
N = 84

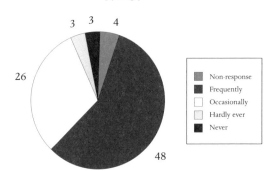

Chronic Low Self-Esteem
The respondents to this survey gave their second highest rank (1.77, standard deviation = 0.75) to the problem of chronic low self-esteem among their pupils. A young person's self-esteem can be deeply affected by their perceptions of self, others, peer group and adults. The fact that the problem of low self-esteem was given such a high rank by teachers in this survey suggests that many of their pupils are at risk of depression and possibly even suicide. Teachers, as significant adults in the lives of their pupils, can promote a positive and strong sense of worth among their pupils by regularly giving affirmation, providing realistic learning challenges and generally developing a positive teacher-pupil relationship (see Fig. 6).

The fact that up to one third of second level schools in Ireland offer little or no time to the Social, Personal and Health Education programme (Morgan and Looney, 2001) can not be ignored when so many teachers are giving such a high rank to chronic low self-esteem as a problem among their pupils.[14]

Figure 6
Teachers' observation of chronic low self-esteem
amongst pupils as a pastoral need
N = 84

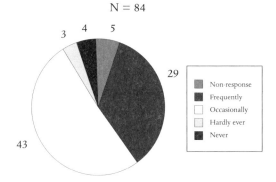

Bullying
Considering the amount of research and attention given to the problem of bullying in recent years it is interesting to note that this problem was given the third highest mean rank (1.86, standard deviation = 0.65) by teachers who responded to this survey (see Fig. 7). This can be interpreted as meaning that despite the various anti-bullying programmes that are available in schools teachers are still observing a very high level of bullying among their pupils.

The questionnaire did not ask how many pupils teachers observed as being bullied but rather which problems had they encountered among their pupils and how often during the previous twelve months. Consequently, it would seem that, even if there were a small number of pupils actually involved in bullying, this is still a frequently occurring problem for teachers in schools which must take up quite an amount of their time and energy.

Figure 7
Teachers' observation of bullying amongst pupils as a pastoral need
N = 84

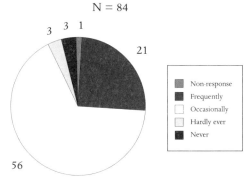

Financial Disadvantage

The teachers in this study gave their fourth highest rank (1.94, standard deviation = 0.80) to the problem of financial disadvantage among their pupils (see Fig. 8). When we consider that the survey was carried out at the height of the recent economic boom in Ireland it is very interesting to note that teachers were frequently encountering financial disadvantage among their pupils. This may be influenced by the fact that almost half of the teachers in this study were working in schools in designated disadvantaged areas.

However, the fact that such a high number of respondents to the survey gave such a high rank to this problem indicates that the economic success that was enjoyed by Ireland in recent years did not touch everybody and certainly many young people in Irish schools are still experiencing financial difficulties.

Figure 8

Teachers' observations of financial disadvantage
amongst pupils as a pastoral need
N = 84

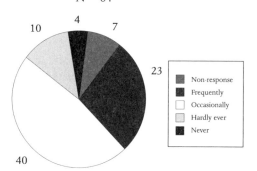

■	Non-response
■	Frequently
□	Occasionally
▨	Hardly ever
■	Never

Death, Loss and Change

The next highest rank (2.01, standard deviation = 0.86) was given to the problem of parental separation/divorce. It is not surprising that this pastoral problem was listed as one of the most frequently occurring problems encountered by teachers among their pupils. The most recent statistics say that parental separation in Ireland has increased by 135 per cent since 1985.[15] Considering that so much of a young person's sense of identity is associated with their parents and family, it can be very stressful for young people when their parents decide to separate or divorce.

Closely associated with the above pastoral problem is the wider problem of bereavement that teachers also ranked as the next most frequent problem that they had encountered among their pupils (2.05, standard deviation = 0.65). Death, loss and change can always be traumatic experiences and this is even more so in the case of young people. Many schools in Ireland have responded to this by setting up bereavement support groups for their pupils. In these groups pupils are helped to recognise that the feelings, thoughts and behaviour that they are experiencing are quite normal and that others can empathise with them.

Figure 9
Teachers' observations of separation/divorce
among pupils as a pastoral need
N = 84

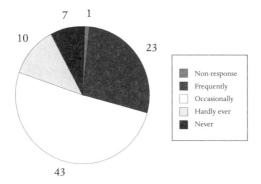

Figure 10
Teachers' observations of bereavement
among pupils as a pastoral need
N = 84

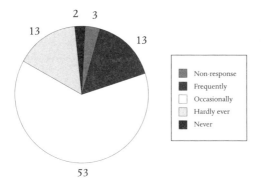

Effect of Pupils' Personal Problems on Teaching

In their work as subject teachers, over half of the respondents (55%) claimed that some of their pupils' personal problems affected their teaching on a daily basis. A further group (24%) claimed that some of their pupils' personal problems affected their teaching on a weekly basis. However, when we break the respondents into groups according to their length of service, it seems that teachers with the longest amount of service, over fifteen years, claim the most (24%) that some of their pupils' personal problems affect their teaching on a daily basis compared to a lower number (10-11%) of teachers with less service claiming the same.

Furthermore, more teachers (64%) working in schools in areas with disadvantage status reported that their pupils' personal problems affected their teaching than those teachers (41%) in schools in non-disadvantaged areas.

The fact that when they were asked to say how often they refer pupils to the school guidance counsellor and school chaplain, only 12 per cent of the teachers actually did this on a frequent basis, indicates that for the most part teachers in Irish second-level schools tend to deal with pupils' pastoral needs themselves and also that they may perceive the guidance counsellor and chaplain as having a more specialist role.

Figure 11
Referrals to non-teaching professionals
(Guidance Counsellor and School Chaplain)
N = 84

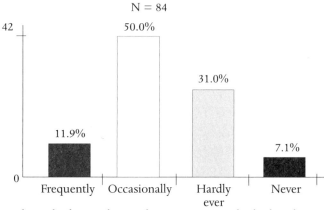

Teachers were also asked to indicate the manner in which the above pastoral issues affected their job as a classroom teacher. The participants in the survey were given a list of possible outcomes and asked to rank them as 1 (Frequently) to 4 (Never).

The teachers in this study claimed that the number one effect of their pupils' personal problems was high absenteeism from school (Mean Rank = 1.26, Standard deviation = 0.44). All of the personal problems, which the teachers listed as frequently occurring among their pupils, could result in a pupil either not being able or not wanting to come to school.

Table 2
Teachers' perception of absenteeism as a result of pupils' pastoral needs
N = 84

Absenteeism	No. ans.	Percent.
Frequently	62	73.8%
Occasionally	22	26.2%
Hardly ever	0	0.0%
Never	0	0.0%
TOTAL OBS.	**84**	**100%**

Mean= 1.26 Standard deviation= 0.44

Another consequence of pupils' personal problems is a lack of concentration, which was also ranked as a frequently occurring symptom by the teachers in this study (Mean Rank = 1.35, Standard Deviation = 0.67).

Table 3
Teachers' perception of poor concentration
As a result of pupils' pastoral needs
N = 84

Concentration	No. ans.	Per cent
Non-response	1	1.2%
Frequently	54	64.3%
Occasionally	29	34.5%
Hardly ever	0	0.0%
Never	0	0.0%
TOTAL OBS.	**84**	**100%**

Mean= 1.35 Standard deviation= 0.48

When a pupil experiences a death or separation, or when there is financial hardship at home, it is very hard for them to apply themselves to school work or to complete homework resulting in low attainment levels which were also given a high rank as symptoms of pupils personal problems affecting the teacher's job in the classroom (Mean Rank = 1.59, Standard Deviation = 0.63).

Table 4
Teachers' perception of low attainment as a result of pupils' pastoral needs
N = 84

Attainment	No. ans.	Per cent
Non-response	4	4.8%
Frequently	39	46.4%
Occasionally	35	41.7%
Hardly ever	6	7.1%
Never	0	0.0%
TOTAL OBS.	**84**	**100%**

Mean= 1.59 Standard deviation= 0.63

Teachers in this study gave their next rank to the issue of disruptive behaviour in the classroom as a symptom of pupils' personal problems affecting the teacher's job in the classroom (Mean Rank = 1.77, Standard Deviation = 0.67).

While many schools and teachers will try to accommodate a pupil who is experiencing a personal problem, sometimes the problem can be so advanced that the pupil will act out in an inappropriate manner. What is often perceived as indiscipline can also sometimes result from a clash between the culture of the pupil's home and the culture of the school.[16]

Table 5

Teachers' perception of disruptive behaviour as a result of pupils' pastoral needs

N = 84

Disruptive	No. ans.	Percent
Non-response	1	1.2%
Frequently	30	35.7%
Occasionally	42	50.0%
Hardly ever	11	13.1%
Never	0	0.0%
TOTAL OBS.	**84**	**100%**

Mean= 1.77 Standard deviation= 0.67

Other symptoms arising from pupil's personal problems were poor communication (Mean Rank = 2.05, Standard Deviation = 0.72) and pupils having to be excluded from the classroom (Mean Rank = 2.63, Standard Deviation = 0.75).

Conclusions and Recommendations

The data from this study reveals that while a small minority do not agree that pastoral care is part of their job, the majority of Irish subject teachers do perceive teaching as having a pastoral dimension.

It is also clear from the data collected from this survey that subject teachers in Irish second-level schools are very sensitive to the needs of their pupils as they arise in the classroom.

The data from this study seems to indicate that the majority of teachers, while not adequately prepared to deal with their pupil's personal problems, are very committed to the pastoral dimension of teaching and to making a contribution to pupils' personal development. Furthermore, the study reveals that for the most part teachers in Irish second-level schools are dealing with pupils' personal problems within their classroom rather than referring them onto the guidance counsellor or school chaplains.

Consequently, it would seem important that in the future the colleges of education and those universities involved in teacher training should include pastoral care as a specific area within the teacher training curriculum.

There will also have to be an increase in the number of pastoral care professionals (such as school chaplains) to supplement the work of the subject teachers with pupils outside the classroom. Research has shown that the contribution of chaplains to pupils' personal development in Irish second-level schools can be very significant.[17]

Furthermore, there will have to be an increase in the provision of in-service for teachers (particularly those who hold pastoral responsibilities as year heads and tutors) by the government and teachers' unions.

Overall, subject teachers in Irish second-levels schools can be said to display a high degree of pastoral concern and experience. However, when we consider the lack of training that they have received in pastoral care, either through their initial teacher training college or subsequently through in-service, it seems that many teachers do not consider themselves to be competent in dealing with their pupils' pastoral needs as they arise in the classroom.

Notes

1. Education Act (1998) 9:d.
2. Boldt, S., 'A Vantage Point of Values – Finding From School Culture and Ethos Survey Questionnaires' in Furlong, C., Monahan, L., *School Culture and Ethos: Cracking The Code* (Dublin: Marino, 2000), pp. 29-58.
3. Norman, J., *Pastoral Care in Second-Level Schools: The Role of the Teacher, A Research Report* (Dublin: Mater Dei Institute of Education, Dublin City University, 2003).
4. See Coolahan, J., *Irish Education History and Structure* (Dublin: IPA, 1981) for a full history of the second-level schooling in the nineteenth century.
5. Dunne, J., 'What's the Good of Education?' in Hogan, P. (ed), *Partnership and the Benefits of Learning* (Dublin: Educational Studies Association of Ireland, 1995).
6. For a more in-depth description of the influences of the nineteenth-century English public school's influence on pastoral care in modern schools see Lang, P., 'Pastoral Care: Some Reflections on Possible Influences', in *Pastoral Care in Education*, 2:2 (Oxford: Blackwell, 1983).
7. See *Charting Our Educational Future: White Paper on Education* (Dublin: Government Publications, 1995); Education Act (Dublin: Government Publications, 1998); Education Welfare Act (Dublin: Government Publications, 2000).
8. Rios-Ellis, B., Bellamy, L., Junichi, S., 'An Examination of Specific Types of *Ijime* Within Japanese Schools' in *School Psychology International*, 21:3 (2000).
9. Giesecke, H., 'Das "Ende de Erziehung". Ende oder Anfang pädagogischer Professionalität' in Combe, A., Helsper, W., *Pädagogische Professionalität* (Frankfurt: Main, 1999).
10. Parks, T., *An Italian Education* (London: Vintage, 2000).
11. Robson, C., *Real World Research* (Oxford: Blackwell, 1993), p. 304.
12. *Ibid*, p.135.
13. *Ibid*, p.138.
14. Morgan, M., Looney, A., 'A Gendered Curriculum? An Investigation of Some Aspects of Curriculum' in *Irish Educational Studies,*, 20 (Dublin: Educational Studies Association of Ireland, 2001).
15. Central Statistics Office, Cork, 2001.
16. Martin, M., *Indiscipline in Schools, A Report to the Minister for Education, Niamh Breathnach* (Dublin: Government Publications, 1997).
17. Norman, J., *Pastoral Care in Second-Level Schools: The Chaplain, A Research Report* (Dublin: Mater Dei Institute of Education, Dublin City University, 2002).

Nurture and the Purpose of Schools

Kevin Williams

Introduction

Over the years it has often struck me that some of the standard criticisms of schools (as being too examination oriented and too competitive, for example) are based on a failure to recognise, firstly, that school has multiple purposes, and secondly, the nature and limits of the notion of nurture in educational institutions. In this chapter I propose to identify the aims of schools and show how nurture has a place in the activity of educating.

Some Aims of the School and One Consequence of Schooling

The first explicit purpose of the school is utilitarian: it is to provide socialisation. This refers to preparation to live in society and to contribute to society. It is both realistic and defensible to expect that the school curriculum should embrace as one of its aims preparation for working life. Even if we lived in a country where no one had to work to earn a living, it would be appropriate to teach young people what it is like for those who have to work in order to survive. This would be a legitimate part of the understanding which school education should be expected to promote. As we do not inhabit this fictional country, the society which supports the institution of formal schooling can reasonably expect that young people should leave school not only with an understanding of the world of work but also with an enhanced capacity to earn a living. This will contribute to the good of society as well as to their own to their personal sense of well-being.

The second purpose of the school is to provide cultural enrichment and this might be called its most conspicuously educational dimension. This refers to the responsibility of schools to introduce young people to cultural activities of a theoretical and practical character capable of yielding satisfaction and fulfilment. The other aims of the school are to provide young people with a nurturing environment, to cultivate moral character and to offer spiritual and religious education. There is little need to labour the fact that these aims overlap considerably and that teachers and chaplains can make an important contribution to realising them.

But organised learning or schooling has another feature, which is an unavoidable consequence of the institution in almost any society. This is its facilitation of positional advantage, i.e. the labour market advantage conferred by the **exchange value** of education. Many negative manifestations of schooling derive from the consequence of its having an exchange value. These features underlie the 'hidden curriculum' of academic competitiveness that is supposed to be a major feature of school life today. The reason why there is such an emphasis on achievement in the academic sphere is due to the esteem attached to academic/professional work in this society. But the narrow focus of some pupils and their parents on academic success is not the direct fault of the school. In any case, I wonder if critics of narrowness of educational focus have different priorities themselves when it comes to the education of their own children. I wonder if those who preach high theories about the 'whole person', the 'disadvantaged' or 'social integration' put these theories into practice when choosing schools for their offspring. I have no evidence on this issue, but I do have some uncomfortable intuitions. If medical faculties decided to accept only those who had done the Leaving Certificate Applied, we would see a transformation in the perception of the less academically oriented curriculum. But unless we have such a dramatic reversal in the requirements for university entrance, the priorities of parents, their children and teachers regarding school are unlikely to change.

I am not persuaded that we can do much about the high valuation placed by many people on the professions and the knowledge that secures access to them. But I do think that schools should not engage in exaggerated fine-tuning of their role in assessing pupil achievement. The impact of the pressure for schools to be 'effective' can have this result. Where examination results are the only criterion for judging the quality of schooling, schools may experience pressure to increase the number and degree of passes at all costs. As Geoffrey Walford points out, one outcome of this process is to make of the school 'an even more effective sorting machine' in respect of allocating to young people their future occupational destinations.[1] What can happen is that a C rather than a D grade in a particular subject can have a wholly disproportionate influence on a person's life chances. Society can justifiably expect schools to offer broad indications of achievement of learners but not fine-grained categorisation based on particular grade differences whose validity and reliability may be questionable.

There is a reprehensible view that where the school has fulfilled its function as a social filter, the kind of curriculum offered to those who do not aspire to university education is not of great importance. This cynical attitude is captured in the words of a teacher reported by Gervase Phinn, an English school inspector. 'They're not your grammar school highfliers…These lads will end up in manual jobs, that's if they're lucky, and not become university professors and brain surgeons'.[2] The teacher in this case is relatively indifferent to what young people are taught but often such pupils can be offered what might be called a tabloid curriculum to keep them occupied and entertained.[3] One reason for this dismissive attitude towards the fate of these young people is due to a view of study at second level as an apprenticeship to further study at university. This is an unfortunate conception because it means that aims within school subjects tend to be intra-subject, that is, that study of a subject at junior cycle at second level is conceived as leading to its continued study at senior cycle and then at university.[4] It should be possible, by contrast, for a period of study within a subject to be conceived as self-contained and also as connecting with wider civic and personal aims than acquiring skills and knowledge within that subject. One of the problems with promoting too close a link between school subjects and universities is that many young people can see their future study and career options as related exclusively to the continued study of the subject they were good at in school. Rather than thinking of the whole range of possibilities, some school leavers can think, for example, only of doing more history or science.

Let us turn next to an examination of the notion of nurture in schools.

The School as a Nurturing Environment

Schools in the English-speaking world are usually conceived as nurturing environments grounded in a broader or thicker conception of children's welfare than that of mere academic achievement. As has been highlighted in the previous chapter this is not the case elsewhere. Observing the education of his two children, British novelist, Tim Parks, has written with some bewilderment about what he perceives as the very different remit of the Italian school from that of its English counterpart:

> For school offers no games, no extracurricular activities. There are no music lessons, no singing lessons, no school choir... no hockey, no cricket, no netball, no basketball, no football, no swimming, no athletics, no sports day, no school teams.[5]

Most of all what strikes him is the absence of any attempt to induce a family atmosphere in the school.

> The school doesn't, as it does in England, pretend to offer a community that might in any way supplant the family, or rival Mamma. That's important. It doesn't, and later on the university won't either, try to create in the child the impression of belonging to a large social unit with its own identity. There is no assembly in the morning, no hymn singing, no prayers, no speech day...[6]

For his two children of six and eight, school is 'no more and no less than reading and writing and mathematics' and other school subjects.[7] Somewhat ironically, though, in spite of the attenuated and circumscribed or thin conception of the school's remit, religion is also part of the curriculum.

The contrast with the spirit of schooling in the English-speaking world could not be greater. Here the school is often perceived as an extension of the home in terms of providing personal support and overall care for young people. This conception of the school is most conspicuous in the case of boarding schools. Here is novelist, Monk Gibbon's, description of the school in England that features in his novel, *The Pupil*. The narrator experiences the school as a 'kind of miniature Plato's Republic', a 'cultured oasis' animated by the conviction of the principal that a 'school should be a large family – a small nation'.[8] The school also assumes a responsibility for character education. In the words of the principal, education is animated by the conviction 'that character is everything, and that everything without character is nothing'.[9] The theme of safety and security surfaces in reminiscence on his schooldays by the English philosopher, Michael Oakeshott. The happiness that Oakeshott experienced at school was 'a kind of serenity' as well as a sense that 'growing up was something to be enjoyed, not merely got through'.[10] What the school provided 'was a feeling of safety and an immense variety of outlets'.[11] It was 'surrounded by a thick, firm hedge, and inside this hedge was a world of beckoning activities and interests'.[12] These emanated from the principal or 'were the private enterprise of members of staff, ...[or were] made for oneself. There was a great deal of laughter and fun; there was a great deal of seriousness'.[13] Notable also in these reflections is the wide compass of activities included within the school. The positive educational experiences to be found even in traditional schools are often much more embracing than those offered by the formal curriculum.

Moreover, commitment to the quality of the experience of school is not confined to teachers in upper middle-class schools. Christopher Winch refers to the 'heroic efforts made by many secondary modern teachers to give their children a worthwhile experience at school'.[14] Here is an account again by Gervase Phinn of the role of the school that would be shared by committed teachers in many schools in the English-speaking world. He arrives in a boys' school in an area of disadvantage catering for children who have failed to get places in the traditional, academic secondary school. By virtue of attending this school the boys are already 'deemed to be failures' and arrive 'under-confident, with low self-esteem'.[15] The task of the school, explains the principal, is:

> first and foremost... to build up their confidence and self-esteem, continue to have high expectations for them and be sure they know, give them maximum support and encouragement, develop their social skills and qualities of character to enable them to enter the world feeling good about themselves.... so they develop into well-rounded young people with courage, tolerance, strong convictions, lively enquiring minds and a sense of humour.... I do really believe... that those of us in education can really make a difference, particularly in the lives of less fortunate children, those who are labelled failures.[16]

He tries, he says, to make the school 'like the good home that I was brought up in, a place where there is work and laughter, honesty and fairness'.[17] Here we find the metaphor of the school as being like a 'good home', reflecting the metaphor of the family in the quotation from Monk Gibbon.

Most schools which I have the privilege of visiting are nurturing and protective environments. Especially, but not only, in areas of social disadvantage, schools can allow young people to be children, secure for a while from the cramped toughness of their world outside the classroom where the demands of a precocious adulthood urge themselves so insistently upon them. This is captured succinctly in the description of the primary school in Roddy Doyle's *A Star Called Henry* where the brother of the eponymous hero cries on being withdrawn from school, missing 'the warmth, the singing, making words, the chalk working across his slate, the woman who'd made him feel wanted'.[18] A positive experience of schooling is not the sole prerogative of the middle class and those bound for university.

Teaching and Nurture

Here I wish to draw attention to the teacher's principal task in nurturing pupils. Fundamentally it is to ensure that the pupils learn. Nurturing is a part of educating; it is not an activity in itself. The defining character of a teacher's job specification is to promote learning. A comparison can be made with the world of medicine. Holistic concern for the patient should be part of any regime of treatment but this concern should not at the expense of competent administration of medical care. Indeed, if I had to choose, I would prefer to be treated by someone who was competent, although curt and brusque, rather than by a person who was 'nice' but unskilled in the practice of medicine. Likewise in education 'niceness' is no substitute for competence. Indeed, 'niceness' on its own can frustrate efforts to reach pupils. In his autobiography, *Another Country: Growing up in 1950s Ireland*, Gene Kerrigan writes of the torment that befell a young 'nice priest' chaplain-teacher.[19] Kerrigan describes him as having a 'fresh, open mind, a soul yearning to enhance our spirituality within a changing, questioning society'.[20] His aim was to get the boys 'talking in the vernacular of the day about eternal truths'.[21] Willing to mingle with the pupils, he sat on an empty desk in the middle of the classroom rather than behind the teacher's desk.

> Smiling, open to dialogue. He wanted to be our friend.
> We ate him alive....
> He wanted nothing but good for us, he wanted to approach us on our terms, he respected us. And we laughed in his face....
> He offered friendship, we smelled weakness....
> We mistook love for vulnerability and we seized him by the throat.[22]

What this young priest did not appreciate was that schools operate within a particular framework and in order to function successfully, teachers must take account of this framework. An essential feature of the framework is an awareness of the adult-child and individual-group character of the teacher-pupil relationship. This requires the exercise of an institutionally appropriate form of authority and the imposition of a certain control. Within this framework, it is possible to provide the nurture that characterises good teaching.

I am not suggesting that all teaching conducted in this context will result in successful learning. Failure to ensure learning may be due to factors beyond the control of the teacher – for example, domestic disharmony or illness. Yet teachers' primary responsibility is to teach their subjects. In some cases, where the resistance of the pupils to school and to learning seems insurmountable, this may prove impossible. But it is simply not good enough to forgo the attempt to teach on the grounds that all efforts are doomed to failure unless we change the whole educational system or indeed the whole socio-economic system. Fashionable theories about re-defining what counts as intelligence may well be sustainable but they are not an excuse for giving up on trying to teach that constituency of the young population described as low achievers. The principal referred to previously invokes no high-faluting slogans about the 'failure of the system', 'narrow conception of intelligence' or the need for 'critical theory'.

In some research I have conducted into the conceptions of good teachers held by student teachers, admiration for structured, orderly and efficient teaching is striking.[23] Young people who experience imaginative, structured and committed teaching are in the process experiencing nurture. Moreover, those who do not aspire to attend university need not be precluded from engagement with the traditional areas of the school curriculum (literature, language, history and science). Here is an account by Gervase Phinn of a teacher giving a lesson based on a novel set during the Second World War to a group of non-academically inclined learners.

> She used well chosen illustrations and probing questions to develop understanding of ideas and motives....She encouraged the boys to explore character in greater depth, whilst sensitively supporting the less able, helping them to stay interested and involved by the use of questions matched to their abilities and interests. She required them to justify a point of view, refer to the text, relate to their own experiences and examine the use of language.
>
> ....
>
> The atmosphere in the classroom was warm and supportive, and the boys responded well to the teacher, clearly enjoying her touches of humour... [She] had a real empathy with, and respect for, the pupils and ...had high expectations of their success. She encouraged, directed, suggested, questioned, challenged and developed the pupils' understanding in an atmosphere of good humour and enjoyment.[24]

The positive attitudes of the teacher are also reflected in the actual classroom environment. This 'was wonderfully bright and attractive with appropriate displays of posters, photographs and artefacts which gave the pupils a feel for the period in which the novel was set'.[25] Striking in Phinn's characterisation of the classroom is the reference to warmth and good-humour – the former also occurring in the extract from Roddy Doyle and the latter in the comments of the principal and in the reference to laughter and fun in the reminiscence from Oakeshott. Regrettably these concepts are not sufficiently foregrounded in educational discourse.

On leaving this class, however, Phinn heads for the final lesson of the day through the school hall. There he finds two aggressive groups of boys shaping up to one another for a fight. So intense does their aggression become that Phinn intervenes, much to the surprise of the boys, and indeed of their teacher, who stands up to inform him that he has been watching a rehearsal of *Romeo and Juliet*. He spends the next half an hour watching 'the most gripping opening' of the play he had ever seen.[26]

The teachers in the two examples provided by Gervase Phinn nurtured their pupils precisely by teaching with energy, commitment and imagination. Teaching of such a character is more important than add-on programmes of pastoral care. I have always been more impressed by careful, consistent and constructive correction of pupils' assignments than by facility at producing theories about holistic education. To be sure, there is scope for nurturing activities of an explicit character within schools. For educators, it is a humbling privilege to be able to offer support and sympathy to young people in times of loss and grief due to bereavement or marriage breakdown. But providing such support is part of what is involved in being an educator: it is not a substitute for good teaching.

Notes

1. Walford, G., 'Redefining school effectiveness', *Westminister Studies in Education*, 25 (2002), pp 47-58, p. 53.
2. Phinn, G., *Over Hill and Dale* (London: Penguin, 2000), p. 159.
3. See some of the contributions to A. Hargreaves, and P. Woods (eds), *Classrooms and Staffrooms: The Sociology of Teachers and Teaching* (Milton Keynes: Open University, 1984).
4. See White, J., *Rethinking the School Curriculum: Values Aims and Purposes* (London: RoutledgeFalmer, 2004).
5. Parks, T., *An Italian Education* (London: Vintage, 2000), p. 287.
6. *Ibid.*
7. *Ibid.*
8. Gibbon, M., *The Pupil* (Dublin: Wolfhound Press, 1981). The quotations are taken from pp. 21, 75, 14 respectively.
9. *Ibid.*, p. 76.
10. I am quoting from a text entitled 'Oakeshott on his Schooldays' published as an Appendix in R. Grant, *Oakeshott* (London: The Claridge Press, 1990), p. 120
11. *Ibid.*
12. *Ibid.*
13. *Ibid.*
14. Winch, C., 'The Economic Ends of Education', *The Journal of Philosophy of Education*, 36 (2002), pp. 101-118, p. 115, note 20.
15. Phinn, G., *Over Hill and Dale*, p. 152.
16. *Ibid.*
17. *Ibid.*, p. 171.
18. Doyle, R., *A Star Called Henry* (London: Jonathan Cape, 1999), p. 79.
19. Kerrigan, G., *Another Country: Growing Up in 1950s Ireland* (Dublin: Gill and Macmillan, 1998), p. 55.

20. *Ibid.*, p. 56.

21. *Ibid.*

22. *Ibid.*

23. Williams, K., 'Student Teachers Remember Good Teaching in Their Schooldays', *Prospero*, 4 (1998), pp. 31-34.

24. Phinn, G., *Over Hill and Dale*, p. 164.

25. *Ibid.*

26. *Ibid.*, p. 167.

Towards an Understanding of the Adolescent Search for Identity

Finola Cunnane

Introduction

Wayne is 17, one of the lads, and beginning to focus on what the future might hold for him. He wonders who he is and questions the meaning and purpose of his life. Sarah's mother died tragically. She is no stranger to suffering and she questions why bad things happen to good people. Tracey's father has entered into a second relationship. Feelings of abandonment, resentment and anger rise to the surface every so often and she wonders if anyone really cares about her. Damien's family have been struggling to make ends meet all through his life. He desperately seeks to be like those who seem to have it all.

My experience is that the above is representative of some of the concerns, struggles and questions for today's adolescents. These young people seek to make sense of the paradoxes of life they see around them: the break-up of family life, the quest for recognition, power and wealth, pressures to be, have and do what would not necessarily be their deepest choice, the injustices in society and in the world and the unselfish dedication of those who strive to make the world a better place. Young people seek identity and a sense of self-worth. Hungering for meaning and purpose, for recognition and connection, for justice and for the holy, they seek a vision that is inviting and deserving of their energy and commitment. Ultimately, they seek a relationship with the Creator and Source of their being and they desire to nourish the hunger for mystery that they experience within. In other words, they seek, what James Bacik calls 'a deeper way of living humanly'.[1]

The Season of Adolescence

There is, indeed, a season for everything, as the Book of Ecclesiastes notes, and there is a season for adolescence. Marking the period from 'puberty until full adult status has been attained', the season of adolescence is one of physical, emotional and psychological upheaval.[2] A more comprehensive definition describes the period of adolescence as:

> a chronological period beginning with the physical and emotional processes leading to a sexual and psychosocial maturity and ending at an ill-defined time when the individual achieves independence and social productivity.[3]

Noting that various activities emerge at specific times during adolescent development, Harvard psychiatrist, Armand Nicholi, has determined that adolescence comprises three stages: early, middle and late adolescence.[4] Early adolescence, generally spanning the 12-14 year age group, is usually associated with puberty where young people are concerned, with their changing bodies and with the physical aspect of their lives. Emotions are in turmoil and expressed erratically, while the capacity to reflect and critically think is developing at a rapid pace. It is as this stage that the religious and philosophical questions regarding the meaning and purpose of life begin to emerge and relationships become more significant.

Middle adolescence is commonly understood as embracing 15-18 year olds. The sexual self is now experienced at a deeper level and emotional involvement is sought with significant others. While the young person becomes more involved with peers and, perhaps, with various causes, this can be a lonely and confusing time as he or she struggles to separate from the authoritarian in the quest for personal identity.

Late adolescence refers to the period from 18 years until independence and social productivity have been achieved. Issues of identity and intimacy can be heightened at this stage, as energies are focused on college, career and, sometimes, marriage choices, as well as concern for the roles that the young person hopes to fulfil in the world. Psychologist Daniel Levinson names this period of adolescence as *Early Adult Transition* and notes two tasks encountered by adolescents as they embrace the adult world.[5] First, young people find it necessary to terminate adolescence and, secondly, young people need to take on the responsibilities of young adulthood. These tasks entail a re-arrangement of existing relationships and re-definition of self, together with exploratory undertakings and provisional commitments to the adult world.

The Question of Identity

Identity is the term most commonly associated with the season of adolescence. This is a time when young people strive for identity and question who they are in relation to themselves, to others and to the world. Struggling with such questions as 'who am I?', 'where am I going?', 'what is the meaning of my life?', adolescents wonder who they are as persons and who they will become. Aware that their self-concept is changing, they seek to harmonise who they were as children with who they are becoming as adolescents. Young people struggle to become comfortable with who they are physically, emotionally, sexually and spiritually and they long for a sense of harmony with themselves, with each other and with the world. They seek, what Craig Dykstra calls, 'a sense of personal identity and a way of life'.[6]

What is identity and why is it so important during the adolescent years? Identity occurs when the young person has an awareness of self that gives meaning to who he or she is as a person, to his or her way of engaging in the world and to the direction his or her life is taking. Several factors contribute to the importance of identity during the adolescent years. First, adolescence represents a critical time in the cognitive development of the young person.

This, according to Piaget, is a time when formal operational thought gives way to a deepening cognitive enquiry that results in the ability to engage in abstract and reflective thinking. As a result, urgent, life-meaning questions seek answers.

A second reason why the quest for identity is crucial for adolescents is that the developing ability for cognitive reflection brings them face to face with their own life story. Conscious of their ability to reflect on the past and present, there is a growing awareness of the need to find and take responsibility for the future direction of *my* life in a way that fosters personal meaning.

Finally, the developing capacity for abstract thinking and reflection, together with the increasing amount of facts and information leads the young person to experience the complexity of everyday life. There are no easy answers to life's questions and problems. The task now is to find a personally meaningful and ethical way of being in the world in the midst of this growing complexity.

In order to understand the season of adolescence and its impact on young people, it is helpful to explore Erik Erikson's psychosocial theory of development. However, it is important to place the generality of developmental theory in dialogue with the uniqueness of each individual, a uniqueness that demands recognition and respect. Adolescent developmental theory is integrative in nature and a spirituality for adolescents should attempt to integrate all aspects of adolescent growth. Erikson's theory of psychosocial development reveals the meaning of identity and illustrates the process of identity synthesis in adolescence. It is to this that we now turn.

Psychosocial Development

In his theory, Erik Erikson expands the Freudian theory of psychosexual development and bases it on the epigenetic principle. Erikson tells us that the idea behind this principle is that:

> anything that grows has a ground plan, and that out of this ground plan the parts arise, each part having its time of special ascendancy, until all parts have risen to form a functional whole.[7]

This principle notes that the various bodily organs develop at specific times in the physical development of the human person. Erikson believes that ego development follows a similar pattern. There is a basic plan for the personality out of which the ego develops as it proceeds through a range of interrelated stages. Each individual stage presents a developmental task that requires successful negotiation, together with an inherent risk when negotiation is unsuccessful.

Erikson covers the life-cycle by proposing eight developmental stages, each of which focuses on an important emotional and social crisis influenced by both biological and cultural factors. Each stage is foundational for and operational in subsequent stages and as the individual resolves each crisis he or she moves to the next higher stage. Erikson's eight developmental stages are identified individually by a conflict with the possibility of two contrasting outcomes. As a result, each stage derives its name from the dual aspect of the pertinent social crisis. Resolving the conflict in a constructive way enables the positive quality presented by the crisis to become part of the ego, thereby promoting healthy development. If, on the other hand, the conflict continues or is resolved in an unsatisfactory manner, the resulting negative quality becomes part of the personality and influences further development.

Occurring in sequential order, the crisis or conflict presented at each stage is emphasised most at the age in which it is placed. While the identity crisis is crucial for adolescents, it is important to note that it is not appearing for the first time and that it will continue to be reshaped at other major points in life. Identity issues re-emerge during times of major change, changes, for example, that occur in relation to employment, marital status, illness or bereavement. The manner in which one embraces any issue concerning a re-definition of identity may well be influenced by the healthy or unhealthy way in which the adolescent crisis of identity was resolved.

The Adolescent Crisis of Identity

The crucial stage for adolescents is *identity versus identity confusion*. Erikson describes identity as follows:

> The wholeness to be achieved at this stage I have called a sense of inner identity. The young person, in order to experience wholeness, must feel a progressive continuity between that which he has come to be during the long years of childhood and that which he promises to become in the anticipated future; between that which he conceives himself to be and that which he perceives others to see him and to expect of him... Identifications with age mates and with leader figures outside the family.[8]

How, then, does identity develop during adolescence? The physiological changes experienced in early adolescence increase the young person's awareness of difference – the difference between who one was as a child, who one is right now and who one is becoming. This takes place in conjunction with the growing ability to question the meaning of self and life. Changes are also experienced in relationships, particularly in familial relations as the young person seeks to detach and separate in order to establish personal identity. In their quest for identity, young people experience more autonomy and freedom. However, the false sense of power that accompanies this stage may lead the adolescent to engage in annoying behaviours in order to be recognised as a distinct and separate entity.[9]

The adolescent dulls the pain of familial separation through attachment to the peer group. However, the sense of security acquired through the peer group can be counterproductive if dynamics within the group demand conformity. In this regard, stress and insecurity may increase if the adolescent attempts to move away from or disagree with the group.

In addition to the above, escalating demands, expectations and responsibilities punctuate the season of adolescence. With an increasing school workload, the responsibility of a part-time job and deepening intimate relationships, new questions, demands and anxieties are presented. The ever-present question of 'who am I?' is constantly in dialogue with the growing responsibility expected by parents, teachers, employers and friends and can frequently clash with internal questioning and self-doubt.

According to Erikson, the process of identity formation 'depends on the interplay of what young persons at the end of childhood have come to mean to themselves and what they now appear to mean to those who become significant to them'.[10] Thus, the task of adolescents in this crucial stage is to establish a sense of identity and to avoid the potential dangers offered by identity confusion and diffusion. Adolescents must work at achieving identity by striving to answer the pertinent questions they have been asking regarding their existence. They also must embrace such critical developmental issues as occupation and career choice, engaging in appropriate role behaviours, including sexual behaviours, and developing a meaningful ideology. Failure to answer these questions and address these issues leads, not only to feelings of isolation and alienation, but also to role diffusion.

Aware of the crucial aspect of this stage, Erikson writes that 'in no other stage of the life cycle are the promise of finding oneself and the threat of losing oneself so closely allied'.[11] An explanation for this lies in the fact that:

> the changes in identity which take place during adolescence involve the first substantial recognition and restructuring of the individual's sense of self at a time when he or she has the intellectual capability to appreciate fully just how significant the changes are.[12]

The Resolution of the Identity v Identity Confusion Crisis

Many factors influence the successful resolution of the *identity versus identity confusion* crisis. One such influence has to do with the manner in which the individual resolved the crises of the previous four stages. For example, if the adolescent does not have a healthy sense of trust, autonomy, initiative and industry, he or she may find it difficult to achieve a healthy sense of identity. Similarly, the way in which the young person revolves the identity crisis will influence the ways in which he or she will embrace the crises of later life.

A second factor that influences the successful resolution of the adolescent identity crisis involves a social process and concerns the young person's communication with others. Through interactions with significant others, young people adopt characteristics that they would like to incorporate as part of their own identity. This can account for the 'hero-worship' that oftentimes characterises adolescence. Similarly, the manner in which young people interpret others' responses to them enables them to identify the elements in their own identities that they would like to hold onto, as well as those elements they would like to discard. Through this process of observation and reflection, the young person seeks to resolve internal questions with external realities.

Identity Achievement

The successful achievement of a sense of identity in any one area of life means that identity has been achieved. This can be manifested through career choice, relationship choice, political ideology or the value system that directs ones life. Once achieved the young person accepts responsibility for a continually evolving self, situated in a relational world. The young adult can now make a commitment to self, others and the world. Once established, a sense of identity is consciously experienced.

> One knows when identity is present, in greater or lesser degree. For the individual, identity is partly conscious and partly unconscious; it gives one's life a feeling of sameness and continuity, yet also a 'quality of unselfconscious living' and is taken for granted by those in possession.[13]

Erikson continues that the most obvious concomitants of identity are 'a feeling of being at home in one's body, a sense of 'knowing where one is going' and an inner assuredness of anticipated recognition from those who count'.[14] Identity achievement, therefore, is characterised by such factors as maturity, stability, consistency in attitudes and behaviour and manifested in effective interpersonal relationships. It is achieved when individuals 'feel in harmony with themselves, accept their capacities, limitation and opportunities... There is a sense of direction and a positive orientation toward the future'.[15] Identity achievers, therefore, have the ability to cope with the various crises they encounter, emerging, usually, with successful outcomes.

Identity Confusion

However, identity achievement may be too difficult a task for the adolescent and thus the young person experiences identity confusion or diffusion. In an article entitled 'Life and the Life Cycle', Erikson describes identity confusion as 'a split of selfimages... a loss of centrality, a sense of dispersion and confusion and a fear of dissolution.'[16] With identity confusion, young people have not made any commitments and are unconcerned about making any. They appear to be ambivalent regarding the past, present or future and as a result tend to be aimless and disorganised. Identity diffused adolescents have no desire to embrace the values and responsibilities of the adult world. Fuhrmann notes that these young people frequently experience poor family relationships and adopt a 'façade of bravado' in order to disguise their low self-esteem.[17] They feel out of tune with themselves, with others and with the world.

When no positive identity is offered or achieved, rather than have no identity at all, adolescents may adopt an identity that is in opposition to parental and social guidance and regarded as undesirable by the wider community. This is done in an attempt to develop an identity in an environment in which they find it difficult to do so. By adopting a negative identity manifested, perhaps, through vandalism or criminal behaviour, the young person gains the recognition he or she desires, but not in a way that fosters positive growth.

Alternatively, the young person may develop an identity that is seemingly the opposite to that of the negative identity by behaving in a very acceptable manner. The aim here is to please whoever is in authority and to engage in whatever it takes to fulfill this aim. While this form of behaviour can be socially acceptable, it can be unacceptable if it is manifested in obedience to the leader of a gang. The problem with this kind of blind obedience is that it is another manifestation of a negative identity in that it is symptomatic of no identity at all.

A similar aspect of a negative identity concerns conformity, particularly conformity to the peer group. While the peer group offers security and a sense of belonging, the fact is that each member of the peer group is also seeking identity and, thus, conformity may not lead to identity achievement. In the event of the group's disbandment, the assumed identity of the young person is in danger of collapsing since it was not built on solid foundation.

Having differentiated between identity achievement and identity confusion, Erikson points out that:

> a sense of identity is never gained nor maintained once and for all... it is constantly lost and regained, although more lasting and more economical methods of maintenance and restoration are evolved and fortified in late adolescence.[18]

This being the case, the successful resolution of the adolescent identity crisis manifests itself in the young person's commitment to a meaningful ideology – an ideology that reflects his or her own values. This commitment is called fidelity and is the essence of identity. Such a commitment is essential for adolescents because it offers young people a clear world-view, a healthy regard for the future and a method of resolving their ideal world with the reality they encounter. In addition, it provides opportunities for young people to experiment with roles, identify with others and a rationale for the values they hold.

James Marcia's Extension of Adolescent Identity Formation
Identity v. Role Diffusion
Psychologist James Marcia extended Erikson's psychosocial theory and identified common factors operating in young people in their search for identity during adolescence. Recognising that adolescent identity achievement rarely occurs without some experience of struggle, he suggests two criteria essential for the achievement of a mature identity – *crisis* and *commitment*.

> 'Crisis', he writes, 'refers to times during adolescence when the individual seems to be actively involved in choosing, among alternatives, occupations and beliefs. Commitment refers to the degree of personal investment the individual expresses in an occupation or belief.[19]

As the adolescent experiences crises, the young person reassesses current viewpoints and modes of behaviour, explores numerous life choices and makes a plethora of decisions with regard to basic life issues. Commitment, then, refers to the personal self-investment that the young person gives to the choices made. Marcia applied these elements of *crisis* and *commitment* to Erikson's *'Identity v. Identity Confusion'* and carried out some research on adolescent identity formation. His study of identity growth led him to identify four major categories in the development of adolescent identity:

1. *Identity Diffusion:* An identity-diffused person has not undergone a crisis of identity nor made any commitment to a system of beliefs or a way of life.
2. *Foreclosure:* Although not having experienced an identity crisis, foreclosure types have values and have made commitments. These values and commitments, however, have not emerged from personal exploration but have been handed on and accepted without question.
3. *Moratorium:* A moratorium is a period of time, devoid of adult responsibilities and obligations, in which the young person actively explores and searches for an identity and for a set of beliefs and values that will depict who he or she is in the world. While this young person may have made some temporary commitments, he or she has not made any permanent commitment to an ideology or a way of life.
4. *Identity-Achievement:* Identity achievement has been reached when the young person has resolved the crises of adolescence and, as a result, has made a personal commitment 'to an occupation, a religious belief, and a personal value system and has resolved his attitude toward sexuality'.[20]

A deeper exploration of Marcia's four categories is helpful.

Identity Diffusion
The person living in the identity-diffused state has not experienced an identity crisis with regard to exploring and evaluating a way of life, religious beliefs and values, a political ideology nor a consistent manner of sexual behaviour. As a result, no obvious personal commitment has been made with regard to these issues. What is important to note here is that the identity-diffused state is an important part of the adolescent developmental process and should not present a cause for alarm. It is only when identity diffusion continues beyond adolescence that help should be sought.

While some form of identity diffusion is a normal aspect of early adolescence, identity diffusion can be narcissistic in character. When this is the case, young people view the world as revolving around them and may use other people in order to enhance their own pleasure and to promote feelings of well-being. According to Muuss, this mode of behaviour may be the result of 'an unresolved ego crisis of Erikson's first stage, *trust versus mistrust,* and being unable to trust people, they use them'.[21] Alternatively, however, there are defense mechanisms put in place by young people in order to avoid the pain of identity-diffusion. In this regard, psychologist Richard Logan identifies some of the ways in which young people seek to dull the pain of identity-diffusion and engage in palliative behaviour aimed to bring immediate relief.[22] For example, the pain of embracing the identity crisis may be too great and, as a result, the young person may turn to alcohol, drugs or other forms of temporary escape in order to ease or deny the confrontation being presented. Temporary escapes may also appear to have a positive nature and may be manifested through over-identification with a specific cause or with a specific role, e.g. athlete, intellectual, leader.

Another approach to the identity-diffused space may be expressed through the young person's desire to become someone. This desire may find expression through activities such as reckless driving, drug-taking and sexual behaviour. It may also manifest itself through competition where the young person strives to become someone either intellectually or athletically. Still other forms include the criticism of others in order to build and enhance one's self-esteem and sense of well-being, the engagement in meaningless activities in an effort to confirm the meaninglessness of one's own existence and the adoption of ways of behaviour that are contrary to the expectations of those in authority.

It is true to say that the identity-diffused person is in a state of psychological uncertainty, with no commitment to a way of life or a personal value system. Subject to a plethora of influences and a myriad of opportunities, the identity-diffused person is liable to respond to the most attractive invitations without sufficient reflection. As a result, the voice that speaks the loudest can be the one that has the most influence causing answers to the question 'who am I?' to become all the more compounded and confused.

Foreclosure
Committed to an occupation, a personal ideology and value system, foreclosure subjects have many of the appearances of identity-achievers. The difference lies, however, in the fact that they have not experienced an identity crisis nor have they explored alternative values for their lives. Rather, the goals directing their lives and the values they live by were designed by people other than themselves – by parents, friends or by religious authorities. Such an example can be seen in the son or daughter who follows in his or her parent's footsteps without exploring other possibilities or who is encouraged to become what the parent was unable to become. Indeed, it is not unknown for parents to live their own dreams through the lives of their sons or daughters. In cases like this it is difficult to differentiate between the young person's goals and those of the parents. The danger with foreclosure subjects is that they become so entrenched in this position that they never achieve identity. What is needed is sufficient challenge and guidance that will enable the young person to re-assess his or her unquestioned values and assumptions, otherwise the foreclosed state may become a permanent fixture.

Identity for the foreclosed adolescent is gleaned through relationship with others or is lived as an attachment of another person. While parents are regarded as having the prevailing influence in the foreclosed state, the peer group is also a swaying force. When the young person yields readily to the role demanded by the peer group, behaviour and manner of engagement is determined by the demands, pressures and expectations devised by this group. This may result in the temporary handing over of a developing identity to the peer group. Consequently, foreclosure occurs as one unquestioningly adopts the role determined by others and allows one's own identity to become subsumed into the group. The young person now defines a way of life and mode of behaviour according to the standards, expectations and demands of the peer group.

Moratorium
However, some young people do experience difficulty in making a commitment or in ascertaining a direction in life. Erikson sees these difficulties as part of the identity crisis and proposes a psychosocial moratorium – a period of time, devoid of adult responsibilities and obligations, set aside for young people to develop fidelity and reflect on their identity in terms of beliefs, values and commitment. The word 'moratorium' refers to a time of postponement when a young person delays making a commitment or taking on a more permanent responsibility. But Erikson stresses it is not only a delay. It is:

> a period that is characterized by a selective permissiveness on the part of society and of provocative playfulness on the part of youth, and yet it often leads to deep, if not transitory, commitment on the part of youth, and ends in a more or less ceremonial configuration of commitment on the part of society[23]

The moratorium period recognises that young people must grow towards adulthood rather than be forced prematurely. While Muuss describes this developmental state as 'the adolescent issue *par excellence'*, it is not without its crises and soul-searching questions.[24] This is a time when the young person explores, searches, experiments and struggles for meaningful answers to his or her life. It is also a time when young people experience the world as unpredictable and undesirable. They seek to right the wrongs they perceive and, therefore, challenge existing structures. While good and effective criticisms may be provided, young people in the moratorium state are unable to furnish solutions due to lack of identity and permanent commitment.

Both Erikson and Margaret Mead describe this period as an 'as-if-period' when young people are enabled to experiment with different roles 'as-if' they had made a commitment to these roles.[25] This has the advantage of affording young people the opportunity to try on various roles, make mistakes, gain experience, change their values and commitments, and become more mature in the process. Facilitating young people in this way contributes to a healthy development of identity, as well as commitments to a personal ideology, vocation and religious beliefs. It is interesting to note that the final commitments made at the end of this period can be less radical than some of the temporary ones experimented with during the moratorium.

The moratorium period, therefore, is a time when the young person psychologically steps aside and grapples with the invitations of the adult world. It is the season of becoming and is, according to Marcia, an essential and crucial requirement for identity achievement.

Identity Achievement
The successful outcome of the adolescent moratorium results in a resolution of the identity crisis, permanent personal commitments and the achievement of identity. Conclusions have been reached, decisions have been made and various choices and alternatives have been considered. While it is not uncommon for the conclusions and decisions of young identity achievers to resemble those of their parents, the essential part of their journey took place through the various options and alternatives that they explored and, consequently, accepted or rejected. In this way, they differ from their foreclosed counterparts whose values also resemble those of their parents but who did not seriously consider other choices or question these values before adopting them.

Individuals who have achieved identity have a sense of direction in life and feel at home with themselves. There is a sense of personal continuity as one emerges from the past and embraces the future. According to Keniston, identity represents a new-found synthesis that 'will link the past, the present and the future'.[26] A new sense of self has now been created providing inner harmony, continuity and consistent values, purposes and goals. Once achieved, identity contributes to 'an increase in self-acceptance, a stable self-definition, a willingness to make commitments to a vocation, a religion, a political ideology and also to intimacy, engagement and marriage.'[27]

**Implications of the Adolescent Search for Identity
for School Chaplaincy and Pastoral Care**
Charles Shelton, in his book *Adolescent Spirituality*, has made several observations in relation to developmental theory and adolescent spirituality.[28] First, it is important to recognise and respect the uniqueness of each adolescent, together with the uniqueness of the young person's relationship with God. Secondly, relationships are key in adolescence and through them adolescents glean a sense of self. The hunger for Mystery is central to all relationships. A third observation acknowledges that adolescence is a period characterised by change and that the young person's perception, understanding and relationship with God is part of that change. Fourth, the capacity to critically think and reflect develops dramatically during adolescence. Values, attitudes and ideas are questioned. It is not unusual, therefore, for a young person to question the existence of God nor to question and criticise the modes of Church practice. Finally, the integrative nature of adolescent developmental theory calls for a spirituality that invites the young person to 'integrate all aspects of adolescent growth in a self that is capable of making a commitment to the Gospel and the forming of a personal relationship with Jesus in the context of a growing sense of adulthood'.[29]

Practically speaking, some suggestions for faith formation with adolescents include the following:

- Invite young people to reflect on their relationship with God by naming some instances when they felt close to God.
- Embrace Scripture. Invite young people to make connections between the Gospel stories and their lived experience. This can be done through a variety of ways – writing the sequel to the Gospel story, writing the story in contemporary times, making an eyewitness report to the Gospel scene, acting out the Word, using Lectio Divina, showing a video or DVD, using music.
- Engage in joyful, participatory liturgies.
- Provide opportunities for young people to explore their faith in ways that are relevant, practical and applicable to contemporary life.
- Invite young people to engage in the work of social justice.

As we leave these pages to journey with young people, may the words of an unknown author guide our steps.

> Our first task in approaching
> another people
> another culture
> another religion
> is to take off our shoes
> for the place we are
> approaching is holy.
> Else we may find ourselves
> treading on another's dream.
> More serious still
> we may forget
> that God
> was there before our arrival.

Notes

1. Bacik, J., *The Gracious Mystery* (Cincinnati, Ohio: St. Anthony Messenger Press, 1987), p. 2.
2. Muuss, R.E., *Theories of Adolescence* (New York: McGraw-Hill, 1988), p. 22.
3. American Psychiatric Association, quoted in C. M. Shelton, *Adolescent Spirituality* (New York: Crossroad, 1983), p. 2.
4. Nicholi, A.M. Jr, 'The Adolescent' in *The Harvard Guide to Modern Psychiatry* (Cambridge, MA: The Belknap Press, 1978), p. 520.
5. Levinson, D.J., et al. *The Seasons of a Man's Life* (New York: Alfred A. Knopf, 1978), p. 56.
6. Dykstra, C., 'Agenda for Youth Ministry: Problems, Questions and Strategies' in M. Warren (ed.), *Readings and Resources in Youth Ministry* (Winona, Minnesota: St. Mary's, Press, 1987), p. 75.
7. Erikson, E., *Identity: Youth and Crisis* (New York: W. W. Norton & Son, 1968), p. 92.

8. *Ibid.* p. 87.

9. Josselson, R., 'Ego Development in Adolescence' in J. Adelson (ed.), *Handbook of Adolescent Psychology* (J. Wiley & Sons, Inc., 1980), p. 194.

10. Erikson, E., *Toys and Reasons* (New York: W. W. Norton & Son, 1977), p. 106.

11. Erikson, E., *Identity: Youth and Crisis* (New York: W.W. Norton & Son, 1968), p. 244.

12. Steinberg, L., *Adolescence* (New York: McGraw-Hill, 1993), p. 255.

13. Kroger, J., *Identity in Adolescence* (London & New York: Rutledge Press, 1989), p. 14.

14. Erikson, E., *Identity: Youth and Crisis* (New York: W.W. Norton & Son, 1968), p. 165.

15. Muuss, R.E., *Theories of Adolescence* (New York: McGraw-Hill, 1988), p. 74.

16. Quoted in B. Fuhrmann, *Adolescence, Adolescents.* (Illinois: Scott, Foreman/Little, Brown, 1990), pp. 122-123.

17. *Ibid.*, p. 314.

18. Erikson, E., 'Identity and the Life Cycle: Selected Papers' in *Psychological Issues Monographic Series 1,* no. 1 (New York: International Universities Press, 1959), p. 118.

19. Marcia, J.E., 'Ego Identity Status: Relationship to Change in Self-Esteem, "general maladjustment" and authoritarianism' in *Journal of Personality*, 1967, 35, p. 119.

20. Muuss, R.E., *Theories of Adolescence* (New York: McGraw-Hill, 1988), p. 66.

21. *Ibid.*, p. 68.

22. Logan. R., 'Identity Diffusion and Psycho-Social Defense Mechanisms' in *Adolescence* 13, Fall 1978, pp. 503-507.

23. *Ibid.*, p. 157.

24. Muuss, R.E., *Theories of Adolescence* (New York: McGraw-Hill, 1988), p. 72.

25. Quoted in R.E. Muuss, *Theories of Adolescence.* (New York: McGraw-Hill, 1988), p. 72.

26. Keniston, K., 'Social Change and Youth in America' in E. Erikson (ed.), *The Challenge of Youth* (New York: Doubleday/Anchor, 1965), p. 212.

27. Muuss, R.E., *Theories of Adolescence* (New York: McGraw-Hill, 1988), p. 74.

28. Shelton, C.M., *Adolescent Spirituality* (Chicago: Loyola University Press, 1983), p. 112.

29. *Ibid.*, p. 113.

The Period of Adolescence and School Discipline

Maeve Martin

Introduction

For those who have chosen to work with young people in schools today both the privilege and challenges associated with this work are daunting. It is worth pondering on what are the privileges and the challenges that stem from this sacred work. As chaplains and teachers we have the opportunity to play a central part in the lives of the young as they go about negotiating the important developmental period of adolescence. Our pupils are in a period of transition from childhood to adulthood. They are no longer afforded the indulgence of a young child nor are they given the freedom or autonomy of adulthood. The main tasks of this developmental period are 1) the forging of a personal identity, 2) achieving independence from parents, 3) making vocational choices, and 4) relating to peers and adults in a mature and respectful manner. As role models and mentors in the lives of pupils, school personnel are vital forces. This is a rare privilege indeed, as our role gives us the opportunity to influence the process of negotiating the developmental tasks, and to help determine the outcome. We have access to the bright minds of our pupils, to their many gifts and talents, access to their idealism, to their enthusiasm, and to their energy. In our gift is the capacity to help them develop and go forth in a way that does justice to these attributes, but alongside that, in a subtler and more profound way, we can influence their value system, their sense of themselves, their choices, and their priorities. Our pupils represent a source of inspiration and hope for us, their seniors. We in turn are significant others in their lives. The reciprocal spheres of influence in which both sets of players operate, are indeed spheres of privilege.

But while there is abundant privilege as an integral part of our role in working with pupils, there is also formidable challenge. Pupils to day live very action-packed lives, and if their life in school is not stimulating, then there is a strong likelihood that they will become disinterested, even alienated, and will detach from the central purpose of the school, namely teaching and learning. Of course there are considerable numbers of pupils who live passive lives that are bleak and barren, and that may be devoid of any kind of social or cultural capital. In the confines of the school setting these pupils may not pose discipline problems. They drift through school in a reasonably invisible way that may mirror how they will go on to drift through life. In a sense their needs may not be detected in the hurly-burly of a busy school. They get lost in the system as their behaviour does not impact either academically or antisocially. Apart from designated duties of a teaching and administrative nature, staff energies tend to be devoted to dealing with problems of persistent disruption, and so the passive, unobtrusive, non-participating pupil may slip through the net.

A Clash of Cultures – External and Internal Challenges

So while schools cater for pupils who live orderly, self-disciplined lives in the security of their caring and responsible families, there are still many pupils who adopt lifestyles that do not seem to be age-appropriate. The out-of-school lives of considerable numbers of our pupils are apt to be filled with the excitement that comes from: connecting with peers, drinking alcohol, experimenting with substances other than alcohol, being sexually active, having disposable income that comes form holding down part-time jobs, viewing questionable video material, listening to music that may contain messages of a violent or sexual nature, using language that is coarse or vulgar, sending and receiving innumerable text messages, and surfing the Internet. There is a real sense in which the throbbing lives that some pupils live may constitute a counter-culture when compared to the dominant culture of schools. School personnel cannot assume automatically that they have a pupil population that is highly motivated and eager to learn. They may find that the norms of behaviour and values which they advocate, and work towards are at variance with those espoused by their young pupils in their off-campus lives. The variation that exists within schools in this small island is great. Many schools do Trojan work in creating school environments that are centres of care, compassion and empathy. They throw lifelines to their pupils who may be battling with issues that could scupper easily their healthy personal development and career ambition. These schools find ways that make school sufficiently attractive to pupils so that they remain in the system until the official school leaving age of sixteen. In fact impressive numbers of the school-going cohort (i.e. 81%) stay on in school beyond this age to participate in senior cycle. This high participation figure is a tribute to schools in how they respond to the challenges that face them. Recent work from the OECD shows that, in the main, pupils in Ireland are content and happy in school, and this accounts for the low attrition rates.

Apart from the challenges from the outside world that are influential in school life in Ireland today, there are pressures within the school that drive much of what happens there. Schools feel that they operate in a system that is very influenced by a mode of assessment that is 'points' driven. There has been a regrettable tendency in recent years in Ireland among some of the national newspapers to publish what approximates to a set of league tables. Schools deemed most successful are those that deliver large numbers of their final year pupils to third-level education institutions. Entry in to the tertiary sector is but one measure of a school's success, and not all schools nor all parents, nor indeed all pupils, see that as the single most important measure of how schools perform. These published tables are not comparing like with like, nor are they tapping into the value-added that schools create for their pupils. Many schools that are meeting the needs of their pupils in an admirable way, and that are succeeding against very convoluted odds, may be disheartened by the publication of these league tables. There is scant regard for, or recognition of, their noble and painstaking work with often difficult cohorts of pupils in challenging and bleak neighbourhoods. Entry into college is a crude but oft cited measure of school effectiveness. Schools that build the self esteem of a floundering adolescent, that listen to him/her, that give their pupils a voice, that offer hope and courage, that provide the skills and dispositions that shape up attainable ambitions and that offer support and guidance in the realisation of these ambitions – these are the unsung schools of our education system. They often plough a lonely furrow, and they may not figure in neon lights in the published league tables that track the numbers of their school leavers who go on to participate in third-level formal education.

Added to the pressure of working within a points driven system, there is the reality of the changing characteristics of the pupil population itself. Our society is becoming very multicultural. This is a phenomenon that has crept up on us very quickly. Some schools that were until recently catering for a homogeneous pupil cohort are now catering for a very diverse pupil intake. Schools welcome the diversity that is associated with our burgeoning multiculturalism, but it poses challenges for school staff as they strive to behave in an equitable and responsive manner in meeting the needs of all their pupils. Many of the *new* Irish pupils may need enhanced language skills in order to engage with the curriculum. Not all schools have teachers with competence in teaching English as a foreign language (TEFL) or teaching English for special purposes (ESP). For those pupils coming from different traditions, their culture may vary in many aspects from the dominant culture of which they now are part. P.J. Boyle has dealt very well with this issue in a later chapter in this book so for now I just wish to highlight how school staff work through all these emerging issues as they seek to be inclusive and responsive to all.

Another feature of the inclusive nature of schools today is the integration of pupils with special educational needs. These pupils who have the right to be educated alongside their peers, may pose challenges for teachers and school personnel who have had little or no professional development in working with children with disabilities. The characteristics of the pupil cohort is changing before the eyes of long-standing staff members, and the attendant challenges of working effectively with them are indeed daunting. Add to this changing scenario the rapid and extensive changes in curricula, the centrality of technology with its infusion in to the teaching and learning process, the new active methodologies that are being advocated, and one cannot but sympathise with teachers, who may feel overwhelmed, at times, by what is coming down the tracks at them in their workplace.

Developmental Challenges

Added to the clash of cultures that exists between the out of school and in school tutors, and the pressures of the system, there is the challenge that comes from the number of age-related issues arising from this period of adolesence. These may include depression, eating disorders, teen parenthood, anti-social behaviour/delinquency, anxiety, and suicidal tendencies. It is true that the school is not the setting in which these issues may be explored or dealt with, but they influence the behaviour of the young adolescent while in the school. If we think *systemically*, we cannot dismiss the seriousness of these issues. They impact on the well-being of our pupils and on their peer group. Schools that are bereaved following the tragic suicide of a pupil are schools that are altered in very fundamental ways. Many of our pupils experience some kind of loss. The fallout from loss can have grave implications for how a young pupil progresses, and adapts to life in school. Considerable numbers of pupils live in households that have experienced parental disharmony that may result in separation or break-up. The legacy of this kind of major disruption in the domestic life of a pupil is pervasive, and the manifestation of how it impacts may be evidenced in ways that violate aspects of the school's code of behaviour. Pupils who find themselves living in reconstituted or blended families often experience difficulty in coming to terms with their altered situations. School may be the forum in which the troubled adolescents give expression to the range of emotions triggered by changes in their young lives. Those who hold designated posts for the care element in schools are dealing with an increasing workload, and the range of difficulties that they encounter were not dreamt of some years ago. These developments, many of them triggered by the changing fabric of society, make the role of a teacher or a school chaplain a very demanding and challenging one. Schools need to have staff who have great sensitivity to the range of needs of its pupils, and who are aware of the issues that dominate their pupils' lives. Many pupils have sad personal scripts, many handle situations that are not amenable to quick-fix solutions. If they feel safe and cared for in the confines of the school, their risk factors are minimised. The real challenge is for schools to help their young people to navigate the troubled waters of the adolescent period, and to set them up with a range of personal resources that prepares them for the next phase of their lives.

Teacher–Pupil Relationship

The concept of resilience is gaining in popularity among those of us who take an interest in why it is that some of our pupils succeed, despite being born in to high-risk environments. It is an attractive concept in that it tends to bring a positive orientation to our thinking, rather than a defeatist or deterministic perspective. There are protective factors that schools can offer their pupils. These protective factors buffer the risk that may be associated with living in areas of urban poverty, or the risks associated with growing up in a family where there may be crime, violence, substance abuse, mental illness, dysfunction or neglect. Schools have the capacity to turn around outcomes for at-risk, or potentially disaffected pupils. The powerful variables within schools that are protective are:

- Caring relationships
- Positive and high expectations
- Opportunity for pupils to participate and to contribute.

The quality of the relationships is vital to the development of resilience. Relationships that are transformational for troubled youth are predicated on respect and on acceptance. Teachers who model acceptance and regard tend not to take personally pupil behaviour that is, in objective terms, offensive. Instead, they use such an incident, or piece of behaviour as a discussion point. They negotiate in a respectful and calm, firm manner. They enter in to a dialogue with the offending pupil/s in a way that allows for an account of the issues to be aired by all parties. Everybody is required to listen, to reflect, and to respond. Behavioural and affective aspects are considered, and possible ways forward are explored. There is no harsh judgement, no rejection, but rather a considerable time investment, based on the belief that all of us can change and grow. Pupils need some introduction in to this way of resolving difficulties, as it may be in contrast to ways of dealing with hurt and offence in their out-of-school lives. They access a world that is not reliant on anger or insult or force as a means of sorting things out. Instead they have a valid place in a world that is mutually respectful and considerate, and that is tolerant of young people who are trying to find their way. The approach is not one that dilutes standards of courtesy or respect for others, but rather one that is pupil-centred in an effort to give pupils the requisite social skills and orientations that will help them to be fulfilled members of a democratic society. Personnel in schools who seek to find win/win solutions for problems that arise are not wimps or soft touches. It is not a weakness to show tolerance and patience when offended by a rude, disrespectful pupil. It is how the matter is handled that counts in the long run. Schools that invest in their relationships at all levels of interaction are safe for those who occupy them. Pupils in these schools manage their anger, and negotiate rather than striking out. The work for teachers, year heads, and pastoral care team may often be uphill, but the dividends for individual pupils, and for society, are unquantifiable. Schools that prioritise healthy, positive, and caring relationships may contribute to breaking cycles of disaffection, despair, and negativity for many of their pupils

Empowering Pupils
Pupils who present with difficulties in schools share some characteristics. They tend to perceive themselves as failures, they are pessimistic about their futures, and their perception is that they are in an inferior or disadvantaged position. Regrettably, some experiences in school may reinforce these beliefs for these disruptive pupils. It is therefore important for schools to be aware of the detrimental consequences of poor self-image and of a defeatist attitude among potentially marginalised youth. Schools need to transmit high and positive

expectations for their pupils. They can help them to build a realistic vision about their future. They can work on pupil strengths, and celebrate minor victories, as these may lead on to more significant accomplishments. Pupils can be helped to set goals and to develop strategies that lead to their attainment. Empowering teachers transmit a sense of optimism and trust to their pupils, rather than, as some teachers do, write them off in subtle ways. Pupils have their sensitivities, and they pick up on the messages that we send them. If we show that we believe in them and in their capacity to grow and to attain, then the self-fulfilling prophecy factor kicks in and success experiences follow. The damage that has ensued from humiliating and oppressive experiences in the past may be turned around by teachers and caring adults who work alongside their pupils in a framework of high, yet achievable expectations. In this supportive caring environment the pupils have a sense of purpose, a sense of autonomy, and a sense of competence.

Schools that foster resilience structure a lot of opportunities for pupils to express their views, to give expression to their creativity and imagination, and to problem solve. In these schools pupils are treated as responsible individuals, and are held accountable for their behaviour. Activities are structured to occur in an environment that is safe both psychologically and physically. Allocated tasks are shared, and there is the opportunity to work collaboratively, and to help each other. The tasks are flexible enough to allow for participation by all. Contributions are valued, and pupils learn a range of behaviours that have applicability in to areas beyond the world of school, i.e. in to the local community, and in to the world of work. The revised curricula in our schools advocate active teaching and learning methods. There is scope to tap in to the inner creativity and gifts of all our pupils, and to develop their multiple intelligences. The failure identity of many of our pupils can be replaced by success identities. An *'I can'* self-concept is much preferable to an *'I'm not going to be able to do it'* identity. Schools that promote pupil participation in the functioning of the school, and that value pupil contributions, are schools that enable the development of resilience in their pupils. The building of resilient people is a long-term process that is based on nurturing, participatory relationships that are based on trust and respect and that strive towards valuable goals.

Promoting a Positive Code of Discipline
One of the recent tasks in which schools have engaged is the development of their School Development Plan. It is customary to devote a section of this to the Code of Behaviour of the school. Engaging in this task offers an opportunity for staff to reflect on the purposes of their behaviour code, and to assess their practices with regard to discipline in the school. It may be that schools come to recognise that the code is outdated, and is not really implemented across the board in schools. It may be that they feel that there should be different emphases for their junior and senior pupils within the code. It may be that they perceive that the code is not in line with recent legislation, and that it leaves their school in a vulnerable position in the event of a legal situation arising in connection

with a discipline matter. A review of the code may point up the reality that the code is very rules based, and does little to develop in the pupils norms of self-discipline that will transfer to situations beyond the life of the school. So why have a Code of Discipline in operation at all? Possible reasons include:

- To allow for the smooth realisation of the core purpose of the school
- To develop self-discipline in our pupils, and respect for the self, for others, and for the environment
- To prepare our pupils to live as responsible members of a demographic society
- To be in compliance with the new legal framework in which we work

The putting together of a Code of Behaviour provides an interesting opportunity for staff in schools to clarify for themselves their views and their values about pupil behaviour. It is not an easy task, as doubtless there will be individual variation among staff regarding what is and what is not acceptable pupil behaviour. There is the tricky task of determining sanctions and how they will be applied. There is a great need for clarity in this area. We live in a world where pupils place great emphases on their rights, but with not so great emphases on their responsibilities. This focus on rights, and immature dismissal of responsibility leave us open to litigation or challenges from partisan parents. So the crafting of the code must be tight enough and loose enough to cater for situations that it is perhaps difficult to anticipate. Central features of a code may include the following:

- An outline of the standards of behaviour that shall be observed by the pupils attending the school
- The measures that may be taken when a pupil fails to observe those standards
- The procedures to be followed before a pupil is suspended or permanently excluded
- The grounds for removing a suspension
- The method of reporting on pupil absences from school

It seems appropriate that the Code of Behaviour should chime well with a school's mission statement. There should be some form of continuity between these two documents, and ideally they should be reflected in the daily business of the school. Codes work well when they are owned by as many of the stakeholders as possible, and when they are implemented across the board fairly and compassionately. Incidents of misbehaviour should be perceived as teaching/learning opportunities. It is best to try to resolve breaches of the code by including the pupils in their resolution. Pupils should be taught conflict resolution skills and peer mediation approaches. It is likely that in their academic programme they will have been introduced to problem solving methods, and to ways of working collaboratively in teams. This learning will transfer to the resolution of difficulties that may result from violations of the

Code. Where pupils are included in the process of addressing difficulties, they learn skills and attitudes that will prepare them for working respectfully and democratically later in the workplace, in their families, and community. An approach that relies on pastoral and conflict resolution methods is much more valuable, and more developmental, than a punitive knee-jerk sanction that gives little scope for an exploration of the underlying issues that may have triggered the unacceptable behaviour. A shared approach that puts the perpetrator and the victim at the centre allows for consideration of the consequences of the misdemeanour for all concerned. In this way pupils inculcate norms of decency and altruism. They learn important listening skills and the value of compromise.

It is inevitable that the Code will be reliant on rules. There are some guidelines that should be noted when drawing up rules. They should be:

- Few in number
- Stated positively in a way that describes the behaviour the school wishes to see
- Reasonable and fair
- Simple and precise
- Explained, discussed, and taught/modelled
- Enforced and enforceable

For the Code to operate effectively, there must be consequences following a violation of a rule, and the pupils must be held accountable. The research in the area of school discipline tells us that there are variables that influence the likelihood of how discipline will play out in schools. Some schools are more deviance prone than others. Schools that insulate themselves against major disruption tend to have some of the following characteristics:

- They are proactive not reactive – in other words, they try to work within reasonable parameters, where boundaries are clearly understood;
- The dominant ethos of the school is pastoral, with an emphasis on positive, participatory relationships, and a climate that is supportive and caring;
- There are planned routines that make for a safe and secure environment;
- There is an emphasis on rewards rather than on punishment – pupils have their efforts and their accomplishments recognised and valued;
- When breaches of discipline are addressed, it is more in the spirit of the code rather than on rigid adherence to the letter of the code. The maxim of 'seek first to understand and then to be understood' is adopted;
- Individual staff members are empowered to deal with unacceptable behaviour, and only in extreme cases is the matter referred to other authorities within the school;
- Responsibility for discipline is a shared responsibility, involving the school, the pupils and the parents.

Conclusion

Working with today's youth requires us to be whole and robust. Working viably and meaningfully in schools is not for the faint hearted, as the demands therein go far beyond the enactment of the official curriculum. But in schools there is a sense of community and a sense of belonging that is difficult to create in other settings. The work is exciting, and there is the throb of being with large numbers of talented young people who will assume positions of responsibility in their families, their workplaces, their communities, and perhaps nationally or internationally in the years ahead. We owe them much. In a sense they give us in large measure essential aspects of our own identity, while they struggle to find their own identity. They are unlikely to forget us whether we are positive or negative forces in their lives. Let us strive in our privileged and challenging work to be good forces in their tender lives.

A Pastoral Response to Adolescent Youth Experiencing Emotional Disturbances

Edward J. Hall

Introduction

This chapter arises out of my work in a residential care home for young adolescents in the United States of America. While I acknowledge that there will be some cultural and contextual differences, it is my hope that these reflections will assist those who work with emotionally disturbed young people in second-level schools. It is my main argument in this chapter that in meeting the challenges presented to us in schools by emotionally disturbed pupils, the young person will benefit most by a response that is underpinned by Christian compassion. Consequently, the school chaplains and teachers who work out of a Christian framework make a very significant contribution to the pastoral care of pupils who are emotionally disturbed.

The Morphology of Emotional Disturbance

What pastoral challenges do school personnel face when they meet young people who live with significant emotional pain? What kinds of empathetic strategies might be useful to help children and adolescents name and claim their personal struggles with woundedness? What praxis is most useful for engaging young people who desire healing and wholeness and who courageously face the hole in their souls? These questions are essential pastoral perspectives when pastoral carers pass over from clinical definitions of emotional disturbance and enable young people to envision alternative narratives.

Biehler and Snowman define emotional disturbance as:

> Personal and social problems exhibited in an extreme degree over a period of time that adversely affect the ability to learn and get a long with others.[1]

The label 'emotionally disturbed' is usually applied to children and adolescents who manifest their pain and suffering through problems or disturbances in living and relating to teachers, parents, classmates and others. It is important to note at this stage that while a label such as 'emotionally disturbed' is useful as a general indicator in the description of a pattern of behaviour, no label can capture the wholeness, beauty and essential mystery that is each person. In fact, at times labels such as 'emotionally disturbed' can accentuate the abnormal, maladaptive or problem-laden dimension of pupils who are emotionally disturbed. Consequently, great care must be taken in our use of this and other psychological labels in the school setting.[2] I would argue further that the use of terms like 'disturbed', 'psychotic' and 'disordered' needs to be preceded by the Christian affirmation that all persons share the same human condition, manifested in different ways, and all have been created in the image of God and given an inherent dignity and intrinsic value simply because we exist. Adolescents living with emotional disturbance have the same human needs for love and acceptance, affection and independence, understanding self-identity and sexuality as others without such impairing problems in the same age group.

In my experience the roots of the suffering of emotionally disturbed adolescents tend to reside in a deprivation of some kind. This would involve neglect or abuse during infancy and early childhood from primary care-givers (usually parents) characterised by unpredictable, unstable and inconsistent fulfilment of basic needs especially love and affection. The parental style of relating to their child(ren) tends to have been rejective in the past and usually such a style continues during adolescence. Research has shown that poor parent-child relationships can lead to behaviour problems and emotional disturbance resulting in peer rejection and sometimes isolation for the young person in adolescence. It is not a surprise then that without appropriate intervention so many emotionally disturbed children leave school early and/or identify with a deviant peer group.

Adolescents with emotional problems manifest their pain in the internal conflict(s) they experience as well as their dramatisation of such conflicts(s) in their relationships with others through particular behaviours, affects and thought processes. While the following description of such styles of relating, behaviours, affects and thought processes is not comprehensive for each adolescent, either in the sense that all apply to one individual or that any combination represent the whole person, it is somewhat indicative of the ways in which emotional disturbance manifests itself. The following five styles are regnant in contemporary dysfunctional behaviour.

Acting Out
In their relationship with others, adolescents are often unable or unwilling to control the expression-in-action of certain impulses, primarily aggressive and sexual impulses. The tendency to satisfy an impulse through inappropriate action is generally called 'acting-out'. Bernard, a fifteen-year-old who lived in the group home where I worked, became quite angry with me when I requested that he turn off his lights for the evening; he defiantly refused to comply with my request, shouted 'F--- you!' repeatedly, and punched a hole in the wall as a way of acting-out his angry/aggressive impulse. Elisa, another fifteen-year-old, acted out her sexual impulse by running away from the group home for ten days to live with a young man she was attracted to.

This type of acting out will be familiar to chaplains and teachers who work with young people who are emotionally disturbed. Simple requests such as asking them to take off their coat in class or to move to a different seat can often be met with acting-out behaviour.

Manipulation

Some adolescents have learned how to get what they want or need from others by manipulating them through deceitful and self-wilful ways. Sixteen-year-old Billy told me that his therapist said it was 'OK' for him to leave the group home that afternoon to sit near his office and read magazines. I had talked with the therapist before Billy's appeal and he had said nothing of this arrangement. It was clear that Billy wanted my permission to leave the house without indicating what he would be doing while away. I told him the therapist had not mentioned such an arrangement to me and that he did not have my permission to leave the group home. Billy decided to leave anyway, but on his way out the door, the supervisor of the home entered the doorway and Billy quickly changed his story, saying he was just going outside for a cigarette. This type of manipulation can often characterise the emotionally disturbed pupil's relationships with other pupils, teachers and parents alike.

Making Demands

Adolescents frequently demand (as opposed to request) the fulfilment of needs or wants with little sensitivity to the needs or wants of others. While adolescence is a time of growing egocentricity in the normal development of identity formation, the particular neediness of emotionally disturbed adolescents can often surface as a demand or assumption for attention, care and support in which the one demanded upon is given little freedom to respond other than in the affirmative. Joel wanted someone to play table-tennis with and approached me one day, saying 'You're playing table-tennis with me'. In addition to demanding quality of relating many emotionally disturbed young adolescents are unable to give back (marginally) to others in their relationships. The pupil who only comes to the after school club when he feels like it or if there is something happening that he is interested in can be said to display this 'demanding' quality in that he fails to see the needs of others at the club.

Defensive Posturing

Young people employ various defences or styles of relating to themselves and others which shields them from emotional pain, hurt and unpleasant feelings like anxiety, guilt, shame, depression or worthlessness. To avoid painful feelings, when in a new and stressful situation or a threatening encounter, the primary defences of these young people are denial, projection, misdirection, displacement and regression. When confronted with a painful feeling or event denial protects the young person from its reality. Projection often comes across as accusation of others. For example, Ernie, aged seventeen, blamed a staff member for 'making him crazy'. Andy said to me, following his angry outburst, 'What's the matter? Are you feeling guilty?' when it was clear that he was feeling guilty for his previous behaviour.

Adolescents who want to cover one feeling can display the opposite feeling (which is more acceptable) as a defence; this is called misdirection. Bernard aged fifteen ran away from the home, sniffed glue, returned later that evening in an intoxicated state and was sent to his room. The next morning he bragged of how proud he was of what he had done. However, in the process of counselling, it became clear that he really felt quite ashamed of what he had done the night before and that his show of bravado and pride functioned to misdirect others from seeing his shame and regret for his previous behaviour.

Displacement occurs when a feeling, usually anger or hostility, precipitated by one person or event is transferred to another person or event. Ernie was angry when his girlfriend ended the relationship. He displaced his anger on various staff members until he admitted his anger and hurt about the loss of his girlfriend. Regression is the return to an earlier, more 'primitive' state of functioning to protect one during a stressful situation. For example, Joanne, aged fifteen, talks like a baby (regresses) when under stress.

Thinking

Most adolescents with emotional problems have a normal to above average intelligence on IQ scales and therefore many can function quite well in academic as well as life settings when other problems do not get in the way. Their thought processes, however, tend to be especially affected during stressful or new situations. Four processes are apposite categories of adolescent thinking:

Obsessive thinking: a particular, sentence, idea or image continually presents itself in one's thinking and resists repression, avoidance and dispelling. This obsessive thinking tends to be the result of anxiety and often centres on those issues most unacceptable to the person. Young people can obsess about many things including violence, sex, food, cleanliness and other people.

Paranoid thinking: Intense projection and great anxiety team together when one thinks in a paranoid manner. Paranoid thinking destroys trust and evidences the anxiety that no one is there to help, in fact, everyone is out to hurt. Wildly paranoid thinking generally occurs in episodes of extreme anxiety and rage. Bernard perceived my efforts to help him with his school work one evening (help he had requested) as suspect and wondered if I was attempting to sabotage his work.

Loose associations: This is where the young person is unable to order his/her thoughts in relation to one another. Bits and pieces of ideas and images are loosely associated and communication is impaired. This can be further compounded for adolescents who come from a lower socio-economic grouping where research has shown that they can have a more limited vocabulary and thus find it harder to communicate complex ideas or feelings.[3]

Hazy reality-testing: Under great stress, some young people have difficulty distinguishing between what they wish, fear, assume or fantasise, and what in reality is actually happening. Their perceptions are distorted and reality-testing (what is actually happening external to their thinking) is often inconsistent and hazy. Joel slapped a female resident one evening and proceeded to beat her until staff members intervened. He fully believed and asserted that the female resident hit him at first. The staff member present watched the beginning inter-action between Joel and the other resident and indicated that she had not hit him at any time that day and that Joel had simply started to assault her.

Thus far I have tried to outline what it means for a young person to be described as emotionally disturbed and some of the consequences for those who work with them in schools and elsewhere. I will now explore how a pastoral response to emotionally disturbed adolescents can be realised.

Pastoral Response to Emotionally Disturbed Pupils

Many teachers, chaplains and other professionals have struggled with the question of how to respond appropriately to young people who are emotionally disturbed. A significant part of any response to an emotionally disturbed adolescent will include psychological and therapeutic interventions. However, the basic needs of these young people are no different from those of other youth. They also need to be loved, to belong, to be respected and to be supported personally. This pastoral response can be offered by any teacher or guidance counsellor. However, the school chaplain will bring an added faith dimension to help the pupil find meaning in his/her suffering and pain as well as in his/her celebrations.

I believe that there are two crucial qualities that pastoral agents offer young people: The first is the ability to be present and to accompany someone. The second is the ability to affirm young people. Being present means making one's self available to others, perceptiveness, listening and relating in the here and now all of which can be inhibited by the business and daily pressures of school life. Affirmation includes unconditional valuing of others, love, articulation, forgiveness and hope. As 'being present' and 'affirmation' are the keystones of any pastoral response to young people with emotional problems I will now spend some time exploring these two aspects of pastoral care.

Being Present

Being present involves the following four qualities or virtues:

Being Available: To be present to adolescents begins with making one's self available to them. For example, to make time to be with them and open to their changing needs and situations in life. Availability assumes that one is predisposed to enter into whatever situations may emerge at any given time. For teachers in schools this will include even the uncomfortable situations of conflict. Verbal battles between young people can be frequent and require the teacher's intervention to prevent an escalation into a physical confrontation. The willingness to make oneself available to adolescents in even the most confusing or anxiety-producing circumstances reveals to the young person that the chaplain or teacher cares enough for them to be there at the most critical of times.

Keenness of Perception: The willingness to be available to youth is complemented by a consistent sensitivity to their needs in any given situation. Perceptivity is the ability to piece together often from little fragments of information what is happening with an adolescent at a particular moment; it includes seeing as well as intuiting the needs of the other and then responding to those needs. For example a pupil may tell a teacher that they are feeling unwell and can't go to a P.E. class. The perceptive teacher will look for a pattern here and will be sensitive to any other reasons why the pupil may be unwilling to got to the class such as the possibility of bullying or not being able to afford the required gym kit.

Listening: Reflective, non-judgemental, supportive and attentive listening enables adolescents to be who they are, feel deeply understood and become connected with another in a trusting relationship. In offering pastoral care the skilled listener, the school chaplain or a class teacher will be able to set aside his or her own agenda and really tune-in to what the pupil is saying. This can be difficult for teachers who have so many curricular responsibilities and who are tied to a busy timetable. In fact, I would say that listening and perceptiveness depend on availability and this is often something that the school chaplain and other pastoral agents will have in abundance. In addition pastoral agents respect confidentiality. A crucial role for the chaplain is to prudently judge the level of appropriate disclosure to other staff so as to enhance their understanding of a pupil's behaviour.[4]

Relating: The former ways of being present to adolescents combine as a style of relating to them in which they may develop a healing relationship with another. Consistent, predictable and stable relationships have often been absent from these young people lives from primary care givers and therefore they especially need the establishment of such relationships. Setting clear behavioural limits and expectations with these adolescents enables them to predict and understand another as well as provides the boundaries to bounce off of (test intimacy) that are essential to their development. The risk of revealing oneself commitments, abilities, values, vulnerabilities – is also evident when honestly relating to adolescence. The chaplain, counsellor or teacher must carefully negotiate the tension between being real and yet not crossing any professional boundaries.

Affirmation

Young people need affirmation. Affirmation of the other implies a *'no strings attached'* relationship of *unconditional valuing* in which the other is valued as intrinsically good. The adolescent does not have to earn love in this dimension of affirmation. If that were the case, love would be reduced to simple cause-effect events and affirmation would mean a reward for doing the expected thing or proving one's self worthy. Unconditional valuing, however, means that God has already given young people worthiness by virtue of their humanity. People do not earn it or prove it. Of course, this is not to say that what adolescents do is of no concern. Certainly, there are more helpful ways of relating than others, and those constructive ways need to be encouraged and destructive ways discouraged. But affirmation insists, before one does anything, that as human beings we are valuable and lovable. Bernard often wears a T-shirt that reminds me of how needy he (and others) are for unconditional valuing and love. His T-shirt reads: 'Accept me for what I am – completely unacceptable.' How much he needs to experience the giftedness of unconditional valuing and love rather than the pain of rejection and unworthiness. Among other things, love is the uniting and harmonising force of affirmation. It enables one to reach out in caring service to another. Where fragmentation, confusion and sadness seemed to have taken over, love enters to cohere all things together.

Articulation: A banner I recently saw proclaimed: 'You may be the only Gospel someone ever reads'. In my work with adolescents, more often than not, I am the only Gospel they will initially read. I am a sign, a 'living reminder' of Jesus Christ and God's compassion in him. Therefore, it is essential that I not only recognise the God-given worth of the adolescents I work with, but articulate that recognition in ways that enable them to see their human beauty as well. Articulation involves translating into word and action the dynamic and redeeming power of God's unconditional valuing and loving of the world and one's place in relation to others and God. It means uncovering the beauty which one cannot see because it is hidden by suffering and pain. It means pointing out the face of God in the midst of one's suffering and pain. The school chaplain will articulate the Gospel to adolescents by simply acknowledging his/her own commitment to Jesus Christ and God's compassion in and through him, by encouraging and praising them not only when they deserve it, but also when they need it, and by expressing appreciation for their presence and relationship. Of course, articulation is not a quick technique to exercise power over adolescents, something they would easily suspect anyway, nor is it an easy gimmick in *'Ten Ways to Win Friends'*, rather, it is the honest and humble communication of presenting what is already given as a gift and simply begs open recognition. Sometimes the school chaplain fulfils this through leading prayer and articulating the needs of the school community.

Forgiveness: So often in our competitive society we expect to receive from others only what we produce ourselves. This utilitarian attitude also spills over into our relationships with others and therefore when we violate or hurt another person the least we can expect is a light punishment. Adolescents need to experience in their own relationships the reality of forgiveness. They often act in ways that elicit punishment when they are feeling guilty about acting harshly towards another. The expectation of punishment blocks them moving beyond an act they can no longer undo except by having someone else hurt them in return. Forgiveness is the possibility of restoring a hurt relationship without further pain or punishment. It is the glad acceptances of another's regret and welcoming acceptance of another's limitations, all the time knowing that the hurt s/he inflicted could easily have been done by one's self. Forgiveness is not cheap grace. It does not mean the justification of sin without the justification of the sinner. It does not exclude preliminary judgments about morality, yet leaves final judgement in the hands of God. Forgiveness enables one to be fully responsible for hurtful actions by the common recognition of such actions and open the way for healing by providing another the free space to show guilt and regret, yet without fear of further hurt. Adolescents often expect more from themselves then do others and harshly treat themselves when they fail to fulfil often rigid expectations. Forgiveness is the way out of compulsive and self-defeating expectations. It recognises the sinful and limited condition that we all share and encourages us to move beyond it. Forgiveness must be the ultimate aim of any school's discipline approach if adolescents are to learn that not everything has to have its match, an eye for an eye, and so on.

Challenges in the Pastoral Care of Emotional Disturbed Adolescents
There are particular challenges which one encounters in a school setting with emotionally disturbed adolescents, tensions which often get in the way of manifesting a pastoral approach. While those who work with young people who are emotionally disturbed or who have special needs will normally have a huge commitment to this type of work and the energy to match their commitment, there are costs involved in sharing the journey of these young people. One of the costs of caring for disturbed adolescents is what psychiatrist Melvin Lewis and psychologist Thomas E. Brown call the *regressive pull*.[5] This is where seriously disturbed adolescents can tend to make others who work closely with them feel a movement towards chaotic and archaic levels of functioning characterised by anxiety in relation to a child who has lost control, rescue fantasies or unrealistic expectations for success and healing alternating with despair, and hostility in the form of punishment. It is not clear whether such adolescents intentionally cause the regressive pull as an attempt to make others close to them feel impotent and themselves omnipotent or whether it results from simply being in their presence. What is clear, is that those who work closely with adolescents with emotional problems need to be supported by their colleagues and employers. One form of support is to have a weekly or monthly de-briefing session in which chaplains, teachers and carers can discuss their experiences and focus on a common approach.

The fact that these adolescents dramatise their conflicts in relation to the adults who work with them often makes relating to them extremely frustrating and emotionally draining, even with the type of staff support outlined above. The emotional intensity of continual conflict for teachers in a school with a high number of emotionally disturbed adolescents and the great neediness of these young people can set one up for emotional burn-out if efforts for personal solitude, staff communication and even prayer are not maintained. I learned quickly that compassion and pastoral care couldn't become a competition between my needs and those of the adolescent. All those who work with young people with this type of special need require an approach that recognises the importance of everyone's needs and seeks to meet them. A failure to respond to personal needs can result in them getting in the way of offering pastoral care to those in our care.

Conclusion
For many reasons, not least of all the change in family life, more young people are presenting in our schools with emotional needs. Some of these emotional needs will be short lived and can be addressed by a caring teacher who takes time out to listen. Others will need more ongoing support from the chaplain,

counsellor or psychologist. Fundamental to any pastoral approach that seeks to meet the needs of these young people is a Christian concern for the person in which the totality of the pupil is recognised. Finally, those who engage in the pastoral care of young people with emotional needs will need to find a healthy mechanism to meet their own needs either through peer support from other teachers and chaplains or through a form of supervision.

Notes

1. Bihehler, R. F., Snowman, *Psychology Applied to Teaching* (Boston: Houghton Mifflin, 1993), p. 194.
2. Ysseldyke, J., Algozzine, R., *Introduction to Special Education* (Boston: Houghton Mifflin, 1990), pp. 175-176.
3. Levine, D. U., Havighurst, A.J., *Society and Education* (Boston: Allyn and Bacon, 1992).
4. Norman, J., *Pastoral Care in Second Level Schools: The Chaplain, A Research Report* (Dublin: Mater Dei Institute of Education, Dublin City University, 2002).
5. Lewis, M., Brown, T.E., 'Psychotherapy in the Residential Treatment of the Borderline Child' in *Child Psychiatry and Human Development,* (Cambridge: Harvard University, 1979).

An Introduction to Counselling in Schools

Noreen Sweeney

Introduction

The purpose of this chapter is to explore some of the areas and issues common to all counselling work done with adolescents. It is hoped to give a flavour of, and some exposure, to the world of counselling adolescents. It provides an overview of what counselling is, the adolescent stage of development, adolescent issues, counselling approaches for working with adolescents, the practice of counselling adolescents, crisis counselling, counselling skills, the spiritual dimension, care of the counsellor, personal and professional characteristics of the counsellor and supervision.

The school chaplain uses counselling skills in her/his work with young people and normally the chaplain has been professionally trained in the use of counselling skills. The counselling aspect of the chaplain's role in schools ranks the highest of all their activities.[1] Many of the issues presented by the student in a session with a chaplain will be similar to those presented to another trained counsellor. However, the chaplain brings an extra faith dimension to the encounter with the student. The nature of the chaplain's helping role in terms of counselling can be termed 'pastoral counselling'. This is a supportive role for adolescents experiencing problems in their life. While the chaplain is a user of counselling skills, he/she is not normally a professionally qualified counsellor, yet her/his work as pastoral counsellor is expected to be as appropriately professional and ethical as that of the professional counsellor. The pastoral counsellor works in a more informal setting to that of a counsellor and refers clients who have deep-seated issues to the professional counsellor. The pastoral counsellor uses counselling skills and strategies that help meet the student's needs. In this chapter the term counsellor refers to all professionals who use counselling skills in working with adolescents including the school chaplain.

Counselling is a contracted relationship between the counsellor and the client where they agree to meet for a set number of sessions. It is a supportive relationship that enables clients to explore issues freely, to understand themselves more fully and to take whatever action that is necessary if they wish to change their problem situation. Responsibility for change rests with the client. The counsellor does not give advice or tell the client what to do.

The Adolescent Stage of Development

In the school setting the chaplain works with adolescents. During their time in second level schooling the young person progresses from childhood to adulthood and from dependency to independence and autonomy. A successful conclusion to this stage of human development requires a parent or carer to recognise, allow and facilitate the adolescent to move out of the dependent role of a child in the family towards independence, autonomy and maturity. Children introject the social and moral values and ways of behaving of their families. Adolescents start to question this imposed value system and it becomes important to them to be in line with their peers rather than be in line with their parents. They search for an identity and a value system of their own. Many adolescents wish to, and need to, belong to a peer group with some level of common ideology and group identity. This need is related to the need for security and acceptability. Adolescents need the support of peer groups at this time of uncertainty and change.

During adolescence young people undergo rapid and extreme biological, physiological and social change. It is a period filled with anxiety for many adolescents. There is a noticeable difference in the rate of growth and sexual development in any group of adolescents. Sexual awareness and interest is high in this stage of the young person's life. Anxiety about their appearance can become obsessional for some. They are also making value judgements about their sexual behaviour. In early adolescence young people tend to form close relationships with friends of the same sex because they feel secure with them.[2] This is also part of their process of moving away from their parents and family.[3] By late adolescence there is a move towards heterosexual relationships for most young people. Some young people discover their sexual orientation at this stage with regard to homosexuality.

During adolescence the rise in sexual hormones may influence the adolescent's emotional state. Hormones act in conjunction with the other major changes that are happening in the young person such as social relationships, changes in beliefs and attitudes and changes in self-perception.[4] At this stage of development cognitive changes are also occurring. The adolescent develops a capacity for abstract thinking, finds out how to think about relationship issues, discusses new ways of processing information and learns to think creatively and question critically.

Adolescents are egocentric, a trait that develops more fully in mid to late adolescence. They feel everyone is watching them as though they were on stage. They may have the idea that they are unique and this makes it difficult for them to believe that another is capable of understanding them or how they are feeling. This has important implications for counsellors working with them. They learn to think critically about interpersonal issues and about other people. Learning to make sense of things helps them to make decisions about how to interact with others.

The most important task for the adolescent is the formation of a personal identity that in turn leads to effective psychological functioning. The process of socialisation is a balance between individuation and the formation of personal identity on the one hand and integration with society on the other.[5] Unless this balance is achieved there are likely to be personal crises for the young person that may result in the need for counselling or other professional help.

The adolescent stage of development is characterised by emotional reactivity and a high intensity of emotional response. A disruptive emotion of early adolescence is shame and adolescents tend to develop strong defence mechanisms like denial, projection and regression to cope with situations and to interact with others. These are areas that counsellors may have to work with in the school context.

Society's expectations pose a challenge for adolescents. Some will find the challenges too much and feel alienated from society because they cannot meet those expectations. Those who feel overwhelmed by society's expectations may revert to antisocial behaviour. This has implications for counsellors and others in the helping professions.

The family is one of the most effective vehicles for promoting values in adolescence, helping adolescents to be successful in school and to have confidence in peer relationships. Steinberg and Steinberg found that the common link between successful adolescents is that they generally have positive relationships with their parents. So an important challenge for the adolescent is to maintain positive relationships with their parents while achieving their developmental goal of separation and detachment from their parents, which is hard to achieve.[6] Research discussed in *USA Today* shows that boys spend less time with their families than girls and girls are more likely to talk about personal issues with parents than boys.[7] Adolescents are more likely to talk when it suits them and when they can take the lead. These traits of adolescents have great significance for counsellors.

Adolescent spirituality is often demonstrated through the adolescent's search for meaning in life's daily experiences. Fowler says that in early adolescence the emphasis is on symbolism rather than knowing factual truth whereas in later adolescence, personal experiences, symbols and rituals can play a major role in the development of spiritual beliefs for the adolescent.[8]

When an adolescent is unable to negotiate and confront a developmental challenge successfully there are likely to be unhelpful psychological, emotional and behavioural consequences. Counselling can be useful in helping the adolescent find new ways to proceed adaptively along the required developmental journey.

Adolescent Issues
Unresolved childhood issues impact on the adolescent. Early attachment problems have an effect on the adolescent's later experiences and influences how he/she deals with stressful situations. Unsatisfactory attachments during childhood have been linked with later substance abuse,[9] eating disorders,[10] early sexual activity and high-risk sexual behaviour[11] and poor self-image[12] in adolescents. Counsellors need to recognise that some maladaptive behaviours in adolescence may be partly the result of poor attachment relationships with primary figures during childhood.

As has been referred to elsewhere in this book unhelpful parenting has a major influence over child and adolescent development and irresponsible parenting may result in antisocial and aggressive behaviours being passed down within a family. Neglect can result in behaviour problems, poor school attendance, weak academic grades and generally low achievement. Children who have been neglected can carry into adolescence angry feelings towards the neglectful carers and are likely to have issues around personal safety, trust, fairness and responsibility.

Adolescents who experience emotional abuse as children often present in counselling with behaviour problems. Children and adolescents exposed to physical abuse may develop symptoms similar to those of post-traumatic stress disorder and many have activity profiles similar to those of children diagnosed with attention deficit hyper-activity disorder also referred to as ADHD.[13]

Children who have been physically abused and continue to be abused may express their feelings by acting out in antisocial ways with high aggression or may internalise their feelings with the consequent development of depression or suicide ideation. Sexual abuse can often be found in the histories of young people with severe mental health disturbances. For children who experience loss the grieving process may extend into adolescence and influence their emotions and behaviours.

It is important for adolescents to work through the grieving process so that their adolescent journey is not affected by grief. Adolescents who suffer the loss of a parent by death report greater shock, disbelief and a greater sense of loss than that experienced by adults. They also reported more anger at the deceased, sleep disturbances, dream activity and irritability than adults.[14] When counselling adolescents it is necessary to examine the impact of early childhood experiences on their ability to negotiate the developmental tasks of adolescence.

Factors such as the family's style of functioning, parenting style, parental relationship, separation and divorce, an alcoholic parent, domestic violence and cultural issues have the potential to cause stress for the adolescent. It is the adolescent's personal responses to the environment that will finally determine the extent of her/his success.

Theoretical Approaches to Counselling Adolescents

Counselling adolescents is different from counselling adults. Counsellors need to tailor their counselling approaches to engage the adolescent directly and actively and to use strategies which will specifically address their needs in a manner that is acceptable to them. The adolescent's internal emotional and psychological needs are best addressed through individual counselling. Family therapy primarily addresses interpersonal relationship issues of adolescents within the family.

The counsellor uses an approach to counselling which helps meet the adolescent's needs as well as a range of counselling skills and strategies.

The *Person Centred Approach* based on the work of Carl Rogers lends itself well to working with adolescents, who, through their experience of the core conditions of empathy, positive regard and congruence offered by the counsellor, are better able to mature and develop. The emphasis here is on the relationship between the counsellor and the client. The counsellor enters the subjective world of the client and communicates that understanding (empathy) to the client. This allows the client to become more open and honest. Feeling safe in the relationship as a result of warmth and caring (unconditional positive regard) of the counsellor, the client reflects this greater openness in deeper levels of self-disclosure. Rogers says that empathy is a healing agent in itself as the client feels that there is at least one other human being who has some understanding of her/his problem.[15] As the counsellor remains congruent the client becomes congruent. On counselling adolescents, intense raw emotions can surface and the challenge for the counsellor is to be able to walk alongside the adolescent as they explore confusion, rebellion and failure. Holding clients in unconditional positive regard means being able to separate the person from the behaviours and this allows clients to confront themselves. The counsellor needs to note that congruence is distinct from self-disclosure, which is an inappropriate sharing of the counsellor's personal life. A counsellor's self-disclosure is a burden for all clients including adolescents.

The *Existential Approach* to counselling is pertinent to working with adolescents. This approach assumes that people need to find ways of making sense of life before they can make sense of their problems. Existential counselling is an exploration of the adolescent's being in the world and how they relate to and understand that world. This approach relies on a questioning attitude to the way one lives life, as well as an acceptance of the need to explore one's relationship to the world. This approach is very appropriate to the adolescent stage of life where there is a search for meaning. The adolescent is helped to explore their 'world' that consists of the natural world, the public world, the private world and the ideal world. The counselling process is an examination of all these interconnected worlds.[16] Meaning helps us to relieve and deal with anxiety that comes from facing a world that does not have a fixed and comforting structure. Meaning gives a framework to the way we live life and helps us develop values that augment our sense of meaning. In a world where people find meaning through striving, creating and achieving, there is no time to contemplate the purpose of life. There is no time to be, it is all about doing. Young people have to come to terms with who they are and how they want to live life as pressure comes from all sides to achieve and succeed. Finding meaning allows the adolescent to engage with life rather than with meaninglessness.

Developed by Albert Eilis, *Rational Emotive Behaviour Therapy* is useful when counselling adolescents. The basic assumption of this approach is that people contribute to their own psychological problems as well as specific symptoms by the way they interpret events and situations in life. A re-organisation of one's self-statements will result in a corresponding re-organisation of one's behaviour. The focus in sessions is to help clients change their cognitions which in turn produces changes in affect and behaviour. Through the therapeutic process clients learn skills that help them identify and dispute irrational beliefs that have been learned and self-constructed. Focus of work is on thinking and acting rather than on feelings. The client learns the need to accept her/himself despite imperfections and stop blaming others. *'Shoulds'* and *'oughts'* are replaced by preferences like *'I choose to'*. Unrealistic beliefs create dysfunctional behaviours.

Egan's *Three Stage Helping Model* is a problem-focused way of working with clients.[17] The model or framework breaks down the counselling process into three stages. In the first stage, the client is encouraged to explore her/his situation and identify problem areas. In stage two the adolescent explores what life might be like if some of the issues could be resolved and sets goals. In stage three the adolescent is encouraged to develop action plans and strategies for achieving the goals set in stage two.

In working with adolescents the counsellor can use a particular approach or use an integrative approach depending on the adolescent's needs. I suggest the *Theory and Practice of Counselling and Psychotherapy* by Gerald Corey, for a detailed study of the above and of other approaches or theories.[18]

The Practice of Counselling Adolescents

The counselling environment should be a place of safety, security, dependability and consistency. A basic requirement of any counselling work is a room that is both private and free from interruptions. In a school environment, this means somewhere discreet away from the noise of the main thoroughfare. The counselling room should be reasonably sound proof so that noises and voices in the corridor will not interrupt the counselling work. The room should be free of distractions. For the protection and safety of all, it is advisable to have a door with a glass panel so that the counsellor can sit in the room where he/she can be seen from outside. This is normal practice for school chaplains.

The process of putting in place the counselling contract with an adolescent is important, but can also have its difficulties. The counsellor takes the time to present the contract clearly while ensuring that the adolescent is a willing and equal partner. Adolescents need to be told that the counsellor does not provide solutions but will help them explore issues and that they will, in turn, find their own solutions. The counsellor will inform them that they have choice around what they want to bring to the session and that they have choice as to how many sessions they want. This will set the tone for the rest of the counselling work. It is good to hear why the adolescent has come for counselling and if they are there on a voluntary or involuntary basis. If they are there on an involuntary basis it would be important to explore how they feel about being 'sent', how they are now that they have arrived and how they would like to use the time.

The counsellor needs to give the adolescent time to understand what is on offer and what is expected of them in the counselling relationship. The freer the adolescent is to say no to counselling without risk of criticism the more likely they are to stay and use the time well. Confidentiality and its exceptions also need to be explained to the adolescent.

Keeping and making appointments is more of an issue with adolescents than other client groups. Some chaplains have a drop-in service and others have a mixture of appointments for a number of sessions and also a drop-in service. A drop in provides a taste of what it is like to talk about a problem and allows adolescents to be seen in an emergency or crisis. They can discuss their problems and express feelings and look at options. Ongoing support can be negotiated for a number of sessions. Some adolescents do not like open-ended contracts so they can be offered a contract of a set number of sessions including a review session. Many adolescents do not turn up consistently for sessions and it is an area to be addressed by the counsellor as absenteeism can be used to express their doubts or concerns about counselling.

Adolescents feel that power in society rests with older people so it is difficult for them to perceive that they will be listened to and that their beliefs, ideas, feelings and opinions will be accepted by an adult including the counsellor. Counsellors and other people in the helping profession are often handicapped by the adolescent's low expectation of any interaction with people from a different age group. It is only by experiencing the counselling relationship that the adolescent will learn to trust and open up. For some this will be a very slow process. Some will try to shock and challenge the counsellor.

In working with adolescents many will act out within the counselling relationship the challenging and confronting behaviour that is a part of growing up and yet is experienced as negative by so many of the adults with whom adolescents come into contact.[19] Counsellors need to be aware of this and of their own responses to it. In working with adolescents it is vital to be responsive rather than reactive. This is asking a lot of the counsellor but supervision plays a very important role here in helping the counsellor separate the personal from the professional and ensuring that an effective service can be provided to the adolescent. Many adolescents respond by going into themselves and by being silent so the counsellor needs to be comfortable with silence, as out of it new awareness can emerge. Some adolescents are withdrawn in the counselling situation because they feel out of their depth in the sphere of feelings. They do not feel good about talking about or expressing feelings. Some feel that their feelings will not be believed or valued so it is only be allowing them space and allowing trust to build that a therapeutic relationship can be developed. For others silence is the only way of being in control in the world. For a few it is a way of expressing resentment and aggression.

Another kind of challenge presented by adolescents is to challenge the counsellor and see her/him as not on their side. The counsellor needs to separate the person and the behaviour, and to challenge the behaviour and not the person's being. Counsellors of adolescents' need to avoid acting in a parental way with their clients. Being aware and having an understanding of the cultural and social context of the adolescent is essential for the counsellor. The pressure to conform to peer group norms is great for the adolescent so an appreciation of these issues is essential for the counsellor.

Young people live in the moment. What is a crisis today is soon forgotten about. Counsellors need to be able to understand and tolerate how adolescents can be notorious for missing appointments and failing to get in touch. Much of the work done with the adolescent is short term, often crisis intervention work so the counsellor needs to stand back and trust the process and the adolescents right to choose when they will address their issues.

Crisis Counselling

Crisis situations are presented to the counsellor, particularly chaplains, in the school context on a regular basis. A stressful event can become a crisis depending on the response of the individual. Stressful events can be divided into two categories.[20] Category one pertains to developmental changes in a person's life. The transition from one stage to another can cause emotional uncertainty, bringing the need for change. The second category of events that can precipitate a crisis consists of probable life events for us all, including bereavement, illness, examination failures, relationship difficulties and other less probable events like accidents and assault. The first category can be a more ongoing type of difficulty and will need to be dealt with over a period of weeks or months. The second category is characterised by suddenness and urgency within the experience. No two people will react to any of these events in the same way. What is manageable change for one person may result in a crisis for another. The crisis lies in the person's perception of and reaction to the event rather than the event itself. When the two categories of events coincide within a person's life, the possibility of crisis reaction increases.

The important thing for the counsellor to do in a crisis is to be calm. By absorbing the panic and grounding the distress, the counsellor can be a calming presence in the midst of chaos. This calmness will help reduce the impact of the crisis and make possible the start of a response to the crisis. A crisis cannot be postponed. It is present now and expects a response now. The counsellor needs to attend to the physical response of the person in terms of a relaxation exercise and/or a drink of water. Next the counsellor's focus is directed on the immediate crisis and the feelings of the person. The discussion will give an indication of what triggered the crisis. All counselling skills are needed to explore the client's perception of the event. The helper next focuses on the support system that may be helpful to the person. Throughout the crisis the client has lost control of his ability to cope with what is going on around and within her/him. If the counsellor can entertain and convey hope for the client then that can enable the client to entertain hope for her/himself. Self-awareness of the counsellor is vital with crisis work where there is a more intense state of distress in the client. There is a need to be mindful that in a crisis there is neither a simple correct answer nor a perfect solution. While aware of their own limitations, counsellors can help as much as is in their power, knowing that they may be the only person available right now. Medical expertise may also be available to the counsellor.

The quality of the counselling relationship is critical in influencing outcomes and client satisfaction. For a successful outcome it is desirable that the following qualities be present: an authentic adolescent–counsellor relationship, the presence of warmth and empathy, understanding and acceptance on the counsellor's part. These qualities are achieved by the way the counsellor and adolescent work together. Where a relationship has difficulties, the counsellor can use supervision to identify reasons and to resolve personal issues around the relationship. The world of the adolescent is uncertain so in order to help the adolescent, the counsellor needs to be congruent, open, honest, sincere and respectful. The presence of these qualities helps create an authentic relationship.

Adolescents strive for acceptance in the world outside the family and believe that no one understands them. The counsellor has to be able to convey to adolescents the message that they are heard and understood and that they are accepted as persons regardless of their behaviour. The presence of empathy and warmth allows the adolescent appreciate that the counsellor is working to understand their world.

Adolescents are generally restless persons who need to be actively engaged. They can quickly become bored and impatient so the counselling relationship needs to be dynamic. The counsellor needs to use skills and strategies in response to the adolescent's immediate needs, as they are identified at any point of time during the session. The counsellor should be active, lively, spontaneous, creative and flexible. It means being able to respond quickly and actively so that opportunities are not lost.

Use of Counselling Skills

The counsellor by making use of a wide range of counselling skills can engage the curiosity and interest of the adolescent. Skills are used either in direct responses to the needs of the counselling process or in conjunction with any of the strategies and approaches already discussed. The list of skills used includes attending, active listening, reflecting back content and feelings, giving feedback, questioning, summarising and challenging.

Observation is an ongoing activity. Being aware that external presentation does not always match what is happening internally is vital. The counsellor in accepting what is presented is creating trust and the adolescent will feel safe in showing what is behind their facade. The counsellor also observes general appearance, behaviour, feelings, speech and language throughout the work.

The skill of *attending* refers to the ways in which the counsellor can be with a person both physically and psychologically. It means paying attention to the person. It tells the other person that one is in a position to listen carefully to her/his concerns. Attending includes facial expression, eye contact, gaze, gestures, posture, physical proximity and time.

Listening means listening actively, accurately and for meaning. It involves listening to the client's experiences, behaviours, feelings, points of view, the context of their story, to what is not being said and observing non-verbal behaviour. It is an activity that requires work. Good listening can comfort, ease suffering, heal psychological wounds, act as a catalyst for moving forward and empower the adolescent being listened to. Effective listeners put the talker at ease, limit their own talking, are attentive, do not interrupt, get a sense of the other person's world and are aware of their own biases. Good listening is essential to the counselling process.

Reflection of content and feelings are skills identified by Carl Rogers as being essential to the counselling process.[21] They let the client know that the counsellor is trying to understand them. The counsellor does not repeat what the client has said but picks out the most important information and using her/his own words feeds this back to the client.

The counsellor matches the adolescent's language. Adolescents will often talk metaphorically. The metaphor might by used to describe feelings and where the adolescent uses a metaphor it is helpful if the counsellor uses it too. *Feedback* includes giving compliments when it is wise to do so and affirmations to reinforce a personal truth that has been described by the adolescent and shared with the counsellor.

Apart from using reflection to feed back information, the counsellor can give feed back through affirmations, cheer leading, normalising, reframing and through statements. *Cheer leading* is a skill used in solution-focused therapy.[22] It uses questions and statements to encourage the adolescent to continue describing the changing process, for example – 'How did you do that?', 'That must have been difficult to do'. This kind of response enables the adolescent to take responsibility for and feel good in the success of achieving change.

Normalising is helpful when working with adolescents who are experiencing high levels of feelings which are new to them. Normalising is useful in cases where unacceptable responses and behaviours are not minimised. *Reframing* is particularly useful when working with adolescents. It is useful to help the person see the bigger picture, and the adolescent is invited to see their picture as part of the bigger picture. Their picture should be incorporated into the bigger picture.

Probing is another skill which makes use of a variety of questions to get clarity and bring focus to the counselling process. Questioning needs to be used sparingly when counselling adolescents as they can be questioned frequently by their parents for information. It is a good idea therefore to limit the number of questions asked and instead make use of other counselling skills which are more likely to encourage the adolescent to open up freely. Open questions are useful in all kinds of counselling. Use questions to heighten the adolescent's awareness, e.g. 'What are you feeling right now?' or 'What is happening inside you right now?'

Circular *questioning* is a non-threatening way of getting information from an adolescent. Instead of asking the adolescent directly how he/she feels, the counsellor could ask how some one else in the family is feeling like 'I wonder what your brother thinks or feels when your parents argue?' Often having answered the circular question the adolescent will continue to talk about how he/she thinks, feels and behaves because they want to make it clear whether he/she agrees or disagrees with the person mentioned in the circular question.

Choice questions help with the exploration of choices and consequences and prepare the person for future situations, for example, 'What would have been a better choice?' 'What would you like to do now?' Guru question allows the adolescent to stand aside and give her/himself some advice, for example, 'Imagine for a minute you were a guru and you could give advice to someone like you, what advice would you give him or her?' Miracle questions allows the adolescent to use their imagination to explore what would be different if their situation changed for the better, for example, 'If the problem was solved miraculously, what would life be like?'

Summarising involves feeding back in the counsellor's own words a brief and concise summary of what the client has said. It lets the client know that the counsellor has heard and understood and also helps the client to clarify and identify what is most important.

Challenging should be done in a way that invites the adolescent to question what they have said, what they are doing or what they believe. Adolescents are usually direct in challenging each other in peer relationships so the counsellor can be direct in a non-threatening way.

The Spiritual Dimension in Counselling

Spirituality is a personal and subjective concept. Bergin is one of many researchers who believe being open to spiritual/religious values will result in a change in the focus of treatment towards more general lifestyle changes.[23] Spirituality is a component of mental health and its inclusion in counselling practice makes the therapeutic process more effective.[24] Spirituality should be addressed if it is a concern for the client. It can be a force that can help the person make sense of the universe and find reasons for living. Spirituality can be a source of healing and give strength in times of crisis and it can help the adolescent ponder on the questions 'Who am I' and 'What is the purpose and meaning of my life?' School chaplains through their professional training and personal faith commitment are particularly well suited to include this dimension in the counselling they offer.

Care of the Counsellor

For many counsellors the danger of what is referred to as 'burnout' is a reality. While counsellors cannot always control stressful events they can control how they interpret and react to them. There is a price to pay for always being available as counsellor and for assuming that one is able to control the lives and destinies of others.[25] The counsellor can develop a strategy for keeping her/himself healthy personally and professionally. The strategy may consider the following: evaluating goals and expectations and checking to see if they are realistic; having other interests besides work; bringing variety to one's work; monitoring the impact of stress on the job; paying attention to ones health, exercise programmes, diet, meditation and relaxation; developing some friendships that are characterised by a mutuality of giving and receiving; learning to ask for what one wants, knowing that one may not always get it; learning to work for self-confirmation as opposed to looking externally for validation; avoiding taking on burdens that are the responsibility of others; keeping up to date in the counselling area; rearranging work schedules to reduce stress; learning to know one's limits with others; engaging in hobbies that bring pleasure; arranging time of spiritual growth; and seeking personal therapy as an avenue to personal development. Two useful questions for the counsellor to ask regularly are, 'What do I have to offer others who are struggling with their life?' and 'Am I doing in my own life what I would want others to do in theirs'.

Personal Qualities of Effective Counsellors

The willingness to struggle to move to being a more therapeutic counsellor is crucial. The list of qualities that follow is intended to stimulate the counsellor to examine her/his ideas of what kind of person can make a difference in the lives of others.[26] Effective counsellors know who they are and what they are capable of and have a sense of identity. They appreciate and respect themselves. They accept their own power and allow others to feel powerful with them. They are willing to leave the security of the known if they are not happy with what they have and are open to change. They are sincere and honest. They commit to living fully rather than settling for mere existence. They are willing to learn from their mistakes. They live in the now and are able to be present with others in the now. They value others and have an interest in the welfare of others. They are able to keep healthy boundaries, they know when to say no and are able to keep a balance in their life. They have a sense of humour.

Professional Qualities of the Ideal Counsellor

Effective counsellors recognise that the client is the most important instrument in the counselling process. They are willing to use existing skills and acquire new ones. They recognise that their learning is ongoing. They are able to enter the world of the client and stay with their frame of reference. They do not impose on clients their view of reality. The client's needs come first. They are able to deal with a wide range of client feelings, thoughts, behaviours and experiences. They are flexible in applying strategies in the counselling process. They get support through adequate supervision and personal therapy. They suspend judgements and values during the counselling process. They take the risk of being self- aware. They constantly strive to be reflective practitioners. They keep professional boundaries and work in an ethical way. The ideal counsellor is aware of the importance of working values which include the following: do no harm, do not take sides, become competent and committed, keep the clients agenda in focus, value the client, value client empowerment, do not over emphasise the role of the counsellor, avoid defensiveness, and challenge one's own blind spots.

Counselling Supervision

Supervision is considered essential for all who counsel adolescents. Inskipp and Proctor define supervision as a working alliance between a supervisor and supervisee in which the later presents an account of her/his work, reflects on it and receives feedback so as to learn to work more effectively with clients.[27] The purpose of supervision is to learn and to enable the supervisee to grow in ethical competence, confidence, compassion and creativity and therefore give the best possible service to clients. Supervision facilitates the personal and professional development of the counsellor. Supervision provides a personal support system for the counsellor whose work is confidential. Given the nature of the problems presented in the counselling context, the counsellor can become over involved. So supervision is the forum where the counsellor can offload and deal with the issues and feelings arising from the work. Working with adolescents can be anxiety provoking. Adolescents are at a vulnerable life stage where difficulties can become crises. Counsellors need help in containing their own anxieties so that they can contain those of adolescents whom they counsel. Ethical issues around the work can be explored in supervision. Good supervision and management reduces the risk of the development of unprofessional relationships. Supervision is an arena where counsellors can continue to learn from reflecting on their practice. The supervisor facilitates reflection on the work.

Group supervision provides insight gained from other members and peer support. One of the advantages of group supervision is that other counsellors' cases can raise issues in one's own practice that might otherwise remain unrecognised. Supervision generates support among counsellors. The volume of supervision should be in proportion to the volume of counselling work undertaken. Group supervision is more cost-effective than one-to-one supervision.

Conclusion

To conclude, those who are engaged in counselling such as the school chaplain need to keep themselves skilled by attending counselling workshops and undertaking further training. Ideally, chaplains are members of the School Chaplains' Association, who abide by its code of ethics and receive regular supervision. The world of counselling is one where the counsellor is always learning. While learning can be gained from reading and training, the most effective learning of all comes from the experience of facilitating the counselling process. The experience of the counselling process is our greatest teacher as counsellors and we learn so much from it through our own reflection and the use of supervision.

Notes

1. Norman, J., *Pastoral Care in Second-Level Schools: The Chaplain, A Research Report* (Dublin: Mater Dei Institute of Education, Dublin City University, 2002).

2. Blos, P., *The Adolescent Passage: Deevlopment* Issue (New York: International University Press, 1979).

3. Geldard, K., Geldard, D., *Counselling Adolescents* (London: Sage, 1999).

4. *Ibid.*

5. Adams, G.R., Marshall, S.K. 'A Developmental Social Psychology of Identity: Understanding The Person-in-Context' in *Journal of Adolescence*, 19 (New York: Elsevier, 1996), pp. 429-42.

6. Steinberg, L., Steinberg, W., *Crossing Paths: How Your Child's Adolescence Triggers Your Own Crisis* (New York: Simon and Schuster, 1994).

7. *USA Today*, Vol. 127, no. 2622, (1997), p. 8 (2).

8. Fowler, J., *Stages of Faith* (Melbourne: Dove, 1981).

9. Gerevich, J., Bacskai, E., 'Protective and Risk Predictors in the Development of Drug Abuse' in *Journal of Drug Education, 26* (Amitville, New York: Baywood, 1996), pp. 25-38; Burge, D., Hammen, C., Davilla, J., Daley, S., 'Attachment Cognitions and College and Work Functioning Two years Later in Adolescent Women' in *Journal of Youth and Adolescence, 26* (New York: Klewur, 1997).

10. Burge, D., Hammen, C., Davilla, J., Daley, S., 'Attachment Cognitions and College and Work Functioning Two Years Later in Adolescent Women' in *Journal of Youth and Adolescence, 26* (New York: Klewur, 1997); Salzman, J., 'Ambivalent Attachment in Female Adolescents: Association with Affective Instability and Eating Disorders' in *International Journal of Eating Disorders,* 21(London: Wiley, 1997), pp. 251-9.

11. Smith, C., 'Factors Associated With Early Sexual Activity Among Urban Adolescents' in *Social Work Journal,* 42 (1997), pp. 334-46.

12. O 'Koon, J., 'Attachment to Parents and Peers in Adolescence and their Relationship with Self Image' in *Journal of Adolescence, 32* (New York: Elsevier, 1997), pp. 471-82.

13. Glod, C., Teicher, M., 'Relationship Between Early Abuse, Post-Traumatic Stress Disorder and Activity Levels in Pre-Pubertal Children' in *American Academy of Child and Adolescent Psychiatry, 34* (Washington D.C.: 1996), pp. 1384-93.

14. Meshot, C., Leitner, L., 'Adolescent Mourning and Parental Death' in *Amiga Journal of Death and Dying, 26* (1993), pp. 287-99.

15. Rogers, C.R., 'Rogers, Kohut and Ericson: A Personal Perspective on Some Similarities and Differences' in *Person Centred Review,* 1 (Boston: 1986), pp. 125-140.

16. Geldard, K., Geldard, D., *Counselling Adolescents* (London: Sage, 1999).

17. Egan, G., *The Skilled Helper* (Pacific Grove, CA: Brooks-Cole/Wadsworth, 2002).

18. Corey, G., *Theory and practice of Counselling and Psychotherapy* (Pacific Grove, CA: Brook–Cole/Wadsworth, 2001).

19. Mabey, J., Sorensen, B., *Counselling for Young People* (Buckingham: Open University Press, 1995).

20. O'Farrell, U., *First Steps in Counselling* (Dublin: Veritas, 1993).

21. Rogers, C.R., *Client Centred Therapy: Its Current Practice, Implications and Theory* (Boston: Houghton-Mifflin, 1965).

22. Walter, J., Peller, J., *Becoming Solution-Focused in Brief Therapy* (New York: Brunner/Mazel, 1992).

23. Bergin, A.E., 'Values and Religious Issues in Psychotherapy and Mental Health' in *American Psychologist,* 46 (Washington D.C.: American Psychologists Association, 1991), pp. 394-403.

24. Corey, G., *Theory and Practice of Counselling and Psychotherapy, 6th edn* (Pacific Grove, California: Brook-Cole/Wadsworth, 2001).

25. *Ibid.*

26. *Ibid.*

27. Inskipp, F., Proctor, B., *Making the Most of Supervision, Part I* (Twickenham, Middlesex: Cascade Publications, 1993).

A Critical Incident in the School Community

How the Chaplain can make an Effective Response

Seán O'Driscoll

Introduction

Bí ullamh is the well-known motto in Scouting: *Be ready*. When it comes to a crisis in the school community this motto also holds true. It is important to have a plan in place and have a step-by-step process to follow. It is quiet normal when a tragedy occurs for those affected to be in a state of shock and this can impede action. In the school community it is imperative that someone stays level headed and knows the best practice in enabling a traumatised community come to terms with what has happened.

Often the chaplain will be the one the principal and other staff turn to because the chaplain is perceived as the one who deals with the everyday mini crises in the school as well as having the professional training to deal with crisis.

The chaplain's ministry is to reach out as a caregiver, particularly to those experiencing deep spiritual pain. Through the medium of *pastoral relatedness*[1] the chaplain is empowered to communicate the love and care of Christ at this crucial time.

The chaplain is well placed to be the initiator in setting up a school *Critical Incident Plan* in cooperation with other key staff. When tragedy strikes is not the time to put together a plan! This is an initiative that is best done in a clearly thought out logical way. I have worked with many schools in putting together their own Crisis Response/Critical Incident Plans and what I share here includes many of the insights I have gained in the process.

A Crisis or a Critical Incident?

It is important to distinguish between a crisis and critical incident,[2] so that we know what level of response to make. For the purpose of this document, a critical incident is one 'where a traumatic death occurs or is perceived', e.g. suicide, murder, major accident with multiple deaths and/or injuries. A crisis is 'a distressing event which can include death in natural circumstances' e.g. death following an illness. It is important to remember that the victims of any of these events, as well as those affected, can be staff or pupils or both.

A Crisis

First, in dealing with a crisis we are scaling down the event. I don't want to demean in any way the shock and sense of loss that a death will bring to the school community. The impact on members of the school community will vary depending on the nature of the death and the relationships and bonds that existed with the victim. If it is a staff member who dies as a result of a long illness, the other staff will have been in some way prepared for the eventuality, whilst needing time to grieve and come to terms with the shock. The impact of this type of death on the pupil body will usually not be as traumatic as a death of a pupil colleague. However, the important thing to remember is that, whoever dies, the whole school community must acknowledge the loss. Be it a pupil or teacher, they are part of the whole community.

However there are sections of the community that will feel the loss greater and provision for their loss and grief must be made. A first year pupil on hearing of the death of a teacher isn't going to be as upset as a pupil that has known and loved that teacher over many years. It is worth bearing in mind, as Evelyn Breen reminds us in her chapter, that any death could act as a trigger for unprocessed grief in any member of the school community.

It is important to note that the majority of the school community will find the resources within themselves to cope and carry on as normal. Identifying those that are not coping and enabling them to receive help and support after the event is the key to a successful Crisis Response Plan. This enables the school community to get back to normal as soon as possible while acknowledging that loss is a normal part of the cycle of life.

Bereavement Guidelines for a Death which Affects the Whole School Community

There are several items to have on the checklist to make sure nothing is overlooked at a time when the school community is in shock. Firstly communication is essential and the staff must be the first to hear the news, whether the death is that of a colleague or a pupil. A brief staff meeting in the morning would communicate the news so that staff don't face a class to be surprised by some pupil who has heard of the event on the local grapevine. Class teachers and others will need support in breaking the bad news to the pupils.

If there were to be an assembly, it would be appropriate for the chaplain to lead some prayers and acknowledge the loss for the whole school community. Perhaps a candle could be lit in the assembly area and a photo of the loved one that has died placed beside it. Opening a Book of Condolences would also be a gesture appreciated by all, as people feel the need to be doing something to express their sense of loss.

It is a good idea to have a room allocated for chaplaincy/counselling/grief work where other staff members can refer pupils showing distress. Both pupils and staff alike will need space to grieve. In the case of a staff member who has died, some colleagues will need to be relieved of their duties, so the deputy principal needs to have an emergency roster to hand. In the case of a pupil who has died, that particular class group may need to have classes suspended for the day, and time given to the pupils to come to term with what has happened. This is where the chaplain will be spending the most fruitful hours. It is preferable to encourage the pupils to stay in school to support one another, even though there are some that will prefer to be at home, provided parents consent to this.

Following the days of the removal and funeral the school should plan a school-based service for the deceased to be held as soon as appropriate. This would enable the school community to bring closure to their loss and also be an opportunity to invite the family of the deceased to the school. I know from experience working with the bereaved that this is very much appreciated. The chaplain could be instrumental in inviting the family to this service, arranging it at a time when the bereaved family are emotionally ready. Another task facing the chaplain is to provide on-going counselling and support to the bereaved (family, as well as staff and pupils) as needed afterwards. Other practical considerations surrounding the funeral would include closing the school on the day of the funeral. This would require a notification letter to parents.

A Critical Incident

Here we are upgrading what has happened to a much more serious level. A suicide is good example of a critical incident that can paralyse a community. This must be handled with much more sensitivity than a death through natural causes and much more skill is required in getting things back to normal. The response required here is much more complex and demanding and requires specialist skills. Training in managing this level of incident is desirable for the chaplain in particular, as he/she will have a key role in leading the school community through the trauma in the wake of such an event.

The religious belief systems of the traumatised will be put to the test, even for those with a strong faith, whilst those on the margins of religious practice will present with anger and many unanswered questions. A tragedy can often be an opportunity for deep meaningful ministry to those whose lives are rarely touched by the chaplain in the normal course of the school year. In my experience it is gratifying to see the most unlikely characters seek me out after a tragedy as they place trust in me to journey with them as they try and make sense of what has happened.

An event that can be classified as a crisis is one that can somehow be managed with the minimum of planning and a school could reasonably stumble through it using all the skills and experience to hand, but a critical incident is another matter. Here there is no place for fumbling. A comprehensive plan needs to be in place so step by step guidelines can be followed. The staff will be in varying degrees of shock. Some will manage brilliantly while others will need as much support as the pupils. We have the issues of breaking bad news, of coping with initial reactions to the shock, to the ongoing distress and trauma that many within the school community will suffer. This is a critical time for stress management and crisis intervention and accordingly a high level of expertise is needed at this time.[3]

I will outline a plan that can be adopted for use on occasions like this. Ideally the staff, parents and pupils should formulate any school plan in order to promote a sense of ownership, keeping in mind local needs and religious sensitivities, i.e. the ethos of the school and the faiths of the pupils/staff members needs to be respected. As in the case of any crisis emergency it is convenient to have a plan to pull out and run through a checklist. Just as one would rush to the first aid cabinet for the necessary remedy in the event of an accident on the sports field, one should think of the Critical Incident Plan as emotional, spiritual and psychological first aid.

Guidelines for School Chaplains: When Confronted with a Suicidal Pupil
The first part of a Critical Incident Plan would be to have guidelines in place for dealing with a pupil at risk of suicide. Being aware of the signs, i.e. withdrawn, changing in mood, feeling down continually, talk of suicide, is the first key to recognising that a pupil my be at risk. Don't be afraid to ask if you suspect that a pupil might be considering suicide. Often it comes as a relief that the subject is brought out into the open. Most importantly don't fall into the trap that you are their saviour. It is not a role that the chaplain can take on alone. If the pupil needs help, then make sure that they are referred on. I always find the GP is a good starting point. After all we may suspect depression, but unless we come from a medical background, this is not our forte. Identifying who is there for the pupil at risk is important, as they need to be reassured who can support them through the crisis.

Being non-judgemental and listening, allowing them to express their true feelings, not pointing out 'all they should be grateful for', and doing all this despite a sense of the helplessness we may feel is the work of the Good Shepherd. Don't suggest anything that could have them feeling guilt/blame, keep dialogue open and don't leave them alone if risk is imminent.

You cannot promise confidentiality if the pupil is high risk, as parents will have to be informed. This is a regular ethical dilemma for chaplains, but there are few cases when confidentiality can't be assured. Parents too will need the chaplain's support as for them it might be their first encounter with suicide and they will feel out of depth. Often as chaplain you will need to be firm with them in insisting they get professional help for their child before they slip into denial.

The school community will need to know too. If the pupil is still attending school and is high risk, all relevant teachers will need to be aware, for purely practical reasons, i.e. pupil cannot be left unsupervised, or visit the bathroom alone, etc.

If friends of the pupil are aware they will need the chaplain to be there to support them to cope. It is a big burden for a teen to take on and some friends of the pupil at risk will feel stressed by the level of responsibility they feel to protect their friend.

Staff too will need support as not all of them will be familiar with this type of situation and might feel very uncomfortable. Obviously if a pupil is deemed to be at serious risk of harming themselves they cannot be in school in the long term, until their mental health professional deems the risk to have passed. The chaplain will need to offer continual support to the pupil once the initial crisis has subsided and they are back to school again.

And finally, self-care: Who is there for *you* as chaplain? Make sure you have your supports in place, whether it is your supervisor or local cluster group of chaplains that meet regularly.

Critical Incident Plan

Critical Incident Team

Forming the Critical Incident Team is the first task. It is important that the team includes the chaplain, guidance counsellor, principal, deputy, and any other key staff members. Those with specialist training in group facilitation or with a background in counselling would be ideally suited to this work. Also, those who volunteer to be on the team should have processed any grief and losses in their own lives and not have suffered a recent bereavement. The tasks that are required to be carried out can be subdivided among the team, with the principal and deputy taking on what would be in harmony with their role in the school. This frees the chaplain and others to concentrate on the more specialist care of individuals.

Intervention Responsibilities

(1) Leadership/Family Liaison/Communication

These are the tasks best suited for management, with the principal and deputy taking responsibility for firstly confirming the death has occurred. Getting accurate information may seem obvious, but it is vital in preventing rumours and misinformation circulating. If the tragedy is presumed to be a suicide for example, it cannot be communicated to others in the school community as such, unless confirmed by the family that this is what has happened.

Obviously the principal will express sympathy to the family, assure them of the school's support and ensure the family know whom to contact in the school. Consultation with the family on school involvement in the funeral is essential. The pupil who has died is a member of the school community, but also a member of their parish and perhaps a member of several local sporting and cultural organisations. They all may want to have some involvement. The school alone cannot hijack the occasion, but the school has the resources that might be welcomed by the family who are finding it difficult enough to get to grips with what has been visited upon them.

There is a need to prepare an announcement for staff and pupils and plan a brief staff meeting outlining the plan that is being implemented. Following this is the distribution of procedures to class teachers in breaking bad news. A process for dealing with telephone enquiries from anxious parents needs to be devised as well as preparing a media statement. If the critical incident is newsworthy, the media may be looking for a comment. (See Appendix 3, p. 272)

Other decisions that the principal must make include notifying the Board of Management; discouraging any pupil or staff from dealing with the media; make decisions on who should attend funeral; should the school be closed on the day of the funeral?

(2) Chaplain/Counselling

The chaplain and counsellor will work as a team to ensure that those who are not coping with the bad news receive adequate support and care. It is important to keep in mind an element of self-care throughout all of this. It is all too easy to burn out, and a burnt out chaplain is of no help to anybody. Setting up the Critical Incident Team room in the school is an important task. This establishes a base where pupils and indeed staff too can come and find space to deal with what is happening to them.

Assisting the class teacher of the deceased's class in breaking the bad news would be the next step for the chaplain. Making sure the class teacher and other staff have guidelines in this process will benefit them greatly in what is for most teachers an uncomfortable role. Having guidelines as well as information on grief responses will help identify those in need of counselling and greater support. Make sure the pupils are aware of the services and help available to them. This may have to be mentioned more then once, as one of the affects of shock is not absorbing very much information once the bad news is broken.

It is important to take time with the most affected pupils in the critical incident room as they will have many concerns they will need to verbalise in a safe setting. Faith issues and anger with God are not uncommon responses at this time. However, it would be wise too to encourage pupils that feel able to return to class and try and keep the normal routine going. There is a danger that some can get bogged down in grief. Normal routine can help, even if thoughts and concentration is not focused on the work of class. Teachers will obviously have to make allowances.

Organising a year group/whole school prayer service for mid morning, or later that day once all pupils have been notified, is a good way to bring calm and focus to the issue at hand. Prayer and faith cannot be underestimated at times like this. The super organised chaplain will have a suitable pre-packaged liturgy at hand for such emergencies, otherwise ask for help from your colleagues in religious education, as your time will have been taken up with distressed pupils all morning.

Whilst the primary concern of the chaplain on this day will be the pupils, support must be given too to colleagues on the staff as well as to parents of friends of the victim who may call up needing guidance. Liaison with local clergy about school involvement in the liturgy once family consent has been given would be the final task of the chaplain, before taking time out for a debriefing.

This brings us to the end of the first day, when the team would do well to meet and support one another over a cup of tea and share how they are feeling and evaluate how things are going, as well as planning for tomorrow. The next day the school should try and run as normal. Normal routine in the wake of a tragedy is very therapeutic, even though pupils or staff may not feel very much like going to class, it is important to go through the motions.

At this stage the chaplain would be concerned with small groups of affected pupils who turn up at school but who are too distressed to face class. Encouraging them to support one another as well as enabling them to tell their story again is the most helpful intervention at this time. Listening skills with a sympathetic ear to hear their pain and confusion and provide support is all that is required for now.[4] It shouldn't be necessary to have a special room allocated today, as the chaplain's office should suffice.

Planning the funeral and the school involvement in it will take some time on day two, while the funeral will most likely by the next day and generally the school will be closed.

Breaking Bad News to Pupils: Guidelines

There is no easy way ever to break bad news. It is a task nobody relishes, but a little preparation and some guidelines can be of great benefit to teachers particularly who have to face this task for the first time. The class of the pupil who has died should be the first to be told, with chaplain and/or counsellor and class teacher present. Other classes will have to be told by their class teachers as the resources of the chaplain will have to be concentrated on those most in need. It is not the kind of news that can be relayed over the school intercom!

Not every class is going to be traumatised, some pupils may not even know the deceased, but it is important to acknowledge the loss for the whole school community. Begin by telling the class you have sad news and it is difficult for you to do this. Let them know the name of the person the news is about. Let them know the facts, as you know them. (It is important to prevent rumours through misinformation.)

Encourage questions after you have relayed the news. Some pupils will not have taken in all you said, and others will have questions you may not be in a position to answer. Assure them that when more information comes to light you will keep them informed.

Let the class know of common reactions to tragic news, the most common reaction being shock. Let them know the symptoms to expect, and reassure those who are already in tears and having other emotional outbursts that this is OK and normal.

Don't allow a pupil to leave the classroom alone and make sure the pupils are supervised within the building while in a distressed state. Let them know that you will support them. Let them know who else is available to support them and don't be afraid to let them know that you are also upset by the news. Allow them time to mingle and talk to one another in groups and explain how they can support one another. There will be natural *helpers* in every class who will be only too glad to assume a caring role.

Be attentive to identifying those who are not coping well with the news, and let them know where the Critical Incident Team (chaplain, counsellor, etc) will be for the morning. Arrange to have refreshments ready and boxes of tissues in this room.

A short prayer for the deceased would be appropriate before the class breaks up and if the pupils appear ready, an assembly may be held to formally acknowledge the loss and hold a brief prayer service at this time.

Some pupils may be able to continue and go to class, while others will need to stay with the Critical Incident Team. It is important in our caring role not to create a dependency on the Critical Incident Team. School break-time can be an opportunity to encourage everybody to leave the room and take some air, not least of all for the chaplain's / other carer's sake who will definitely need a break by this time.

Common Reactions on Hearing Bad News
For teachers and others breaking bad news it is well to know some of the common symptoms that may present themselves. These include mental and behavioural as well as physical and emotional reactions. The person in shock can be confused, have poor concentration, be disoriented, withdrawn, be restless, feeling very let down, and can feel uncertain about the future too. The emotional content of shock can present itself in tears, panic attacks, denial, anxiety, depression, anger and emotional outbursts. Guilt feelings are also very real, particularly if it is a friend of a suicide victim. Nausea, fainting, pain, dizziness, weakness, breathing difficulties and palpitations are just some of the more common physical signs to look out for when someone is in shock and overwhelmed by grief.

Getting Back to Normal
While for some the funeral will bring a certain closure to the traumatic event, for others the grief will be all the more acute. As they see some of their friends go back to the routines of teenage life, it will be even more distressing to remain stuck in the tragedy. Grief has no time limits or format and despite the identification of the stages of grief by Kubler-Ross and others, it takes no set pattern. This is the crucial time for the Critical Incident Team to make appropriate interventions. After the funeral the team should meet again to plan their ongoing response to those still deeply affected by the trauma and those not coping. This should involve input from class teachers and year heads that may be able to help identify those most affected. The best practice following a critical incident is a debriefing which is a structured group process to help those most affected to acknowledge what has happened in a safe setting.

Critical Incident Stress Debriefing
Critical Incident Stress Debriefing (CISD) is the widely used format for the debriefing of survivors of global disasters, i.e. 9/11, airline crashes, bombings, hijackings, etc. I have used this process many times in schools following a traumatic incident (suicide, murder, etc) and it has been successful for the participants. Primarily it enables the majority to get back to normal as soon as possible. The process is structured and non-threatening, but needs trained skilful facilitation giving all participants an opportunity to acknowledge the impact the tragedy has had on them.

Participants are not put on the spot to speak, but are encouraged to do so. Those reluctant to go to the debriefing are asked to attend to support their colleagues as their presence will be supportive. The group also serves to highlight the small number who will need on-going counselling in a one-on-one context and it aims to prevent to onset of Post Traumatic Stress Disorder (PTSD) which can sometimes follow after a person is exposed to an extremely traumatic event.[5]

CISD is a worthwhile closure to what will have been a stressful and traumatic time for all in the school community. Acknowledging the process as a form of spiritual, emotional and psychological first aid can prevent grief being buried, only to resurface more painfully later. From the Christian perspective, as the chaplain reflects theologically, the first rays of light of the resurrection can be glimpsed in the midst of darkness.

Notes

1. Quinlan, J., *Pastoral Relatedness* (Lanham: University Press of America, 2002), p. 25.
2. Everly, G. S., Mitchell, J. T., *Critical Incident Stress Management: The Basic Course Workbook* (Baltimore, Maryland: International Critical Incident Stress Foundation, 1998), p. 17
3. Everly, G. S., Mitchell, J. T., *Critical Incident Stress Management: Advanced Group Crisis Interventions* (Baltimore, Maryland: International Critical Incident Stress Foundation, 2000), p. 7.
4. Ward, B., et al., *Good Grief: Exploring Feelings, Loss and Death With Over 11's And Adults* (Barbara Ward, UK 1992).
5. *Let's Talk About Post-Traumatic Stress Disorder – Information Leaflet* (Arlington, Virginia: American Psychiatric Association, 1999).

Partnership in Schooling

The Role of the Chaplain in Promoting Community

Marjorie Doyle

Introduction

In this chapter, I propose that partnership, one of the educational principles on which the Education Act 1998 was formulated, is also the key to forming and sustaining a Christian faith community in a school. I further propose that the chaplain has a unique role to play in helping to create and sustain that partnership which creates the ethos or spirit necessary to facilitate:

> Christian communities that are marked by a sense of caring, sustained by an experience of belonging and missioned by a spirit of justice?[1]

Reviewing the history of education in Ireland one is struck by the absence of any structures to facilitate the promotion of partnership in second-level schools, despite the fact that the majority of these schools are Catholic and the ideals of Catholic education as outlined in Church documents strongly favour its pursuit. The Education Act, the Irish Constitution and legal framework strongly support partnership with parents yet parents are still the outsiders, the token voice, in the formation of educational policy and the day-to-day happenings in the school. At this time, when the institutional Church in Ireland is under intense scrutiny and has been found wanting, the case for new approaches to building and sustaining the Christian community is strong and requires urgent attention. All this points to our schools as the ideal foundation for building Christian communities, but without the ethos of partnership, which will impart a sense of identity to our young people, this identity will find it hard to survive the vicissitudes of our present culture.

In reviewing the history of education, I will highlight circumstances which may militate against the pursuit of partnership in our schools, but by examining the ideals of Catholic education as outlined in Church documents, and the findings of prominent educationalists, we will see the case for the pursuit of that partnership. An examination of the Irish Constitution and legal framework will further support the case for partnership in the educational system, and the story of the Educate Together Movement is one story of how schools may approach the pursuit of partnership.

What is this Ethos or Spirit, which facilitates the Growth of a Christian Community?
In every community of people the daily lived experiences may give rise to particular customs and practises which in turn permeate the daily-lived experiences of all those in that community. These daily experiences create the atmosphere or ethos of the institution, or in other words the spirit of the Christian community. In Book II of his *Ethics*, Aristotle proposes that:

> Moral goodness... is the result of habit... the moral virtues... are engendered in us neither by nor contrary to nature; we are constituted by nature to receive them, but their full development in us is due to habit.[2]

Anyone who has watched babies grow and develop will be aware of the way they develop speech, and behaviour very similar to their parents or siblings because of continuous contact, or habitual interaction. So too in a school, the ethos which is the result of the daily, weekly or yearly practices, interactions and relationships will affect the learning, character and behaviour of the young people experiencing it. Therefore, the traditions and rituals which are observed and the behaviour of the different participants will influence the character and behaviour of all who are part of the school community. This atmosphere or spirit cannot be forced. Any parent will testify to the old adage that children learn from what they [and you] do, not from what you tell them to do. They very quickly sniff out hypocrisy or deceit. Adolescents are not designed to comply unquestioningly with rules and regulations; their fundamental challenge is to develop a healthy personality which calls into question the values and mores of present and past generations, in order to define their own identity. It follows then that their experience of an atmosphere 'marked by a sense of caring, sustained by an experience of belonging and missioned by a spirit of justice,'[3] an atmosphere which tolerates and accepts different viewpoints, an atmosphere of partnership, will enable them to freely create their own identity and in turn contribute and partake freely in the partnership of the Christian community. I propose therefore, that the principle of partnership, while not a strong part of our educational tradition can make a very positive contribution to that process, strengthen the democratic system and significantly enable the building of a truly Christian community.

The Evolution of the Irish Education System
The OECD report of 1991, stated that the educational system in Ireland:

> Was not planned methodically but expanded in piecemeal fashion in order to respond to importunate pressures.[4]

These pressures were closely bound with the struggle for nationhood and an Irish identity.

From as early as the sixth century CE, the provision of education has almost entirely been under the auspices of denominational authorities. The establishment of the monasteries at that time facilitated the monks sharing their knowledge of scripture and philosophy with the communities in which they lived. However, the present involvement of the Church in education has been greatly influenced by its reactions to the Penal Times when Catholics were forbidden to teach, priests and bishops were outlawed, and the second-level schools were private, catered solely for Protestants and were modelled on the English Grammar School. This suppression of Catholicism was part of the Government policy to anglicise the Irish population. It rebounded however, as Catholicism became entwined with the cause for an independent national identity, and the alliance of the native Irish population and the native Catholic clergy led to the Church having a powerful voice in secular affairs. From this time, the Catholic hierarchy maintained a distrust of government involvement in education, a fact that greatly contributed to tension between Church and State and was not conducive to the promotion of partnership.

In his efforts to build a strong and powerful Church, capable of opposing government attempts to proselytise Catholic children, Paul Cullen as Archbishop of Armagh (1850) invited dioceses and religious congregations to establish second-level schools. The Catholic population welcomed this as a means of maintaining its own Irish identity. CORI outlines the mission of these schools in the late eighteenth and early nineteenth centuries as being one of empowering the poor, excluded and marginalised in Irish society, in order that they might take their place in the society of the future.[5] However, Louis O'Flaherty maintains the schools 'were managed in a benevolent autocratic manner',[6] by the denominational authorities who jealously asserted and guarded their ownership of them. Reports in 1899, 1905, and 1918 all highlighted various defects in the system.[7] They included an unbalanced curriculum, cramming, lack of sanitation, unhealthy rivalry and competition, unqualified teachers and neglect of the academically weaker student. The small numbers of lay teachers were badly paid and lacked security of tenure. The denominational authorities refusal to cooperate with the state, in its efforts to improve the educational system by the inspection of schools and payment of teachers, meant that Irish schools were markedly inferior to their English counterparts. These facts influenced the future development of the secondary teachers union the ASTI, and contributed to tension between this union and the management authorities, a fact which also militated against the pursuit of partnership.

The educational reforms, which came about as the result of the establishment of the Irish Free State, were largely administrative. In his treatise *Framework of a Christian State,* on which the 1937 Constitution of Ireland is widely acknowledged to have been based, Fr Edward Cahill recognised:

> It would be an error to suppose that the system as it stands is perfect or free from danger. Neither the present system of primary education, nor the technical or vocational schools, nor (indeed much less) the Irish University system, nor even the Secondary system... realise the ideals of

Catholic Education… hence one may hope that they now be gradually refashioned in accordance with the full Catholic ideal.[8]

The full Catholic ideal, outlined at that time by Pope Pius XI, regarded Christian education as the responsibility of the Church, the family, the school and the State in partnership. Yet, teachers were badly paid, lacked security of tenure and were excluded from policy discussions. Parents too, were excluded, a throwback to the Cullen era when an Irish Bishops statement claimed they had no desire to be involved:

From the conviction, which we regard as, on the whole, sensible on their part, that these things are somewhat outside of their competence.[9]

Cahill's call for reform and development did not fully materialise until the introduction of discussions before the passing into law of the Education Act 1998. This Act was the culmination of almost ten years of consultation, debate and dialogue in which parents, teachers, denominational authorities, and the public at large participated. They were all invited to present their points of view at a National Education Convention, which aimed to be transparent and respectful of every viewpoint. For the first time in the history of the State, the Act proposed a clear statement of aims and a philosophical rationale for educational policy in Ireland. It is based on the principles of pluralism, equality, partnership, quality and accountability, and its fundamental aim is to serve the educational needs of individuals so that the quality of life in society and the economic well-being of the nation will be enhanced. It has significantly changed the face of the education process by democratising it and denominational schools are now required by law to balance their foundational aims and objectives with the requirements of legislation. John Walshe maintains, 'the principle of partnership has become firmly rooted in the educational landscape.'[10] Our system of education is no longer the preserve of the wealthier middle classes, so, more than ever before, if we are to integrate the culture, faith and daily-lived experiences of an increasingly pluralist Irish society there is an onus on educational authorities to develop and sustain that partnership in practise. The problem in the past has been a lack of communication and dialogue between the partners; the Act provides encouragement and a framework for the development of that partnership ideal. However, in order that it would make a positive and productive contribution to the education process, teachers, parents, management and trustees might benefit from education in the theory and rationale of partnership and community building, and the goodwill to surmount past tensions.

Partnership in Official Church Teaching
The Book of Genesis in one account of creation tells us that God created man and woman in his own likeness; while another account tells us 'it is not good that man should be alone' (Gen. 2:18), so, from one person, God created another and the two could be as one. Two different accounts, which relate the same truth that

we are made to live together, in partnership with each other and with God. Ideally then, the Church sees society as based on a network of personal relationships bound together with love, which give meaning to our lives because, as the *Pastoral Constitution on the Church in the Modern World* states:

> God, who has fatherly concern for everyone, has willed that all men should constitute one family and treat one another in a spirit of brotherhood.[11]

The story of the Israelites journey to the Promised Land in scripture highlights the communal aspect of God's relationship or covenant with humankind. They were called to be 'the people of God' not as individuals but as a group, interdependent on each other. This interdependence on each other, so necessary for the people of the Old Testament, is just as necessary when building and sustaining a faith community today. As Groome points out, 'each person has non-negotiable responsibilities to live the covenant faithfully and thus contribute to the faithfulness of the whole people.'[12] This points to the responsibility we each have in building a faith community, and it calls for a spirit of inclusion and welcome in our approach which takes account of the pluralist nature of today's society, and the partnership which the members of the school community share. Jesus, the *first chaplain,* built on the Hebrew understanding of God's relationship with humankind and invited people into a community of disciples, with the radical call to, 'Love thy neighbour as thyself.' St Paul exhorted these communities to act as a body:

> For as in one body we have many members, and all the members do not have the same function, so we, though many, are one body in Christ, and individually members one of another. (Romans 12: 4)

This is a powerful analogy for our understanding of the requirements of a faith community. The implications of it are that we are called to value and respect each other equally, while recognising that we each have a separate role to play according to our talents, but that we work in communion or partnership with each other.

In essence, the benefits derived from a consultative/partnership approach in schools are consistent with the ideals espoused by the Catholic Church, and are well embedded in educational theory. The works of Wolfendale, Bastiani, Macbeth and Macleod, advocate the benefits, to the development of the child's whole personality, of parents and teachers working together, because through their exposure to the school parents will learn more about education, while teachers will gain from hearing at first hand the practical implications of home life. By stressing the value of each individual to the faith community, Groome further contends that:

> They find their Christian identity only by functioning together as Christ's body in the world... the Church.[7]

In other words, we realise our identity as Christians in a believing community, which is 'founded on truth, built on justice, and animated by love,'[13] and which, although interdependent, recognises the talents and contributions of each individual to that believing community. It is this desire to impart a Christian identity to our students, which again points to the benefit of partnership in our schools.

Vatican II's *Declaration on Christian Education* recognises the dignity of the human person and the importance of a spirit of community which engages the participation of all and fosters mutual understanding as being central to the education process. In recognising the importance of the family to the development of the child, this document, and the later encyclical *Familiaris Consortio,* by Pope John Paul II urges the State and the Church to support and 'give families all possible aid to enable them perform their educational role properly'. This points to the need in our educational system of a partnership, which takes account of the innate parenting skills of parents while at the same time providing education around the needs of the child. The recent document, *The Catholic School on the Threshold of the Third Millennium,* identifies the importance of community in the Catholic school. It calls for initiatives to encourage communication and dialogue between all those involved in writing on the 'very spirits of human beings',[14] in order that the culture, faith and daily life of the young person would be integrated and balanced. Therefore, ideally the Catholic school develops a framework, which supports and includes parents as part of the community. In practice, however, as we have seen from our historical review this has not been the case in Catholic schools in Ireland.

Granted, parents have been involved in fund raising, and they attend parent-teacher meetings, but in my opinion parental involvement and parental partnership in the education process are not the same. One is involved in the process by just bringing one's child to school, and being concerned with one's own child. Partnership however, is characterised according to Wolfendale, as parents being:

> Active and central in decision making and its implementation;
> Perceived as having equal strengths and equivalent expertise;
> Able to contribute to as well as receive services (reciprocity);
> Able to share responsibility so that they and professionals are mutually accountable.[15]

Pugh offers a definition of partnership as a 'working relationship that is characterised by a shared sense of purpose, mutual respect and the willingness to negotiate. This implies a sharing of information, responsibility, skills, decision making and accountability.'[16]

Many parent representatives on boards of management and in parent associations are active in working out policy, and developing mission and vision statements. However, the general body of parents need to be drawn into these developments by an interactive process of communication that will educate and disseminate information and be open to dialogue. This will enable the general body of parents to contribute to and feel a part of the building of a school community in which their children will witness the value of respecting each other and of working in partnership for the good of that community:

The constant aim of the school, therefore, should be contact and dialogue with the pupils' families, which should also be encouraged through the promotion of parents' associations, in order to clarify with their indispensable collaboration that personalised approach which is needed for an educational project to be efficacious.[17]

A Vision for Education

We have arrived at a point where the benefits of partnership in a school community have been outlined. The work of Thomas Groome emphasises the importance of this partnership in the building of a faith community. He reinforces with the help of modern scholarship and science the fundamental truths that 'humankind is essentially communal, and both humanly and spiritually, we have our best possibilities in community.'[18] He calls on educators, both parents and teachers, to create a spirit in which the proper education and development of our young people can take place in community. For the Christian this community is imbued with the spirit of God and is a faith community. For that reason, in whatever community he/she serves, the chaplain has a role in fostering and sustaining the community in relationship with God. This community offers an identity to the participants by its strong and empowering rituals; consequently, it generates a sense of identity for the adolescent. The chaplain has a pivotal role to play in developing and sustaining these rituals in order to create an atmosphere 'enlivened by the gospel spirit of freedom and charity'[20] which will enable the young person to view the world from a Christian standpoint and to bring their own Christian perspective to bear on the world. This involves synthesising the Christian faith with the culture of the young person. That culture involves the local community, family and society working in partnership. As Aristotle said, good moral development is the result of the interactions of good people with each other, therefore the atmosphere that exists between the significant adults in the young persons life greatly influences his/her development and ability to contribute to the common good. For this reason the manifestation of a spirit of partnership between the participants in the school will benefit not alone the young person but society as a whole, and the chaplain, as a significant faith presence among the community, is pivotal to its development and sustenance.

The Education Act specifies that the trustees have the right to insist on their ethos prevailing in the school. However, I would agree with the opinion of Kevin Williams when he says:

Whatever kind of ethos characterises a school, it is not something which can be imposed upon it... the dominant, pervading spirit or character which informs the habits of behaviour to be found among participants in the institution must be voluntarily accepted.[21]

This is why legal and constitutional provisions about ethos will not enable the building of a Christian faith community. The stance, therefore, of the denominational authorities in demanding a right to impose an ethos on a school and enshrining it in the Education Act is called into question. The ethos or spirit necessary to foster and sustain a genuine faith community grows freely and is sustained in partnership by that community. The Israelites journey to the Holy Land was freely undertaken and despite all their shortcomings, God was with them all the way. The chaplain, by journeying with and caring for the spiritual dimension of each participant in the school can understand their different perspectives and together they can build up rituals and traditions, which will give a Christian identity to their community. The imposition of an ethos will not plant the seed of love and respect that is required for working out the principle of partnership and the building of a faith community in a school.

Partnership in the Irish Constitution and Legal Framework

Our examination of the Irish educational system has highlighted the absence of any framework for parental involvement in the pursuit of partnership, up until the enactment of the Education Act 1998. An examination of the constitutional and legal provisions that underpin the principle in the Act will highlight the rights of parents enshrined in the Constitution of Ireland 1937, and upheld in recent Court decisions. We have seen that the Constitution strongly reflects the Catholic social teaching of 1937, but it also provides for the natural rights common to all human beings. There are several provisions that are relevant to the position of parents as legitimate partners in the education process. Article 41.1.1 recognises 'the family as the primary and fundamental unit of society, and as a moral institution possessing inalienable and imprescriptible rights, antecedent and superior to all positive law.' It guarantees to protect the family ... as the basis of society. The state must therefore acknowledge the family as a legitimate partner in the educational process, with a legitimate right to participation. According to Article 42 on Education:

> The state acknowledges that the primary and natural educator of the child is the family and guarantees to respect the inalienable right and duty of parents to provide according to their means for the religious and moral, intellectual, physical and social education of their children.[22]

The Education Act of 1998 gives expression to this clause, by strengthening and legalising the position of parents in education. The Act defines their entitlements and rights. Parents are entitled to form Associations in schools, and their national Parents Council has been given statutory recognition. However, this does not guarantee a partnership. John Walshe's analysis of the consultation process,[23] which led to the Education Act, discloses unease in teacher's union circles with the cultivation of parent power, as they feared it was an effort on the part of the government and management bodies to curtail the power of the unions. The reaction of the teachers unions to parent's comments concerning the industrial dispute (2001-02), and their reported intolerance of parents at the ASTI conference 2002,[24] are testament to the deep unease about the role of parents that exists in the teaching profession. On the other hand, parent's efforts to establish their right to be involved in the education of their children have often contributed to this unease on the part of teachers, due to the fact that their representatives may present extreme or insensitive views, thereby alienating both teachers and the general body of parents. This calls for a common structure of education, training and dialogue, which would encourage sensitivity and a willingness to trust each other's viewpoints and thereby aid the development of the partnership ideal.

High Court and Supreme Court Decisions
In 1988, the Campaign to Separate Church and State Ltd (CSCS) and Jeremiah Noel Murphy initiated a legal action against the Minister for Education and the Attorney General, challenging the right of the state to pay the salaries of chaplains in comprehensive and community schools. They maintained it was contrary to the constitutional provision of not endowing any religion. The issue of endowment of religion, while relevant to the case, does not concern us here. It is relevant, however, that in both the High Court and subsequent Supreme Court ruling the rights of parents to assistance in the religious development of their children was upheld. This religious development included religious instruction and formation. The role of the chaplain is to help provide the ethos or atmosphere in which this formation or habitual behaviour may take place, in accordance with the wishes of the parents. Ultimately the judgements broadened the interpretation of the constitutional rights of parents with regard to the education of their children, 'especially in the matter of religious and moral formation.'(Art. 44.2) They also recognised the valuable role the chaplain plays in counselling and helping young people, regardless of their faith, with 'moral, social, educational, personal or family problems...'[25] thus recognising the integration of the culture and faith of the young person. In essence, the judgements recognise the important role the chaplain plays in the maintenance of an ethos or atmosphere conducive to the formation of the young persons character, and recognises the constitutionality of that role as far as it is in accord with the wishes of parents. This again places an onus on the chaplain to work in partnership with parents and the whole school community.

In the case of Jamie Sinnott v The Minister of Education and the Attorney General (July 2001), Mr Justice Hardiman referred to the alteration of the legal scene relating to education as the result of the Education Act, 1998, the Education Welfare Act, 2000 and the Equal Status Act 2000. Collectively these three statutes have conferred a legal structure on education that underpins the principle of partnership and the rights of parents in the education of their children. They have affected a considerable transfer of power from denominational authorities to boards of management where parents, teachers, the community and the denominational trustees are represented. For the first time in the history of the state, the principles of democracy and partnership are part of legislation, but, as already argued, legislation alone will not produce partnership. It is fostered and sustained by habitually encouraging an ethos of partnership and by developing a framework for its implementation.

Theory into Action

We have explored some Church documents and educational literature in order to ascertain the philosophy behind the Catholic Church's involvement in education, and have found that the principle of partnership between all the participants in the school is constantly emphasised. The Irish Constitution and legal framework supports and gives legal definition to this aspiration. The implications undoubtedly point to the importance of fostering and sustaining partnership in the school community. Unfortunately, our review of the history of the Irish Catholic Church's involvement in education has highlighted the lack of a framework for partnership and the existence of possible tensions, which will militate against its implementation. In my experience, the schools that give fullest practical expression to the principle of partnership in Ireland today are the schools in the Educate Together sector. It is valuable therefore, for the chaplain and those concerned with denominational schools to become acquainted with the model of partnership in the Educate Together schools. Adapted appropriately, this could serve as a model for the fostering and sustenance of partnership in denominational schools.

The Educate Together Movement

The Educate Together movement has evolved as the representative organisation of individual schools throughout Ireland who espouse the founding principles of being multi-denominational, co-educational, child-centred, and democratic. This account of their growth offers a model of partnership and participation which is rooted in the community and which the chaplain could emulate in the building of a faith community in a school. The governing spirit or ethos is defined as multi-denominational, co-educational, child-centred and democratic,[26] and all activities both inside and outside the classroom constantly reinforce these principles. While they do not teach a particular faith, they do follow a core curriculum that teaches appreciation and respect of social, cultural, and other human difference. It examines the tenets of all religions, and celebrates the major religious festivals of the world. The background and ethical preferences of every family is respected and cherished within the school and parents are facilitated to organise religious instruction for their children outside the main school programme.

Each school is co-educational and committed to encouraging all children to explore their full range of abilities and opportunities, and to develop programmes to counter gender stereotyping and inequity in all aspects of school life. They are committed to the creative development of the educational programme through genuine dialogue between teachers and parents for the common good of all children attending the school.

Because all Educate Together schools are set up by groups of parents, parents have unparalleled access and involvement in the running and development of the school. The patron body or executive is a charitable company governed by a constitution, which is set up by parents in the locality. All policy decisions are passed at general meetings and officers are elected annually. The executive establishes a Board of Management for the day to day running of the school which is constituted in accordance with the Education Act.

At all times the professional role of the teacher is recognised and supported in an effort to build a genuine partnership between the professional and the parent in the interests of the child. The guidelines appreciate 'the intense and personal involvement of the parents in the education of their children, their detailed knowledge of them as individuals',[27] but they also emphasise the importance of parents recognising and respecting the professional training of teachers, the teacher's objective experience of each child, and the long-term career and conditions of employment of the teacher. The guidelines of the Board of Management stipulate that:

> At the very heart of the uniquely Educate Together educational experience lies the creative partnership between the professional role of the teachers and the democratic involvement of parents... [the relationship] is one of genuine partnership, mutual respect and support and equality. Neither role should be allowed to predominate to the expense of the other as the full development of both is essential if we are to harness the full potential of this partnership for the benefit of the children's education.[28]

This partnership evolves within the school community as a consequence of working together on a daily basis to manage the school. It is not imposed because of legislation or the imposition of an ethos statement. It grows from the daily interactions of the partners in the school, and the responsibility for providing an environment conducive to protecting and maintaining it in high esteem lies with the Board of Management. To facilitate and sustain partnership, training courses are provided for the management bodies with particular reference to communication, conflict resolution, decision-making, finance, and curriculum. We have already referred to the need for partnership training and education in the denominational schools and here we see it receives high priority as a means to sustain partnership.

The schools constantly communicate the principles that govern the school to all members of the school community including the students. Denominational schools have traditionally taken it for granted that people know the ethos of the school and are at one with it. In the more pluralist environment of today this can no longer be taken for granted. Along with the written communication of policies, now required by law, the chaplain can facilitate the communication of information and governing principles to all the school community. The rituals associated with the liturgical calendar are powerful tools with which the chaplain as a faith presence in the school community may make present the spirit of God in the lives of the community.

Typically, in an Educate Together school parents are asked to contribute their talents and skills to building the school community, therefore professional and unskilled alike can feel a sense of ownership and belonging. They may provide extra attention for individual children during the arts, crafts, music or science lesson, they may challenge the status quo and haggle with the politicians, or they may get involved with the major task of fundraising. Many women in particular have discovered dormant skills and have 'emerged as leaders; as entrepreneurs who spearheaded successful fund-raising ventures; as public relations and marketing executives, "selling" the new school and finding potential pupils; as excellent negotiators with officialdom at both local and central level; as counsellors and mediators who helped to resolve conflicts as they arose.'[29] By working together parents and professionals learn to resolve any conflicts because if they walk away the school falls apart. The community, which develops in partnership, is based on mutual respect and care for the good of all the children in the school and is in my opinion, a reflection of the early Christian communities efforts to build a community based on the words and life of Jesus. The role of the chaplain in a similar community could incorporate the message of Jesus into the enterprise.

The story of Educate Together to date has been a success story, writes Aine Hyland:

> It is a story of change and development from the bottom up – a story of ordinary people from a variety of different backgrounds – religious, cultural and social – working together to provide an educational system where their children can be educated together.[30]

It illustrates the changed social landscape; some parents are prepared to take responsibility for the education of their children and they may not necessarily choose religious denominational schools. Foras Patrúnachta na Scoileanna LanGhaeilge has adapted this model in its efforts to establish and promote schools teaching through the medium of Irish, and it has experienced similar success. The success of both Educate Together and *gaelscoileanna* illustrates that parents are prepared to participate as partners in an educational process, in which they contribute to the ethos and in which they can have a level of participation and a creative partnership with the teaching profession. It indicates that when the required structures are in place parents, teachers and local community are willing and able to work together to promote an ethos whereby each family and child are valued and respected and where the pursuit of partnership leads to a greater understanding of each others viewpoint. The implications of this model for the growth of a Christian community in a school is relevant because as a result of the Second Vatican Council the Catholic Church is committed to changing its structures from primarily an authoritarian decision-making process to one where co-responsibility and shared decision-making are all important.

Conclusion

This chapter set out to examine the principle of partnership as it manifested itself in the Irish educational system, with the expressed intention of examining its benefit to the chaplain in fostering and sustaining a faith community.

Our review of the history of the Irish educational system has shown that the school system we have inherited is predominantly Catholic, and that it is strongly influenced by the commitment of religious orders to the provision of schools. Historically, the ethos of these schools was taken for granted as the key personnel, all subscribed to a shared value system. Today, the lack of religious personnel combined with the growing pluralism of Irish society calls for a framework whereby the ethos of the school community can grow and develop in partnership. Unfortunately, contrary to the principles governing Catholic schools, the system that has evolved has created tensions between the various participants, and structures and models of practice exist which militate against the partnership ideal. Today, these are challenged by the introduction of legislation and the interpretation of our constitution by the courts. However, because of our history, all participants may need some time to understand and work out a model of partnership. I propose that the chaplain is in a unique position to influence and facilitate this partnership, ministering as he/she does to all the participants in the school community.

The role of the chaplain in the school is no longer the preserve of ordained clergy, who was often part-time and appeared on occasion to celebrate the sacraments. The *Guidelines for the Chaplain in a Community School* drawn up in 1976 between the Department of Education and the Dublin Archdiocese clearly indicate that the chaplain should exercise a pastoral role through personal contact, liturgy, and apostolic, cultural and social activities with students. However, it also requires the chaplain to be available to staff, and forge a bond between the home and school. This clearly indicates a role for the chaplain in the development and sustenance of partnership between all the participants in the school as he/she accompanies and supports them with their spiritual and pastoral needs. In fact, research reveals that the more pastoral presence of the Church in community schools, in the person of the chaplain working with students and staff, reflects the educational aims of the Church more successfully than the voluntary secondary schools.[31] I refer to this research in order to illustrate the success of the chaplain working in partnership with staff, students and parents to create an atmosphere whereby the young people experience caring structures and feel valued. It further illustrates the value of partnership as an aid to the growth of a faith community.

We have seen partnership defined as 'a working relationship that is characterised by a shared sense of purpose, mutual respect and the willingness to negotiate',[32] and that it is the aspiration of all Catholic schools to develop models of partnership which will contribute to the building of the faith community. However, history shows that the Catholic authorities have treated with suspicion and distrust any attempt by laity, teachers or parents, to be involved in partnership and in my experience the remnants of that mindset still exists. For example, the tone of the Bishop's submission to the National Education Convention was legalistic and reflected a view that they alone were the guardians of the Christian message. The resulting framework provided by the provisions of the Education Act 1998 for the pursuit of partnership in our schools militates against its true spirit. Partnership is not about ownership or trusteeship. Legislation will not guarantee its presence. It is about the presence of a spirit or atmosphere, which recognises and respects the contributions of all the participants in the school community. The Educate Together schools are an example of this partnership in operation. The school community own the school, and the school community works together to maintain and develop it. There is a genuine attempt to reach decisions by consensus. The denominational authorities have safeguarded their ethos in legislation; and have continued to guard their custodial position by maintaining a majority representation on Boards of Management, and trusteeship of the schools. I would agree with the view of the Association of Managers of Catholic Secondary Schools that this control may militate against other partners getting involved, due to a belief that the trustees/managers carry the responsibility for the school community. Alternatively, it may be a cause of resentment, in the minds of teachers, the amount of power and control the trustees/managers have over their professional lives.[33] I believe that legislation alone will not guarantee the living out of an ethos, which is imposed by trustees, and agree with Kevin Williams, who contends,

> A school ethos must emerge from the genuinely held convictions and aspirations of parents and teachers and pupils. It cannot be imposed by legislative *fiat*.[34]

Jesus' example of partnership with all humankind and with God did not need to rely on legislation or trustees. It was based on the simple premise: love God and your neighbour as yourself. It is the example that the chaplain seeks to emulate in building a faith community. I do not propose to provide a model for the development of this partnership or the building of a faith community. That is a matter for local negotiation and is perhaps the subject of further study. However, the example of partnership in operation in the Educate Together schools does offer a practical framework for the partnership that Catholic Church documents aspire to.

By emphasising the importance of partnership to the development of a faith community, this paper seeks to highlight the need for all the participants in the school community to develop an understanding and respect for each other's point of view. It also calls on the Church authorities and the Religious Orders to trust and respect the role that the people of God play in the Church. I would also call on parents, teachers and Church members to participate in the partnership, which is communal. This involves a commitment on all their parts to a process of training in communication skills, conflict resolution, decision-making and the curriculum for all involved in decision-making positions.

To conclude, we have seen that while the Education Act legislates for partnership, and the maintenance of a democracy demands it, it cannot control the interactions and relationships of different groups in society. The chaplain is in a unique position to facilitate dialogue and interaction between the participants in a school and thereby increase the level of partnership. In addition, because the school community consists of people of diverse perspectives and traditions, the challenge for the chaplain is to welcome and learn from these traditions while cherishing his/her own particular identity. The promotion of the principle of partnership will guard against the exclusive and sectarian approach to the building of the faith community, which marked the Catholic school pre-Vatican two, and will contribute to the building of a faith community living in the spirit of the Gospel, in today's world.

Notes

1. Lane, D., *Catholic Education and the School: Some Theological Reflections* (Dublin: Veritas, 1991), p. 96.

2. Aristotle, *Ethic Book II,* trans. J.A.K. Thomson, (Middlesex: Penguin Classics, 1976), p. 91.

3. Lane, D., *Catholic Education and the School: Some Theological Reflections* (Dublin: Veritas, 1991), p. 96.

4. O.E.C.D Report 1991, p. 36.

5. Conference of Religious of Ireland, *Religious Congregations in Irish Education: A Role for the future?* (Dublin: CORI, 1997), p.16

6. Louis Flaherty, *Management and Control in Irish Education* (Dublin: Drumcondra Education Centre, 1992), pp. 1-23.

7. Intermediate Act Report 1899, Dale and Stephens Report 1905, Killanin and Moloney Report 1918, see J. Coolahan, *Irish Education: History and Structure* (Dublin: Institute of Public Administration, 1991), pp. 52-81.

8. Edward Cahill, *Framework of a Christian State,* p. 376.

9. *Statement of Irish Bishops,* Maynooth, 22nd June 1904, in B.E. Titley, *Church, State and Control of Schooling in Ireland 1900-1944* (Dublin: Gill and Mac Millan, 1983), p. 20.

10. Walshe, J., *A New Partnership in Education: From Consultation to Legislation in the Nineties* (Dublin: Institute of Public Administration, 1999), p. 209.

11. Second Vatican Council, *Gaudium et Spes,* ed. Walter M. Abbott, S.J., *The Documents of Vatican II* (London: Chapman, 1966), p. 223.

12. Groome, T., *Educating for Life: A Spiritual Vision for Every Teacher and Parent* (Allen, Texas, Thomas More, 1998), p. 176.

13. *Ibid.,* p. 81.

14. Second Vatican Council, *Gaudium et Spes,* ed. Walter M. Abbott, S.J. *The Documents of Vatican II,* (London: Chapman, 1966), p. 225.

15. Congregation for Catholic Education, *The Catholic School on the Threshold of the Third Millennium* (Boston: Pauline Books, 1998), par. 20.

16. Wolfendale, S., *Parental Participation in Children's Development and Education* (New York: Gordon and Breach Science Publishers, 1984), p.15.

17. Pugh, G., 'Parents and Professionals in pre school services: Is Partnership Possible?' in S. Wolfendale (ed.), *Parental Involvement: Developing Networks between School, Home and Community* (London: Cassell, 1989), Ch.1.

18. Congregation for Catholic Education, *The Catholic School on the Threshold of the Third Millennium* (Boston: Pauline Books, 1998).

19. Groome, T., *Educating for Life: A Spiritual vision for every teacher and Parent,* (Allen, Texas, Thomas More, 1998), p. 175.

20. Second Vatican Council, *Gravissimum Educationis* (1965), ed. Walter M. Abbott, S.J., *The Documents of Vatican II* (London: Chapman, 1966), p. 646.

21. Kevin Williams, 'Understanding Ethos – a Philosophical and Literary Exploration', C. Furlong, L. Monahan (ed.), *School Culture and Ethos: Cracking the Code* (Dublin: Marino, 2000), p. 81.

22. *Bunreacht na hEireann*, Art. 42.

23. Walshe, J., *A New Partnership in Education*, (Dublin: Institute of Public Administration, 1999) p. 115.

24. *Irish Times*, April 2001.

25. Barrington, J., *Supreme Court 1996*, No. 36.

26. Educate Together, *Basic Information on Educate Together Schools* (Dublin: Educate Together, 2000).

27. Educate Together, *Guidelines for Boards of Management/Executives of Educate Together Schools* (Dublin: Educate Together, 2000), unpublished document, p. 2.

28. *Ibid.*, p. 1.

29. Hyland, A., 'Educate Together Schools in the Republic of Ireland: The First Stage 1975-1994', www.educatetogether.ie/Info/reference_articles/Ref_Art_001.html, 16th March 2004.

30. *Ibid.*

31. Norman, J. *Ethos and Education in Ireland* (New York: Peter Lang, 2003).

32. Pugh, G., 'Parents and Professionals in pre school services: Is Partnership Possible?' in S. Wolfendale (ed.), *Parental Involvement: Developing Networks between School, Home and Community* (London: Cassell, 1989), Ch.1.

33. The Secretariat of Secondary Schools, *The AMCSS & The Catholic School*, unpublished document, p. 2.

34. Kevin Williams, 'Understanding Ethos – A Philosophical and Literary Exploration' in C. Furlong, L. Monahan (eds), *School Culture and Ethos: Cracking the Code* (Dublin: Marino, 2000), pp. 81-82.

Understanding the Pastoral Needs of Asylum-Seeking Pupils

P.J. Boyle

Introduction

Irish society is now a multi-cultural reality. Those working in Irish education are in a unique position to experience at first hand the advantages and challenges that evolve as a result of the intercultural process. Nowhere is this more evident than in the school sector. Schools in Ireland can be envisaged as microcosms of wider Irish society where new multicultural experiences, interactions and relationships are evolving and developing on a continuous basis. As change has been identified as a concept that can be challenging and difficult, it is therefore timely to explore the concept of interculturalism and its impact on the Irish school sector and Irish education in general.

This chapter will outline a number of essential issues for addressing multiculturalism in schools. Firstly it will explore the nature of how Ireland's demographics have changed in recent years as a consequence of the increase in ethnic minorities seeking asylum in Ireland.[1] Secondly, it will focus on the concept of interculturalism and the importance of engaging in this process from a pastoral care and educational perspective. With the aid of a case study from my own experience I will outline some specific issues that asylum-seeking children may present as a consequence of their personal and legal status. Asylum-seeking and refugee children may manifest behaviour in school as a consequence of some social problems that warrant sensitive and responsible intervention by school staff. Very often these problems will require a pastoral response.

Particular attention will be given to the children of asylum seekers and 'separated children' due to the fact that this group makes up a significant proportion of the multicultural population that exists in Irish schools today. In addition the fact that 'normal' social integration for these families and children can be interrupted by their precarious legal status in Ireland, it warrants attention and observation by those entrusted with a statutory mandate to care for such people, i.e. educational staff, healthcare staff, etc. This is not to say the only pupils of ethnically diverse backgrounds in Irish schools are refugees or asylum seekers. Indeed there has been cultural diversity in the pupil population in Irish schools for decades. However, the fact remains that in twenty-first century Ireland the perceived phenomena of increasing multiculturalism continues to challenge society. This chapter will attempt to address some of the issues as they relate to Irish schools.

Multiculturalism and Irish Schools – The Case of Asylum Seekers

Approximately half of the worlds 13.2 million refugees are children, yet consideration of the needs and rights of refugee and asylum-seeking children is frequently absent from the national social and political agenda.[2] Such observations accurately reflect the situation in Ireland when it comes to catering for the needs of this vulnerable group. In addition the United Nations Convention on the Rights of the Child (UNCRC) obliges states to address the needs of all children within their jurisdiction. In specifically addressing the rights of asylum-seeking and refugee children the UNCRC mentions the right to family reunification, rehabilitative care and social integration. The challenge exists for Ireland to honour its obligations as a signatory to this convention. Fanning also points to the government's National Children's Strategy[3] as having the scope to address such matters. The Strategy could be used to enable the promotion of equality and contribute to social inclusion of children regardless of ethnicity or cultural background. Furthermore it could promote the notion of cultural diversity as a concept that is broader than just issues of race and ethnicity by including children with special needs, e.g. children with disability. As schools are one of the first places of socialisation for children outside the family home, they (schools) are in an ideal position to address and implement strategies and plans concerning integration and interculturalism.

According to the Office of the Refugee Applications Commissioner approximately 12 per cent of newly arrived asylum seekers in Ireland in 2002 were of school-going age.[4] This figure constitutes a significant proportion of the overall numbers of newly arrived asylum seekers, which totalled 11,600 applications in the same year. If we compare this to the number of total applications in 1993, when only 362 applications were made, we can begin to see the overall consequences of such an increase. For local communities the consequent delivery of services such as education, accommodation, health and social welfare must be carefully thought out and planned. An awareness of what is 'cultural diversity' must also be considered and examined. The tendency to view groups as 'monocultural' continues to prevail and can contribute to negative stereotyping of particular sections of society. Within the asylum-seeking population alone in Ireland there are approximately over 156 ethnic groups represented, each with their own unique language or dialect and in some cases people having more than one. Such cultural diversity can contribute enormously to personal and professional development if facilitated in a genuinely committed and structured fashion, for example through a whole organisational development plan or strategic plan of an organisation or community.

Currently in Ireland multiculturalism is regarded as a relatively new phenomena. However, Ireland has always had some degree of heterogeneity when it comes to social demographics.[5] For centuries the Irish Travelling community has experienced difficulties around the acknowledgement of their ethnic identity by the majority indigenous community of 'settled' Irish. There is also an established Jewish history in Ireland tracing back to the eleventh century. Ireland, in more recent times, has seen other communities seek refuge during times of conflict. For example, in the 1950s some Hungarian nationals sought asylum here, while in the 1970s some Chilean and Vietnamese refugees came to Ireland to escape wars in their homelands. Unfortunately the cliché of 'history repeating itself' continues and since the 1980s each decade has seen people flee persecution and seek refuge in Ireland from many areas of the globe. The 1980s brought a group of Iranians, and, in the 1990s, world media focused on the emerging civil and political unrest in the Balkans. Images of ordinary people in extraordinary situations were beamed across international television and news reports highlighted the trauma of many people's lives. Soon Ireland was receiving government welcomed 'programme' refugees from the Balkan wars. These people required careful and sensitive attention and an opportunity to integrate with Irish society. An essential component of this integration process would have been the education of their children. Through attending schools, meeting staff, parents, other pupils and community members these asylum seeking children were helped to 'normalise' their lives after the trauma and bereavement experienced by leaving their homelands.[6] For many newly-arrived asylum seekers today the provision of education continues to be a vital element in enabling their families to integrate into society.

The concepts of *multiculturalism* and *interculturalism* have come to the fore in social and political debate in recent times in Ireland. I will now offer a brief explanation on the subtle but important difference between the two concepts of multiculturalism and interculturalism. The word 'multiculturalism' is mentioned frequently in discussions and debates about cultural diversity. However, the word multiculturalism in itself is minimalist in its explanation of different cultures. As a definition the word 'multiculturalism' only acknowledges the existence of many cultures. Consequently, in discussing issues in relation to cultural diversity, the concept of interculturalism is more appropriate and in recent times has replaced the concept of multiculturalism in cultural diversity discourse. The National Consultative Committee on Racism and Interculturalism defines interculturalism as:

> the acceptance not only of the principles of equality of rights, values and abilities but also the development of policies to promote interaction, collaboration and exchange with people of different cultures, ethnicity or religion.[7]

This definition clearly calls for more than tolerance and points to the challenge for those concerned with and entrusted with the development of society.

The challenges posed by the arrival of asylum-seeking/refugee families and consequently pupils from other countries has resulted in calls for an examination and evaluation of services in relation to current needs. In general the introduction of Ireland's Equal Status legislation in 1998 with the Equality Employment Act and in 2000 with the Equal Status Act and the establishment of the Equality Authority has been the catalyst for raising awareness of equality issues in Irish society. More specifically, in education the effects of these demographic changes have not gone unnoticed. The 1998 Education Act and the Education (Welfare) Act 2000 recognise the State's responsibility in promoting the overall development of the pupil. This development will include the spiritual and cultural dimension of education. Furthermore, Ireland's obligations under the UN Convention on the Rights of the Child (ratified by Ireland in 1989) emphasise that education should be directed to the development of the respect for children's own cultural identity, language and values. Ó Cuanacháin points to the fact that all of this rhetoric is important but not necessarily enough. He stipulates that further provisions should be undertaken to include factors such as additional funding for school staff to undertake specialised training on anti-racism, clear policy guidelines and the recruitment of teachers from the ethnic minority communities.[8] In addition the National Council for Curriculum and Assessment has embarked on planning specific policies and procedures for interculturalism in the primary and secondary educational systems as have the Irish National Teachers Organisation with its publishing of *INTO Intercultural Guidelines for Schools – Valuing Difference & Combating Racism*. Now that Ireland is an increasingly multicultural society the aforementioned legislation and guidelines provides a strong legal and moral framework in which to promote social integration and for an ethos of interculturalism to develop.

However, as the next section of this chapter will outline, there is also a need for teachers and other staff to be aware of some of the specific personal needs of pupils of diverse ethnic backgrounds which may require a pastoral understanding and response within and beyond the school environment.

Case Study

Claude (not his real name), a sixteen-year-old boy from a West African country, arrived at the health centre for his voluntary health assessment three days after his arrival in Ireland. On meeting Claude his demeanour displays a shyness and politeness that could also be interpreted as a slight anxiety. Claude speaks French and English. Claude was travelling alone having left those remaining of his family at home in his country. A family friend had arranged for Claude to escape from the appalling circumstances he, his family and community found themselves living in. Claude had witnessed the murder of some of his family and neighbours as a consequence of the ethnic conflict in his country. He was the oldest boy in his family and his parents desperately wanted him to survive. Claude was doing well in secondary school prior to the start of the conflict in his homeland and had ambitions similar to any child of his age. Claude was told he was going to another country. He was told he had no choice. He had no idea where that country would be and he had been very frightened. However, Claude explained to me that, like many of those who seek asylum in Ireland, he had a strong Christian faith and that this faith would see him through. He stated that he was already grateful to God that he had arrived safely and had this opportunity to seek refuge. On arrival in Ireland Claude was initially placed in adult accommodation. Following intervention Claude was later accommodated in a facility more appropriate for his age. Claude was a separated or unaccompanied minor as defined by the United Nations High Commissioner for Refugees (UNHCR). He was now happier to be living with peers of his own age. He was also happy to have sourced a school and commenced education. In addition he was further motivated to make contact with other supports such as church, choir, home-work club, and so on. My first encounter with Claude took place shortly after he arrived in Ireland. About twelve months later Claude came to visit the health clinic again. During this visit he explained how he was getting on in Ireland. Claude stated that, although he was attending school over the past year and felt supported to some degree by staff members, he still felt lonely in school. He found it difficult to make friends. He was more conscious of his 'colour' than ever before in his life and felt that it was a barrier to his forming relationships with other pupils. Claude stated that he felt lonely for a number of reasons. Firstly he *was* alone. He had no family in Ireland. He had left all he had known at home in Africa. He had experienced the loss of his family, friends, community, his language and his way of life as he knew it. He stated he had no close 'wise' adult-figure to guide him. Simple everyday things like food, music, communication and weather became factors that began to get him down. He stated he was feeling increasingly sad. Other issues that were more serious, like the lack of privacy in his accommodation, uncertainty with his refugee status and other normal adolescent peer pressure issues, became major obstacles for Claude to deal with. He stated he was doing his best to be a good person, but was experiencing a range of difficulties that included thinking about his people back home, grappling with pressure from peers about dating, smoking and drinking alcohol, and more seriously his not knowing if his future in Ireland would be secure. Claude has been waiting over one year for a decision on his refugee status and he remains apprehensive. Eventually Claude stopped attending school and his church choir – something he had previously been proud of and enjoyed very much. It was all too much for Claude and he decided to opt out for a while.

A Pastoral Response to the Social and Personal Needs of Asylum-Seeking Pupils

This case study clearly illustrates how asylum-seeking children or children of ethnic minority in a new country can experience difficulties due to the challenges posed by the acculturation process and asylum procedures. However, it is worth bearing in mind that the experiences of social exclusion by asylum-seeking children and families in Ireland are to a considerable extent akin to those of many children from indigenous communities in a number of respects. What is unique to the emerging problems for asylum-seeking children is the fact that they are more likely to experience poverty and social exclusion than other groups in Irish society due to higher levels of dependence on social welfare and higher levels of housing deprivation.[9] It would appear that policies currently in existence for asylum-seekers, such as the direct provision of food and accommodation, appear to be exacerbating this problem. Claude's need for privacy and personal space in his hostel was causing him great anguish. So much so that his attendance and overall motivation for school and other social activities was effected. However, the likelihood of Claude finding an alternative type of accommodation is very small primarily due to the inflexibility of such policies. There is a need for school staff to be aware of the external factors that affect children like Claude and to familiarise themselves with current statutory policies that impact on pupils in this predicament. I would suggest that further to this some school staff are in a unique position to be able to advocate on behalf of pupils like Claude who in many ways find themselves voiceless and under-represented. Claude felt powerless and consequently excluded from many decisions about important aspects of his life.

Furthermore, it is clear that Claude needed to talk and be listened to. His situation is indeed different when compared to that of a pupil who after the school day shares the support of family and friends and all that is familiar around them (i.e. their culture). The lack of this type of support adds to the stress experienced by Claude. Claude had the added complication of being alone and trying to 'go it alone' in a strange country and culture. Adolescence in normal circumstances is a time of separation and individuation; for asylum-seeking and refugee children further separations, losses and grief lie at the core of their experience.[10] While a large percentage of asylum seekers will have experienced loss through death, a significant proportion will have experienced loss and bereavement due to other reasons. Such reasons may include the leaving behind of family members and friends, home, belongings, roles, lifestyles and to a large extent their culture. In this case Claude identified some of these issues as the cause of his current difficulties. Likewise Vekic, in his study, acknowledges similar experiences and indeed elaborates on how additional factors such as fear, financial constraints and the practical difficulties of making contact with family for some young asylum seekers compounded their feelings of loss.[11] For most young asylum seekers the manifestation of post-migratory symptoms (insomnia, headaches, abdominal pain, feelings of fear, loneliness, confusion and poor concentration) is common place. If children are attending school it is likely that a child may present with one or more of these symptoms. Consequently school staff will need to familiarise themselves with the issues that confront asylum-seeking children in schools and be alert to those who may require intervention and special care. The National Health Strategy acknowledges the contribution of educational services to the health and social well being of all citizens.[12] In keeping with such recommendations some school staff may need to develop professional working relationships with local community care staff such as social workers, community nurses, GPs and psychologists. Lynch in her summation on working effectively with refugee children also points to the fact the health of refugee children must be considered beyond ensuring access to health care to include issues such as housing and education.[13]

Claude also identified that he found it somewhat difficult to make friends and made a passing but significant reference to his colour. Schools need to be alert to the possible barriers that these children may encounter in their daily lives both in school and in the wider community, e.g. bullying due to racism. As school is central to the child's asylum-seeking experience, there is an onus of responsibility on the school to steer away from traditional assimilatory trends and develop more inclusive intercultural models by developing partnerships with key members of ethnic minority community groups. In addition, where anti-bullying policies exist they should be explicit in their approach to combating racism and other forms of discrimination such as homophobia.

From Claude's case we are aware that the normal adolescent concept of exploring his 'identity' is proving problematic due to the many extra stresses experienced by asylum-seeking children. Claude is grappling with normal peer pressure issues and is uncertain how to respond. While most adolescents grapple with this concept, children of ethnic minority who are removed from their own culture may experience further difficulties. For an adolescent who is an asylum seeker or refugee and alone in a different culture it will be even more difficult. For many refugee and asylum-seeking children, constructing a new identity after their arrival in their new place of residence can be extremely challenging and difficult. If a child has had a traumatic encounter as a consequence of their seeking asylum (e.g. experienced the death of a loved one, witnessed or experienced torture or endured a lengthy and dangerous journey to 'freedom'), then the process of escape also intensifies their awareness of change in self, others and the outside world. On the other hand, it may also be the case that they perceive that their own culture has failed them and is now irrelevant and no longer their own. The greatest threat to identity in refugee adolescents then is not the feeling of belonging to two cultures but of belonging to none.[14]

It is not only unaccompanied minors that may require specific attention. Also worth bearing in mind are the circumstances of some children of ethnic minority who are living with their parents in a host country. These children too can experience difficulties during their adolescent years. However, these difficulties can be further compounded by additional family stress factors associated with the migratory or the asylum application process. For example, intergenerational and intercultural conflicts can erupt in ethnic minority families due to differences in attitude and behaviour between children and their parents. This can occur when both parties are experiencing adjustment problems associated with acculturation. Rice and Dolgin refer to cultural conflicts that can exist between parents and children in this context. One conflict that exists can be 'role reversal'. This can take place when children have a degree of fluency and comprehension of the spoken language of the host country and parents do not speak or comprehend the language. In effect children become 'cultural brokers'. This added dependence by parents on their children for communicating needs can result in prolonged family stress as a result of role reversal. This stress may manifest in adolescents by feeling angry or resentful towards their parents and can result in children blaming parents for their own difficulties with integrating in school or outside. Such cultural conflict within families can include many other issues such as changes made by adolescents on important lifestyle matters including dating, marriage and career choices. In these circumstances the lines of demarcation between parental roles can be altered. In Ireland these cultural conflict situations encountered by people of ethnic minority (particularly those living in hostel type accommodation) have been identified. Fanning refers to this as the 'infantalisation' of parents. In his study parents described how parental authority and respect was undermined by hostel life due to the loss of autonomy in day to day matters such as deciding what their children will eat or wear and for what length of time can their children play. Many parents of children in hostels stated that their parental authority was undermined by their lack of control or influence over matters which affected the day to day lives of their children. Parents stated that at times they feel prevented from providing positive role models for their children.[15] As a consequence of these types of situations children attending school from hostels may be experiencing related stress.

In many respects Claude is no different from any other sixteen-year-old male adolescent. Adolescent development at the best of times can be complex and harrowing for many children. Negotiating and confronting changes from the physical and intellectual to emotional and spiritual, the adolescent finds themselves in a whirlwind of uncertainty and change. Therefore it is acknowledged that adolescents will require resolve but also support from those around them. For asylum-seeking children, including children of ethnic minorities, these years can be particularly difficult, particularly if they are facing such formative years alone. Vekic in his study clearly outlines how for a percentage of unaccompanied minors in Ireland their normal adolescent development has been hampered by their refugee experience and lifestyle while living in Ireland. In Claude we have a clear illustration of how an asylum-seeking pupil may experience these stresses

For interculturalism and integration to be successful in schools or in society in general, it must be acknowledged that the acculturation process is a bilateral one requiring equal commitment from both parties. From a practical standpoint the school is an ideal place to pioneer new methods and programmes to address interculturalism. Schools can provide a safe and secure environment where learning and negotiation can take place. The emerging dynamic among pupils, staff and the wider community will be multifaceted, involving changes in values and attitudes, not to mention the development of skills and knowledge for all involved. In the school context this may require additional funding, extra personnel and a change of, or re-negotiation of, school policies and practices. It may even require a re-examination of the school culture and ethos. In addition to this our understandings and definitions of education and the purpose of school may also need to be further explored.[16]

Conclusion

In conclusion, it is essential that while working with refugee and asylum-seeking children in schools we acknowledge the resilience and resourcefulness that these pupils display on a daily basis. Claude's case study illustrates a number of issues requiring attention for those working in schools. The need for school staff to fundamentally re-define their own understandings of what it means to educate pupils has to be considered. It presents for all concerned the dilemma that can exist for some staff between where the teaching role ends and the caring role takes over.[17] The duty of care in advocating on behalf of more vulnerable pupils has traditionally been associated with the Irish education system. As global conflicts continue to impact locally on Irish schools and the Irish education system through the arrival of more asylum seekers, there will be a continued need for staff who care in our schools. Furthermore, the professional skills and knowledge of pedagogy and teaching methods may also need to be combined with pastoral skills training and education in order to serve the future pupil populations of Ireland in the twenty-first century. The emergence of Ireland as a multicultural place will continue to be a vibrant and welcome phenomenon. When national policies are fully implemented and local projects are resourced effectively in addressing cultural diversity and social integration we can raise to the challenge of creating not just a multicultural country but an intercultural country – a country with an education system that will be characterised by acceptance, tolerance, care and understanding in terms of the needs of all pupils.

Notes

1. Asylum refers to those people who due to fear of persecution in their home country are seeking to be allowed refugee status in another country. Refugee refers to those whose asylum applications have been granted.

2. Fanning, B., Veale, A., O'Connor, D., *Beyond the Pale: Asylum Seeking Children and Social Exclusion in Ireland* (Dublin: Irish Refugee Council, 2001).

3. Department of Health & Children, *National Children's* Strategy (Dublin: Government Publications, 2001).

4. Office of the Refugee Applications Commissioner, 2003.

5. See Cullen, P., *Refugees and Asylum Seekers in Ireland* (Cork: Cork University Press, 2000).

6. O'Regan, C., *A Report of a Survey of the Vietnamese and Bosnian Refugee Communities in Ireland* (Dublin: Irish Refugee Agency, 1998).

7. *National Consultative Committee on Racism and Interculturalism* (Dublin, 2001).

8. Ó Cuanacháin, C., 'Intercultural Education in Irish Post-Primary Schools' in *Intouch 52* (Dublin: INTO, 2003).

9. Fanning, B., Veale, A., O'Connor, D., *Beyond the Pale: Asylum Seeking Children and Social Exclusion in Ireland* (Dublin: Irish Refugee Council, 2001).

10. Rice, P. F., Dolgan, K., *The Adolescent: Development Relationships and Culture* (Boston: Allyn & Bacon, 2002).

11. Vekic, K., *Unsettled Hope: Unaccompanied Minors in Ireland, From Understanding to Response* (Dublin: Marino, 2003).

12. Department of Health & Children, *National Health Strategy* (Dublin: Government Publications, 2001).

13. Lynch, M., 'Providing Healthcare for Refugee Children and Unaccompanied Minors' in *Medicine, Conflict and Survival 17:2* (June 2001).

14. Rice, P.F., Dolgan, K., *The Adolescent: Development Relationships and Culture* (Boston: Allyn & Bacon, 2002).

15. See Fanning, B., Veale, A., O'Connor, D., *Beyond the Pale: Asylum Seeking Children and Social Exclusion in Ireland* (Dublin: Irish Refugee Council, 2001).

16. Boyle, P.J., 'Engaging with Ethnic Minorities' in N. Prendergast, L. Monahan, *Reimagining the Catholic School* (Dublin: Veritas, 2003).

17. See chapter two by Kevin Williams in this book.

The Role of the School and Education Programmes in Nurturing the Spirituality of Young People

Marian de Souza

Introduction

> The great malady of the twentieth century, implicated in all our troubles and affecting us individually and socially, is 'loss of soul.' When soul is neglected, it doesn't just go away; it appears symptomatically in obsession, addiction, violence, and loss of meaning. Our temptation is to isolate these symptoms or to try to eradicate them one by one; but the root problem is that we have lost our wisdom about the soul, even our interest in it.[1]

A recent news report in Australia described the plight of an elderly person who tripped and collapsed on the side of a busy road in a big city. She lay there for some hours, ignored by passing motorists until a young woman stopped and tried to help her. The elderly woman was not badly hurt, she was just unable to get up without assistance after the fall. A few hours later she died, not from the fall but from hypothermia due to the hours of exposure as she lay in the road. This was not an isolated regional incident. Incidents bearing similar characteristics of disinterest and non-involvement happen time and again in large cities the world over with equally tragic results and, for many of us, they raise some sobering questions: How could this possibly have happened? What is it that has brought us to this point in our evolutionary process that persuades us to look the other way when we see someone in need or shelter in the shadow of fear and anxiety rather than get involved? Perhaps this troubling symptom reflects a society whose members have become quite disconnected from the *Other* in our communities. It is precisely this disconnectedness that implies perhaps a flawed spirituality or, indeed, a spiritual immaturity where an individual becomes absorbed, or even obsessed with the interests and desires of self[2] and remains detached from the interests and desires of others except when they may have some relevance to or meaning for the self.

That this is the only context that our children and young people know and have experienced is of some significance, and given current statistics indicating the rise in the number of young people suffering depression and other illnesses related to mental health, alienation and marginalisation might be one of the consequences.[3] An emerging factor from discussions that seek to promote the wellbeing of young people is the recognition of the need to develop amongst them the qualities of resilience, belonging and connectedness.[4] On another front, the number of recent conferences and papers devoted to trying to find ways to address this issue is some indication of its seriousness[5] and it is pertinent to this discussion to note that the term *spirituality* has crept into the language of many of these professionals who work with young people.[6]

This chapter will discuss new understandings of the nature of spirituality as expressed in terms of the connectedness that the human person has with Self, the Social Other (in community), the Physical Other (in Creation) and a Transcendent Other. Further it will explore the implications such an understanding of spirituality may have for school environments and educational programs.

The Nature of Spirituality: An Expression of Connectedness

For many years, particularly in the Western world, spirituality and religion have been closely interlinked so that, very often, the terms have been used interchangeably. In his discussion of New Age spiritualities as a secular religion, Hanegraaff claims that religion may manifest as a 'spirituality' when it is:

> ...any human practice which maintains contact between the everyday world and a more general meta-empirical framework of meaning by way of the individual manipulation of symbolic systems.[7]

Hanegraaff further attributes 'spiritualities' and 'religions' to the individual and institutional poles within the broader area of 'religion' and claims that a 'religion without spiritualities is impossible to imagine but a spirituality without a religion is possible in principle.'[8]

A further elaboration on the link between religion and spirituality is also observed by Tony Kelly who argues that while spirituality is not a fully expressed faith, it is the 'condition for the flourishing and radiance of such a faith'.[9] However, Kelly makes the point that without a spiritual dimension, religious faith becomes a 'series of strangely coded answers to unasked questions' and suggests that spirituality is:

> ...being in touch with the real questions of life as they arise out of our most genuine sufferings and, for that matter, our most precious joys. It is the center where we do not surrender to some lesser version of ourselves, where we break out of all the 'little boxes', speak with our own voice or keep our own silence rather than follow the scripts that others have prepared for us. It is the challenge of finding the real center and the ultimate connection.[10]

The relational dimension of spirituality that Kelly points to has been recognised by other theorists and researchers.[11] Harris refers to spirituality as 'our way of being in the world in the light of the Mystery at the core of the universe'[12] and discusses seven components of contemporary spirituality. To begin with it is both *personal* and *communal* and these traits lead to the next two which are a strong interest in issues related to *justice* and the *non-human universe*. Then there is *age* as in the different ages of life which implies a lifelong learning aspect leading to ongoing development and maturation, and the *Age* in which we live which would provide a particular context for spiritual development. Finally, Harris mentions *experience*, *ritual* and *new understandings of the Sacred* which she regards as important components of human spirituality.

Elaborating on the relational theme, Nye coined the term *relational consciousness* to describe children's spirituality because they identified a:

> ...distinctive property of mental activity, profound and intricate enough to be termed 'consciousness', and remarkable for its confinement to a broadly relational, inter-and intra-personal domain.[13]

Nye went on to describe the children's awareness of being in a *I-Others, I-Self, I-World* and *I-God* relationship and suggested that it is this relational aspect of childrens' lives that led to 'meaningful aesthetic experience, religious experience, personal and traditional responses to mystery and being, and mystical and moral insight'.[14]

Groome alludes to the *spiritual journey* thereby recognising both the relational and the lifelong learning aspects, and he argues that our capacity to live as spiritual beings is the soul's preeminent expression, with the soul drawing us inward and outward through our own depths into relationship with others and with The Other.[15]

Most relevant to any discussion on contemporary spirituality is the literature that has emerged in the past few years. This has raised some new insights into the biological nature of spirituality as an essential and distinguishing human trait. These perspectives have drawn on recent advances in brain research which have involved exploring the functions of large areas of the cerebral cortex.[16] Ramchandran has shown that when a person responds to or discusses things that have religious or spiritual significance for them, there is a corresponding increase in activity in their temporal lobes. As a result they have dubbed the area of the temporal lobe the *'God spot'* of the *'God module'* which they claim has evolved to fulfill some evolutionary purpose although this does not offer any real proof about the existence of God.[17]

Newberg, D'Aquili and Rause have also investigated the activity in the brain when people move into deep meditative states or when they are involved in prayer. In a discussion of mysticism and the neurology of transcendence, Newberg claims that there is nothing magical about mystical experience, that it is 'nothing more or less than an uplifting sense of genuine spiritual union with something larger than the self'.[18] More relevant is Newberg's reference to research which indicates that those who have experienced genuine mystical states appear to enjoy much higher levels of psychological health than the general public in terms of 'better interpersonal relationships, higher self-esteem, lower levels of anxiety, clearer self-identity, an increased concern for others, and a more positive overall outlook on life'.[19] Newberg goes on to argue that if, as some would claim, mystical experiences were a product of a confused or disordered mind, it would be hard to explain why such minds generally demonstrate high levels of mental clarity and psychological health.[20] He finally concludes that 'humans are natural mystics blessed with an inborn genius for effortless self-transcendence'[21] and that like all experiences, moods, and perceptions, these unitary states are made possible by neurological function. More specifically, they are the result of the softening of the sense of self and the absorption of the self into some larger sense of reality that we believe occurs when the brain's orientation area is deafferented, or deprived of neural input.[22] Thus, Newberg's work has also has highlighted spirituality as a relational dimension of self.

Also pertinent to this discussion on spirituality is the claim from a new field in medical research, *neurocardiology*, that a major brain center is situated in the human heart which functions in dynamic with the fourfold brain in the human head.[23] The four which are contained in the head represent the whole evolution of life preceding use: reptilian, old mammalian, and human and Pearce draws on these findings to claim that 'outside our conscious awareness, this heart-head dynamic reflects, determines, and affects the very nature of our resulting awareness even as it is, in turn, profoundly affected' and it is within this mutually interdependent system that lies the key to transcendence.[24]

A different perspective on the relational dimension of the human person is offered by Albright and Ashbrook who cite research conducted by Hubel and Wiesel to argue that to be human is to respond to a human presence.[25] In their discussion on the neurobiology of faith they suggest that 'people experience and express their relatedness to the physical world as well as to the social world in terms that convey personal meaning' and claim that:

> When we lose the ability to personify, to experience and express the human and humane dimensions of our reality, then 'we have lost part of our humanity'. That essentially human part is the origin of transforming experience. The symbolizing capacity frees us from the constraints of a totally deterministic environment. This capacity to imagine, to construct, to play, which comes with the emergence of our new brain – the neocortex – is a central ingredient in religion.[26]

While much of these research studies into the functioning of the brain and the biology of spirituality are still relatively new and controversial, they do raise some pertinent questions about the relational nature of spirituality which may be an innate element in the build up of the human person. Equally, they do suggest that when the problems affecting young people are being investigated, perhaps, attention should be given to their expressions of spirituality.

The concept of spirituality as a distinctly human trait which is expressed through the individual's sense of connectedness to the human and non-human world was an important factor in a pilot study conducted in regional Australia.[27] It investigated the perceptions and expressions of spirituality of twenty-two young people, aged sixteen to twenty. The sample included young people who came from a religious background and others who did not belong to a religious tradition. In general, the findings suggested that there were different levels of connectedness that were apparent for each participant which were expressed through their attitudes and behaviours, and which contributed to their sense of identity and self-worth. For most of the participants the relational dimension of their lives was mostly concerned with the 'Other' in their immediate world, and their actions for justice and their perceptions of the important times in their lives were related to issues and rites of passage within these familial and communal frameworks. Some, however, indicated a level of connectedness to the 'Other' in the wider world. This was shown through their display of concern, compassion and empathy, and their action for people in less fortunate circumstances, for instance, refugees and victims of disasters. Finally, most spoke of their sense of a Supreme Being or transcendent presence outside the material world, and their concern with the Big Questions was often linked to an awareness of this presence.

Thus, the findings did suggest that levels of connectedness are linked to the spiritual expressions of young people which provide them with a sense of self-worth and which help them to find some meaning and purpose in their everyday. The findings also suggest that while a religious tradition may affect the spirituality of a young person, the development of their spiritual lives is more dependent on the positive relationships that they form from their very early years.

One factor that emerged from the study by de Souza et al. was that the different levels of connectedness that were expressed by the respondents reflected the understanding that spirituality may be described as a journey towards *Ultimate Unity*. This supports Newberg's discussion of the neurology of transcendence as a movement towards *Absolute Unitary Being*, that is, when the self blends into other and mind and matter become one and the same.[28] Newberg suggests that there is a *'unitary continuum'* where, at one point, a person may interact with others and the world but experience it as something from which s/he is apart. However, as s/he moves up the unitary continuum, that separateness becomes less distinct.[29]

From the respondents' comments in the study by de Souza et al. it became apparent that there appeared to be a movement through different strata of connectedness beginning with the relationships that were formed within the individual's immediate environment. These relationships were significant in shaping the individual's sense of identity and their perceptions and actions. With each accruing layer, the sense of connectedness was extended to the wider world and beyond and, sometimes, this was achieved through their educational experiences. Each layer brought with it a learned wisdom, empathy and compassion which was expressed by the way in which the individual interacted with others and the wider world. Importantly, the movement appeared to be a spiralling motion which moved forward but also could falter and fall back depending on the context of the individual's experiences and responses. It would be logical to assume that the forward movement that was evident for some of the participants may have had the potential to ultimately lead to the deepest level of connectedness where an individual would experience an all-consuming oneness with the Other. There is also the possibility that, sometimes along the journey, the individual may reach a mystical state where s/he may glimpse and/or experience moments of deep sacredness and transcendence in their everyday.

Education and spirituality

Given these new understandings of the nature of spirituality, there are clearly some implications for the design of school environments and educational programs in today's world. Contemporary Australian classrooms would tend to reflect classrooms in other Western countries where there is an emphasis on competition and a distinct pressure on the achievement of outcomes which will equip young people for the workplace within society, one which is dominated by a shrinking world so that global problems and concerns may sometimes override the problems and concerns of the local community. Indeed, many young people have experienced a sense of frustration and alienation through their experiences of conventional educational frameworks which do not always have a positive effect on the relational dimension of their lives. In addition, a powerful, sometimes destructive, force that combines media and telecommunication invariably invades private living spaces and dominates topics of conversation, attitudes and behaviour. Many of our young people have grown up with this invasion. They actually know no other way of being in this world. Others face endless choices related to lifestyle and, particularly at senior secondary level, career. Under such circumstances, it is not surprising if we find young people experiencing anxiety, tension, disillusionment and, sometimes, despair.

In response to this scenario, educational policies and practice have identified those young people who are *at-risk*, and various attempts to address their problems result in alternative programs that focus on the development of life-skills, resilience, and the promotion of a sense of connectedness. However, that these characteristics may reflect the spiritual dimension of learning and living has not always been considered. It is true that there has been a move in some countries over the past decade towards recognising a spiritual dimension in education,[30] however, most school programs have been influenced by a concept of rational intelligence as indicated by IQ tests developed in the early part of the last century. Thus, a pupils' ability in particular areas such as language and logic, with particular skills such as verbal and mathematical, and in processes such as comprehension, reasoning and memory have been used to determine their success in education. Gardner's (1983) Multiple Intelligence Theory began to change this thinking since it gave credence to a concept of different kinds of intelligence. This was something to which many educators responded positively since it offered wider access to success for learners. Moreover, it provided potential for greater flexibility in the process of teaching, learning and assessment.

Other recent theories that focus on the concept of emotional intelligence also have some implications for education.[31] Goleman argued that intellectual and emotional intelligences were not opposing competencies but were separate ones. He suggested that the logic of the emotional mind is associative; it takes elements that symbolise a reality, or trigger a memory of it, to be the same as that reality. That is why similes, metaphors and images speak directly to the emotional mind, as do the arts – novels, film poetry, song, theater, opera. Great spiritual teachers, like Buddha and Jesus, have touched their disciples' hearts by speaking in the language of emotion, teaching in parables, fables, and stories. 'Indeed, religious symbol and ritual makes little sense from the rational point of view; it is couched in the vernacular of the heart'.[32] Ultimately, Goleman pointed out that emotional intelligence is a basic requirement for an effective use of our rational intelligence – that is, our feelings play an important role in our thought processes.

Yet another perspective on intelligence was offered by Zohar and Marshall who have drawn on Ramchandran's studies and the possible existence of the 'God spot' to argue a case for a spiritual intelligence that enables a person to consider questions of meaning and value. They suggest that the spiritual quotient (SQ) complements the intellectual quotient (IQ) and the emotional quotient (EQ) in human intelligence. It is a process that:

> ...unifies, integrates and has the potential to transform material arising from the other two processes. It facilitates a dialogue between reason and emotion, between mind and body. It provides a fulcrum for growth and transformation. It provides the self with an active, unifying, meaning-giving center.[33]

They further argue that SQ is essential for the effective functioning of both our intellectual quotient (IQ) and emotional quotient (EQ):

Neither IQ nor EQ, separately or in combination, is enough to explain the full complexity of human intelligence nor the vast richness of the human soul and imagination... SQ allows human beings to be creative, to change the rules and to alter situations. It allows us to play with the boundaries, playing an 'infinite game'. SQ gives us our ability to discriminate. It gives us our moral sense, an ability to temper rigid rules with understanding and compassion and an equal ability to see when compassion and understanding have their limits. We use SQ to wrestle with questions of good and evil and to envision unrealised possibilities – to dream, to aspire, to raise ourselves out of the mud.[34]

Given the above discussion, the question for educators is how can this spiritual dimension in education be addressed? I would suggest that the concept of these three intelligences may provide a useful framework for the learning and teaching process so that cognitive and affective learning can be complemented by a spiritual dimension. To this end, I have introduced a learning model to my pupils which recognises that the rational, emotional and spiritual factors are necessary elements in a learning program (Figure 1). The first deals with the thinking aspect of learning, the second with the feelings involved, and the third recognises the inner reflective/intuitive processes that complement the first two processes in assisting young people as they attempt to make meaning from their interactions with their environments. Such an element has been identified by Merton as the *intuitive and interior way of knowing*.[35] Del Prete adds:

> ...to activate and grow in our capacity to know the living dimensions of truth requires practice in an intuitive way of knowing that Merton views as natural, though neglected in Western society.[36]

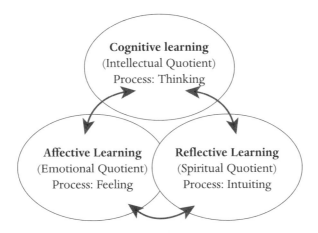

Figure 1
A model for learning – thinking, feeling and intuiting

Consequently, educators should consider the potential of all learning activities to promote not only knowledge, interest and participation amongst their pupils but which will engage pupils at a deeper, more personal level. Some of the factors that may lead to this are:

1. Exploring how the activity may address the relational dimension of the pupils' lives since it is a vital ingredient in their spiritual, emotional and, therefore, their intellectual learning. Story telling and personal narratives are useful strategies that may allow a pupils' personal story to resonate with the story of another thereby creating a sense of connectedness.

2. Ensuring that class and school community remain inclusive and open to dialogue so that differences are not merely accepted but celebrated in real and meaningful ways. This may help pupils develop feelings of compassion for and empathy with the 'Other' in their community.

3. Including time for silence, solitude and contemplation in the school day so that pupils may focus on their inner selves.

4. Creating sacred spaces in the school which are prayerful, aesthetic and accessible to all regardless of their backgrounds, cultures and religious beliefs.

5. Offering opportunities for pupils to develop their creative imagination and to experience joy, awe and wonder. This may be achieved by using an arts approach to teach across the curriculum as it engages the pupils at different levels.

6. Persuading pupils to share their gifts and talents, to accept responsibility for one another and to commit to action for the common good.

7. Encouraging pupils to become aware of a transcendent dimension and to respond to a divine presence in their lives.

Educators may further consider Palmer's description of the spiritual quest in relation to education:

> To know 'the rapture of being alive' and to allow that knowledge to transform us into celebrants, advocates, defenders of life whenever we find it. The experience of aliveness must never degenerate into a narcissistic celebration of self – for if it does, it dies. Aliveness is relational and communal, responsive to the reality and needs of others as well as to our own...
>
> ....
>
> We need a spirituality which affirms and guides our efforts to act in ways that resonate with our innermost being and reality, ways that embody the vitalities God gave us at birth, ways that serve the great works of justice, peace and love.[37]

Palmer also suggests that it is vital that an educational community should be a 'community of truth' and suggests the following virtues that give an educational community its finest form:

- *diversity*, not because it is politically correct but because diverse viewpoints are demanded by the manifold mysteries of great things;
- *ambiguity*, not because we are confused or indecisive but because we understand the inadequacy of our concepts to embrace the vastness of great things;
- *creative conflict*, not because we are angry or hostile but because conflict is required to correct our biases and prejudices about the nature of great things;
- *honesty*, not only because we owe it to one another but because to lie about what we have seen would be to betray the truth of great things;
- *humility*, not because we have fought and lost but because humility is the only lens through which great things can be seen – and once we have seen them, humility is the only posture possible;

- *freedom through education*, not because we have privileged information but because tyranny in any form can be overcome only by invoking the grace of great things.[38]

Conclusion

With the new knowledge that educators have today about spirituality, they would be remiss if they did not consider the implications for the development of their learning programs and the design of their school environments. More attention needs to be given to activities that promote positively the relational aspects of young people's lives rather than continue to propagate the highly-charged competitive climate that encourages the individual to work against their co-pupils thereby generating a de-humanising effect. Basic human virtues of love and compassion, truth, courage, humility, honour and integrity should be modeled regularly to counteract the values of greed, deceit, power, non-involvement and self-obsession that frequently dominate in the media. Schools should develop structures that allow pupils to have a voice which may encourage in them a sense of belonging and a cause for action.

Most importantly, there must be a realisation that teachers need to nurture the spiritual dimension of their own lives if they wish to address the spiritual lives of their pupils. Professional development programs need to be offered regularly to provide teachers with strategies that will raise their potential to be successful in this area. Only then will the spiritual dimension be recognised and addressed appropriately thus raising the potential of schools and educational programs to offer hope and meaning to all pupils and increasing their chances of developing as whole people.

Notes

1. Moore, T., *Care of the Soul: A Guide for cultivating Depth and Sacredness in Everyday Life* (New York: Harper Collins, 1992), p. xi.

2. In this chapter I shall refer to 'self' as the outer identity of an individual with corresponding expressions and behaviour. 'Self' will refer to the inner person.

3. A recent US report (September 2003) of the Commission on Children at Risk, *Hardwired to connect: The scientific case for authoritative communities* has identified the rising rates of mental problems and emotional distress amongst US children. In Australia, Mission Australia reported the findings of a survey undertaken in 2002 where depression/suicide was indicated by 52.6 per cent of a sample of 2,657 of young people aged between 12 to 25 years.

4. *Commission for Children at Risk 2003* (Victoria: Department of Education and Training, 2003).

5. For instance, the topic for the 10th Annual conference for Suicide Prevention in Australia (2003) was 'Finding meaning to sustain life: The role of spirituality in suicide prevention'. A 2001 conference in Ireland on 'Mood Swings, Depression and Suicidal Behaviour in Young People' which was opened by the Minister for Children, Mary Hanafin TD, mirrored this concern. Finally, there is a planned conference, 'The spiritual dimension in therapy and experiential exploration', at the University of East Anglia, Norwich, UK in 2004.

6. For instance, O'Connell Consultancy, *Evaluation of The Community Response to Six Incidents of Youth Suicide in Hume Region, June – September 1999: Community Document* (Victoria: Human

Services;, 1999); Lindsay, R., *Recognizing Spirituality: The Interface Between Faith and Social Work* (Western Australia: University of Western Australia Press: 2002); *Commission for Children at Risk 2003* (Victoria: Department of Education and Training, 2003).

7. Hanegraaff, W.J., 'New Age Spiritualities As Secular Religion: A Historian's Perspective' in *Social Compass 46* (2) (London: Sage, 1999), p. 147.

8. *Ibid.*, p.151.

9. Kelly, T., *A New Imagining: Towards an Australian Spirituality* (Melbourne: Collins Dove, 1990), p. 8.

10. *Ibid.*

11. Harris, M., Moran, G., *Reshaping religious* Education (Louisville, Kentucky: Westminister, John Know Press, 1998); Hay, D., Nye, R., *The Spirit of the Child* (London: Fount Paperbacks, 1998); Groome, T. H., *Educating for Life* (Texas: Thomas Moore, 1998).

12. Harris, M., Moran, G., *Reshaping religious* Education (Louisville, Kentucky: Westminister John Know Press, 1998), p. 109.

13. Hay, D., Nye, R., *The Spirit of the Child* (London: Fount Paperbacks, 1998), p. 113

14. *Ibid.*, p. 114.

15. Groome, T. H., *Educating for Life* (Texas: Thomas Moore, 1998), p. 325.

16. Persinger, M.A., 'Feelings of Past Lives Expected Perturbations Within Neurocognitive Processes That Generate The Sense of Self: Contributions From Limbic Liability and Vectorial Hemisphericity' in *Perceptual and Motor Skills,* 83:3, Part 2 (Missoula, Mont: Ammons Scientific ,1996); Ramachandran, V.S., Blakeslee, S., *Phantoms in the Brain* (London: Fourth Estate, 1998).

17. Zohar, D., Marshall, I., *SQ: Spiritual Intelligence, The Ultimate Intelligence* (London: Bloomsbury Publishing 2000) p. 95; Fontana, D., *Psychology, Religion and Spirituality* (Malden, USA: BPS Blackwell), p. 80.

18. Newberg, A., D'Aquili, E., & Rause, V., *Why Gods Don't Go Away: Brain Science and the Biology of Belief* (NewYork: Ballantine Books, 2001), p. 101.

19. *Ibid.*, p. 108.

20. *Ibid.*, p. 109.

21. *Ibid.*, p. 113.

22. *Ibid.*, pp. 113-114.

23. Pearce, J.C., *The Biology of Transcendence: A Blueprint of the Human Spirit* (Vermont: Park Street Press, 2002), p. 3.

24. *Ibid.*, p. 4.

25. Albright, C.R., Ashbrook, J.B., *Where God Lives in the Human Brain* (Naperville, Illinois: Sourcebooks Inc., 2001), p. 16.

26. *Ibid.*, p. 26.

27. de Souza, M., Cartwright, P. & McGilp, E.J., An Investigation into the Perceptions of the Spiritual Wellbeing of 16-20 year-old Young People in a Regional Centre in Victoria, unpublished report (Ballarat: Australian Catholic University, 2002).

28. Newberg, A., D'Aquili, E., & Rause, V., *Why Gods Don't Go Away: Brain Science and the Biology of Belief* (NewYork: Ballantine Books, 2001), p.156.

29. *Ibid.*, p. 145.

30. In Britain, the National Curriculum Council (1993) released a document entitled *Spiritual and moral development: A discussion paper,* which described spiritual growth as 'a lifelong process of encounters in which people respond to and develop insight from experiences which are, by

their very nature, hard to define'. Aspects of spiritual development were further discussed in a paper from the School Curriculum and Assessment Authority (SCAA, 1995). Also the Office for Standards and Education in Britain (Ofsted) (1994) articulated spiritual development as relating to that aspect of inner life through which pupils acquire insights into their personal existence, which are of enduring worth. It is characterised by reflection, the attribution of meaning to experience, valuing a non-material dimension to life and intimations of an enduring reality. 'Spiritual' is not synonymous with 'religious'; all areas of the curriculum may contribute to pupils' spiritual development'. In the US and Canada, various educators such as Moffett (1994), Miller (2000) and Kessler (2000) also have written extensively on spirituality and education.

31. Salovey, P., Mayer, J.D., 'Emotional Intelligence' in *Imagination, Cognition and Personality*, 9 (Amityville, New York: Baywood, 1990), pp. 185-211; Goleman, D., *Emotional Intelligence: Why It Can Matter More Than IQ* (London: Bloomsbury Publisher Inc., 1995).

32. Goleman, D., p. 294.

33. Zohar and Marshall, p. 7.

34. *Ibid.*, p. 5.

35. Cited by Del Prete, T., 'Being What We Are: Thomas Merton's Spirutality In Education' in Miller, J., Nakagawa, Y., *Nurturing Our Wholeness* (Rutland, Vermont: Foundation for Educational Renewal, 2002), p. 171.

36. *Ibid.*, p. 171.

37. Palmer, P., *The Active Life: A Spirituality of Work, Creativity and Caring* (San Francisco: Jossey-Bass Publisher, 1990), p. 8.

38. Palmer, P., *The Courage to Teach: Exploring the Inner Landscape of a Teacher's Life* (San Francisco, Jossey-Bass Publisher, 1998), pp. 106-107.

Relationships and Sexuality Education

Guidelines for Good Practice

Edel Greene

Introduction

The Foreword to the 1995 *Expert Advisory Group Report on Relationships and Sexuality Education* (RSE) emphasised that 'any programme which seeks to educate the whole person must have due regard for Relationships and Sexuality Education as part of the total programme'[1]. All schools in Ireland are required to provide some form of RSE now. This chapter explores the guidelines for good practice in bringing this about. We shall be looking in turn at policy development, parent involvement, teacher training, pupil participation and modular teaching of the programme.

The RSE programme is part of the new era of reform in Irish education, which through whole-school development planning requires delegation, collaboration, consultation and communication if it is to be effective. In this way, every member of the school community has a contribution to make in the process of developing the school's RSE programme whether as parents, teachers or pupils. Their different roles are defined and their contribution is highlighted in this chapter. What emerges is that through dialogue the RSE programme becomes an evolving rather than a static aspect of school life as evaluation and feedback permit growth in adapting to the needs of all members of the school community. This remains a condition of the school's ability to implement the RSE programme in a satisfactory way. Over the next few years it is envisaged that all schools will have an RSE policy and will be implementing the RSE programme. The difference between authentically addressing the relationship and sexuality aspect of a young person's development and having a document that testifies to the idea, rather than the fact, is dependent on good practice from the start.

Policy

The school policy document provides the foundation for the implementation and teaching of the Social, Personal and Health Education/Relationship and Sexuality Education programme (SPHE/RSE). In his evaluation study of the implementation of the RSE programme Mark Morgan has reported that:

> Despite the increase in the percentage indicating that they were drafting/completing the [policy] document, there is still a substantial number of schools where apparently little has happened. [2]

His research indicated that 49.9 per cent of the schools in the study had finalised the policy document in 2000 and that 44.7 per cent had circulated it. The development of the school policy is now a matter of urgency and schools need to move forward with the policy committee in producing a document that defines the school policy on RSE. A suggested policy statement on RSE could include the following structure. The introduction of the policy should give a detailed description of the socio-economic background of the school, a profile of pupils (age and gender), the trusteeship of the school and the school philosophy. The partners involved in the development of the policy should be identified: parents' representatives, teachers, principal and board of management representatives. A clear description of the collaborative process, including any questionnaires to parents, teachers, or pupils used to gather information, could be referenced in an appendix. The policy should state the aims and objectives of the school's RSE programme clearly and unambiguously. A brief summary of the moral framework the school will adopt should include the mission statement and a description of the content of the curriculum for both the junior and the senior cycle. The school's stance on topics such as abortion, contraception and homosexuality should be outlined together with summary information on what will, or will not, be taught and guidelines for teachers and staff practices. In this way the teacher is protected by the policy and the staff understand their collective responsibility in a whole-school approach to RSE. The RSE *Curriculum and Guidelines* emphasise that:

> An effective programme of RSE must be supported by the school climate marked by gender equality and a healthy respect for sexuality... In this regard every staff member has a role to play in the delivery of the school's RSE programme. [3]

The policy statement should explain how RSE will be organised in the school, a job description of the RSE co-ordinator, number of classes allocated to RSE and how the school will facilitate teacher training and in-service in RSE. The policy statement should include the school strategy for evaluating and assessing the implementation and teaching of RSE. This might well include the encouragement of reflective practice by teachers, group evaluation sessions and, if possible, a whole staff evaluation at least each year.

The suggested policy statement needs to be understood within the context of the whole-school plan. In this way it is connected to other school policies. Thus, the RSE policy requires that further policies be developed by the school and that they are referred to in the RSE policy; for instance, the school policy on disclosure and reporting sexual abuse, sexual harassment, bullying, guidance and counselling. The RSE policy should also include the school's procedures for dealing with a pregnant pupil. This should outline the informing of parents, an identification of support groups who assist in crisis pregnancy, the different procedures that are followed if the pupil is over eighteen, guidelines on how teachers deal with pupils who seek their help, and the informing of staff members that a pupil is pregnant. Another area that needs to be developed in conjunction with the RSE policy is the school's approach to sexual orientation. The school must include in its policy a commitment to combating homophobia, thus reaffirming its mission and vision statement in meeting the holistic development of all its pupils. Teachers again must be provided with guidelines on how to support a young person who discloses that they are gay or lesbian. The school must protect both pupils and staff members from prejudices and discrimination on the grounds of their sexual orientation.

A whole-school approach to RSE necessitates the inclusion of the ancillary staff in the policy development, implementation and evaluation of the programme. Ancillary staff often have to deal with pupils in sickbay, the school office or in extra-curricular activities. They must be familiar with the school policy, understand all school procedures and receive some level of training to assist young people in their development. The ancillary staff, especially those in the office, handle sensitive information often disclosed by parents over the phone, or by upset pupils. This responsibility should not be ignored or overlooked. Ancillary staff need to work closely with teachers, parents and principals in meeting their own needs and the needs of the school. The school policy should recognise the role of the ancillary staff and allow for their input into the writing of guidelines and procedures and in the evaluation of whole-school approaches to RSE.

Role of Parents

The RSE programme's emphasis on co-operation and collaboration with parents empowers parents and gives them a unique role in curriculum development. Morgan highlighted that in his study:

> The parents took the view that schools and parents have complementary roles with regard to relationships and sexuality education, part of which involves consultation and partnership with parents in the development of the programme within schools.[4]

Parents should therefore be participants in the development of the school policy on RSE, right through to the implementation and the evaluation of RSE in the school. They must be informed of new initiatives that arise out of the evaluation of the programme and be encouraged to continue to give feedback to the school on the programme. It must be remembered that parents can feel uncomfortable coming into schools. Some parents have had negative experiences of school and this can make them defensive and nervous in the school environment. Some only come to the school because of their child's discipline or behaviour problems. While there are many parents who are comfortable coming into the school the opportunity to do so is often limited and focused on events such as the school play, a graduation night or a fund-raising event. It is often parents of pupils that have problems that are most reluctant to come to the school. This strengthens the argument that all schools should have a home-school liaison teacher on staff, to meet parents in their home, identify their needs and explain programmes like RSE to them. Schools need to organise information nights for parents to review resource material, discuss their concerns and opinions on controversial issues, and create provisions for their active role in policy and implementation development. Mark Morgan noted in researching parents attitudes to information meetings on RSE, that among the parents who were 'motivated and interested enough to come' there was a 'great deal of satisfaction in having their questions answered and in getting an explanation of the rationale of RSE.'[5]

Getting a sub-committee of parents to work with a group of teachers in exploring aspects of adolescent development and examining issues that arise in teenage sexuality and relationships could enhance the development of the RSE programme. This sub-committee could report back to the parent body and parents with professional expertise should be invited to assist on such sub-committees. Giving parents the opportunity to share their experience of dealing with teenagers in post-primary school can be a learning experience for both teachers and parents. School parents' associations should not be viewed solely as fund-raising bodies but as forums for parents to run information evenings and workshops. Morgan reports that one fifth of parents who attended an advance information night on RSE did not feel that they had enough time to examine the resource material.[6] This issue could be addressed by running small workshops over the year for parents of each year group.

Schools cannot ignore parents who are opposed to the introduction of the RSE programme. Helen Davies, in an article entitled 'Sex Education: Are they safe in their hands?', voices opposition to the introduction of sex education and questions whether it is education or manipulation. She regards it as an infringement on the rights of parents. Writing in the *Catholic Medical Quarterly* she argues that:

> Lip-service is paid to the rights of parents. They may be told that there will be a sex education programme in the school, but it will be difficult for them to find out exactly what will be taught and the resources that will be used. They will be told that none of the other parents have complained, or even that it is part of the religion programme so it will not be possible to withdraw their children. What the sex educators have conveniently forgotten is that children of the same age will vary considerably in their levels of emotional maturity and come from differing home and family backgrounds. They may also be exposed to influences both within and outside the school which these same educators will be unable to control, for example bullying or exploitation.[7]

Schools need to address the fears and legitimate concerns that are expressed in standpoints like this. Parents have the right to withdraw their children from the RSE programme. The problem is that there is no provision for supervision of these pupils and this raises issues in regard to insurance cover for the school. The supervision of pupils is a continuing issue of debate within schools and a solution to the problem will require much serious negotiation between teachers, school management and the Department of Education and Science.

The RSE programme encourages schools to give parents advance warning before commencing the teaching of certain topics. Letters should be sent to parents giving them a date when the lessons will begin, an outline of the topics to be taught and a time to contact the school or the teacher to discuss concerns. Permission slips should accompany the letter for speakers or videos that will be used during the lessons. Parents' representatives could be invited to sit in on the speakers and report back on their assessment of the talk. Morgan's study found that 'while parents wanted consultation they did not consider that the objections of small minorities should result in the programme not being implemented'.[8] But in any case collaboration with parents is dependent upon the school's efforts to be open, welcoming and transparent in procedures and policies. Parents' voice on the education of their children is a right and not a privilege.

School Ethos
The RSE programme adopted by schools contains a moral framework that is informed by the inherent values and ethos of the school. This has to be translated into reality by schools. In a Catholic school, for example, this means exploring the theology of sexuality and understanding Church teaching on relationships and sexuality and on sex education. The American Bishops state:

> We do not accept the rationale that underlies sexuality education programs that offer only the 'quick fix' – an easy solution. Programs that facilitate easy access to contraceptive devices or that are focused primarily on preventing unwanted pregnancies or sexually transmitted diseases are short-sighted and foster irresponsible behaviour.[9]

Denominational schools cannot assume that teachers have been brought up in the religious tradition of the school, or that those who have, have an informed understanding of the Church's teaching on such matters. The school has to make teachers aware of how the ethos informs the values within the programme, while maintaining the teachers' right to their own personal convictions, religious belief and professional autonomy. Teachers on the staff of a denominational school need to sit down and examine the values inherent in the ethos and identify how they will teach the RSE programme. This is where religion teachers, school chaplains and church advisors can provide expert assistance and guidance. The *Resource Material* for RSE must be examined in light of the school ethos by both parents and teachers. These materials often arrive into schools and become the definitive teaching resource. This is largely because ease of access and lack of time mitigate against the refining and redesigning of material to represent the school ethos. Greater effort on the part of the denominational school needs to ensure that the RSE programme is faithful to the inherent values and ethos of the school. Mark Morgan concluded that the parents in his study overwhelmingly supported a moral framework for RSE, 'there was broad consensus that RSE should be... linked with attitudes and values'.[10] The American Bishops consider that the information in sex education programmes 'ought to be communicated within the context of formation, guided by the values and responsibilities of the whole person...'[11] The moral framework is regarded by the Church as essential:

> In addition to providing accurate information, sexuality education programs, to be adequate, must do more than teach *about* values and beliefs. They must promote and encourage behaviours reflective of these values.[12]

Parents who send their children to a denominational school have the right to expect that the values of their religious tradition be endorsed. Parents from a liberal democratic tradition need to be aware of this as a reality in choosing to send their children to a denominational school and schools for their part should make this abundantly clear.

Teacher Training

After all the policies are written and the parent information seminars are over the task falls to teachers to teach RSE. Morgan concludes that post-primary schools regard the optional training in RSE/SPHE for teachers as most important in continuing to develop RSE.[13] Teacher-training he points out, is central to the successful implementation of RSE and for its endurance as a viable part of the curriculum. Morgan highlights that 'RSE is likely to become an inherent part of the curriculum over the next few years, given the continuation of support'.[14] The number of post-primary teachers who participated in the RSE training had reached 1,700 in 2000. This is not a sufficient number for the implementation of RSE in all schools and to all classes. There are a number of important factors that have to be considered in the continued provision of RSE in-service and the encouragement of teacher participation. Firstly, while the Department of Education and Science has sanctioned that teachers' attending in-service training will be covered at the Department's expense, there is a great shortage of substitute teachers available for this work and they are not necessarily matched in subject speciality. Secondly, the teacher attending the RSE in-service is missing school time and possibly exam classes. This creates pressure for the teacher to make up for lost time and can result in their reluctance to attend the training. Thirdly, pupils and parents are often unaware of teachers' participation in in-service training. This can give rise to complaints about their absence especially if the in-service falls on the same day over a couple of terms. In-service programmes should therefore be held on alternative days and it would be an idea if schools included in their information letters to parents the dates of in-service and the names of teachers attending. Fourthly, time is required in school for the teachers who have attended the in-service to plan the implementation of their training, discuss strategies and brief teachers teaching RSE who did not attend the in-service. This allows for professional collaboration where there is a sharing of resources and an exploration of areas of concern or satisfaction that could be voiced at the following in-service course. Finally, the RSE support service needs to maintain contact with teachers between in-service sessions and to visit schools to establish the socio-economic and cultural needs of particular schools.

SPHE/RSE should now become a compulsory module in all teacher-training programmes. Universities and teacher training colleges must equip pupil teachers with the necessary skills and methodologies of the programme. As the in-service training in RSE aims to support the personal development of teachers, with regard to relationships and sexuality, so too should teacher training colleges. An emphasis needs to be placed on the personal development of the young teachers' self-esteem – listening skills and communication skills would form an essential part of this. Provision should be made in training young teachers to deal with sexual abuse disclosure and other sensitive issues. Training should include stress management, an index of support services and a guide to professional advice available to teachers. Where teachers have not received training in SPHE/RSE school policy should include an introduction to the programme by an experienced teacher on the staff in the school's induction of new staff. This allows schools to highlight the influence of their school ethos and explain the schools tailored programme. The school should also make provision in its policy to send untrained teachers on RSE in-service courses and to ensure that newly qualified teachers are not given SPHE/RSE until they have completed formal training.

In the area of teacher-training it is important to acknowledge that there are members of the school staff who have a wealth of experience and expertise in the area of pastoral development and SPHE/RSE. Teachers need to perfect and in some cases embrace the climate of collaboration fostered by the development of whole-school planning. Indeed, teachers on the staff of any particular school could be the best people to run training programmes for the new members of staff. This however needs to be embraced, recognised, encouraged and financed by the Department of Education and Science. Interested teachers could attend workshops for being RSE trainers and be certified as school trainers. Professional recognition of teachers' participation in further training, in-service and in-career development programmes like RSE needs to be provided by the Department of Education and Science through certification. Not only can the teachers within the school be utilised more effectively, so to can the teachers from neighbouring schools.

Cluster meetings of both primary and post-primary teachers should be held to enable them to become familiar with the totality of the programme, understanding how it begins and where it leads. A new perspective on the programme can be obtained through understanding the work of all teachers in all stages of a child's life. Community action and development projects could inform these meetings and look at the specific requirements of a given community. Input from help agencies, the Gardaí, the Rape Crisis Centre, Alcoholics Anonymous and other relevant Groups, especially parents' organisations, would create a unique forum for professional advice, discussion and information.

Undertaking to develop strategies in training and perfecting teachers' expertise requires commitment from teachers and schools. Time, money and resources are needed from the Department of Education and Science, all of which can be slow in coming. One thing that schools need urgently is the allocation of a counsellor for the Staff. Teachers are people with their own personal problems. They often work with pupils who have problems that affect them personally. If teachers are to effectively support pupils in crisis they need to be supported themselves. While there is the argument that this is outside the job description of a teacher and it is true that they are not counsellors, a young person spends up to fifteen years in school and a very significant point of contact they have with the adult world is the person of the teacher. During those years they face many life experiences that they are ill-equipped to deal with alone, for instance, the death of a parent, suicide of a friend or a crisis pregnancy. These experiences are not left at the door of the school, they are brought into the classroom and to the attention of teachers directly or indirectly. This can be happening more often in a class such as RSE because of the content of the course.

Pupils' Voice
In David Tuohy's and Penny Cairns' book, *Youth 2K: Threat or Promise to a Religious Culture?* they found that young people's experience of school centred on their relationships with peers and with teachers. They identified the 'social climate, as defined by friends and one's social standing within the peer group, was a key ingredient in making school enjoyable'.[15] The skills necessary to develop and maintain quality inter-personal relationships are fundamental to a pupil's overall positive development and socialisation within the school environment. Pupils are therefore relational and sexual people. Sexuality is an integral part of the human person and the school in addressing the holistic need of the young person must help them to comprehend their sexuality. This should be done in collaboration with pupils, allowing them to voice their needs and concerns in all aspects of their learning but especially in the area of relationships and sexuality.
Luke Monahan concludes that:

> Many areas of school life impinge on the effective learning for example: *curriculum development; behaviour code; exam policy; special needs provision; extra-curricular activities; home-school relationships.* The voice of the pupils needs to be heeded in respect of these areas. It is important to acknowledge that the pupil is not only at the receiving end of learning – the pupil also contributes to the learning of others in the school community.[16]

The Education Act 1998 recognises that pupils have a legitimate voice in education through the establishment of the Pupils' Council. Schools need to consult pupils in developing, implementing and evaluating the RSE programme. This can be done in a number of ways: questionnaires, small focus groups of pupils, class discussions on the structure of the lessons, an anonymous suggestion/question box for pupils to ask questions that they may be too embarrassed to ask in class, consultation with pupils on their own learning, what way they like the classroom set up for RSE class, their opinion of speakers or material used, their suggestions for future classes. The RSE programme highlights the importance of the pupil by encouraging that through negotiation the teacher works out a class contract with the pupils establishing the ground rules for the class. Pupils assume ownership of the contract because they have been instrumental in designing it. Referring to the class contract and reminding the pupil that they undertook to follow the rules reinforces positive discipline. Teachers need to be aware of the level of development each individual pupil is at and to understand the influences that affect this development. Pupils are the best source of information in identifying these influences and can also be a resource in suggesting ways of combating peer pressure and handling conflict at home or in school from their own experience. Peer leadership, peer mediation, twinning (fifth year pupil mentors a first year pupil), the prefect system and the Pupils' Council give pupils responsibility, training and confidence to communicate as assertive young people in an environment that listens and values their contribution. All of these initiatives serve to enhance the RSE programme and allow the aims and objectives of the programme to come to fruition.

Structuring a RSE module
In the teaching of the RSE programme one of the drawbacks to the effectiveness of the programme is the limited time given to the lessons. The programme recommends that RSE be taught in five or six timetabled periods. While RSE is a module within the SPHE programme, not all schools have the SPHE programme up and running, and many have difficulty finding the space on the timetable for the additional one period a week required. RSE is often taught as a module within the religion programme, or the six classes are part of a pastoral care class. Six lessons of RSE in isolation from the developmental programme of SPHE are limited in their effectiveness. It is questionable that issues such as sexual development and relationships could be explored at any depth over such a short period and in a class that occurs only once a week. Although RSE has cross-curricular links the material is often covered in isolation from other subjects with little or no cross-referencing. There is even the difficulty that pupils coming from the experience of formal learning in their subject classes are expected to adapt and be comfortable with the informal structure of the RSE class. It takes more than six weeks to get pupils accustomed to the approach of the RSE programme, the methodologies, the role of the teacher and the classroom setting it attempts to create. The very fact that it is limited to a class period per week means that pupils move from exploring their feelings and emotions, to sitting a class test or attending a subject class that is unaware of the content of the previous class. The concern

is that not enough time is available to debrief pupils and that unearthed feelings and emotions are left often for pupils to deal with alone.

One recommendation that would facilitate cross-curricular links, and make teachers more aware that RSE is taking place, would be for the school to identify a particular week in the school year when each year group would undertake the RSE programme. This date could be decided at the beginning of the school term, allowing the subject teachers of home economics, religion and biology to plan to cover or revisit the material that is linked to the RSE programme. Teachers, in this way get the opportunity to reinforce the RSE programme during their subject time and on a pastoral level because they will be aware of the pupils needs and sensitive issues that might arise during the week. Luke Monahan's definition of pastoral care provides a context for understanding the importance of attending to the pastoral dimension of RSE:

> School pastoral care ... influences all aspects of the life of the school, in particular policies, curriculum, roles and structures in order to sustain and enrich the educational experience of each pupil and consequently that of every person in relation to the school.[17]

Planning an RSE week means that parents can be given plenty of advance warning, including a list of speakers that might be booked and information nights that might be held for parents during the week. Time could be set-aside for pupils to meet with the guidance counsellor, chaplain or an outside counsellor. Teachers could also be given time for planning, to see parents and evaluate the programme as it progresses. This week could work only if it is run in conjunction with the developmental work of the SPHE programme and that there would be follow-up classes to continue to reinforce the skills, attitudes and values developed by the pupils.

Evaluation

A school's policy on RSE is a working document and it is envisaged that it will be reviewed and amended following the evaluation of the programme's implementation. The context for such an evaluation is the development of whole-school evaluation (WSE). This is a collaborative process where teachers, pupils and parents evaluate the school. The report on WSE 1999 explains that: 'the purpose of WSE is to evaluate collaboratively the work of the school as a unit and to foster and promote the development of school activities as a whole'.[18] Teachers are thus encouraged to evaluate their own practices, methodologies and implementation. This is done through reflective practice, collaboration with pupils and the inspectorate. There is also the possibility that, should WSE become a reality in schools, there will be an RSE inspector. If this happens teachers would have to become more open to external inspection and the role of the inspector would need to be understood as an external assessor in the consultative, collaborative work of the school. In the meantime teachers' evaluation of the RSE programme should include an evaluation of the aims and objectives of the programme, the identification of the strengths and weaknesses of the school's programme, pupil and parent evaluation of the programme and recommendations for the future development of RSE. Teachers' own evaluation of their practices would be enhanced by external appraisal from the RSE support team or a trusted colleague.

Post-primary schoolteachers, unlike primary teachers, are not familiar with external inspection, nor are they used to having other teachers in their classroom while they teach. Many find the prospect of inspection, or a colleague evaluating their class, to be a fearful prospect and an encroachment upon their autonomy. However, it could also prove a fruitful and rewarding exercise in reinforcing the work of the teacher and sharing professional advice and good practice. RSE teachers need to evaluate the content and the resources they use in the programme. This would involve exploring effective methodologies for certain topics, highlighting areas where difficulties arise for teachers in dealing with a particular topic or where pupils did, or did not, respond well to the material. This information needs to be recorded and suggested changes, or improvements, need to be discussed. The idea of team-teaching could assist the programme in the event that a teacher found a particular topic too difficult to teach. The evaluation of RSE should include teachers from other subject areas for instance, home economics, religion and science to review the cross-curricular links. An overall evaluation of the whole-school approach to RSE would examine pastoral care provision, information seminars, in-service attendance, allocation of resources, financial budget and staff participation in the programme. The evaluation of the RSE programme should be presented at a staff meeting, and details of the findings furnished to the board of management.

Conclusion
It has to be acknowledged that schools are limited institutions and that while there are high expectations from parents, the government and society in general, they are first and foremost places of learning. The existence of the points race and the use of the Leaving Certificate for selection means that schools, in attempting to address all the developmental needs of pupils, are often forced to prioritise academic as distinct from deeper educational goals. Although SPHE/RSE was considered to be not only important but urgently required by the Expert Advisory Group, it made no attempt to reduce the already over-crowded junior cycle curriculum. As society continues to turn to the school for the socialisation of young people there is a need for greater co-operation between the school and the community, more resources are required, professional assistance from community members such as the Gardaí, doctors, nurses, psychological services and parent organisations. The delivery of an effective RSE programme would certainly be aided by a reduced teacher-pupil ratio. Smaller classes allow teachers give pupils more individual attention, thus establishing good interpersonal relationships and enabling teachers to understand the personal issues that might be affecting pupils. Time is the most sought after commodity within the teaching

profession. Teachers need time to meet pupils, liaise with parents, listen to pupils, plan, evaluate and train. Despite the limitations, parents, teachers and pupils are engaged in collaborative work that has produced policy documents and witnessed the training and implementation of the RSE programme. It has come from the commitment, dedication and hard work of people who seek to make real the belief that education embraces the heart and the mind. It comes from a conviction that the young people are the future and that while debate remains as to the best way to meet their needs in the area of relationships and sexuality within the school environment, the school has as an obligation to try to genuinely address these needs within an educational framework. One dynamic aspect of the RSE programme is that it encourages schools to create structures that facilitate communication which is rooted in mutual respect for all stakeholders; it attempts to create a climate of open, honest, direct and focused communication between parents, teachers and pupils. Good practices in schools are identified in the school's ability to communicate effectively and continuously with the various participants, i.e. teachers, pupils and parents. Only through such communication can it become a community of inter-personal relationships sharing a common vision and mission. In this way relationships and sexuality education can be promoted not simply as a class subject but as a fundamental part of the everyday life of the school.

Notes

1. Government of Ireland, *Report of the Expert Advisory Group on Relationships and Sexuality Education* (Dublin: The Stationery Office, 1995), p. 2.

2. Morgan, M., *Relationship and Sexuality Education: An Evaluation and Review of Implementation: Summary of Main Findings* (Dublin: Government of Ireland, 2000), p. 102.

3. National Council for Curriculum and Assessment, *Relationships and Sexuality Education: an aspect of Social, personal and health education: Interim curriculum and guidelines for post- primary schools* (Dublin: National Council for Curriculum and Assessment, 1996), p. 8.

4. Morgan, M., *op. cit.*, p. 74.

5. Morgan, M., *op. cit.*, p. 84.

6. Morgan, M., *op. cit.*, p. 84.

7. Davies, H., *Sex Education: Are they safe in their hands?*, Catholic Medical Quarterly, Vol. XLVIII, No. 1 (1997), p. 7.

8. Morgan, M., *op. cit.*, p. 74.

9. United States Catholic Bishops, *Called to Compassion and Responsibility: A Response to the HIV/AIDS Crisis* (USA: Origins 19, 1989), p. 35.

10. Morgan, M., *op. cit.*, p. 74.

11. United States Catholic Bishops, *op. cit.*, p.36.

12. *Ibid.*, p. 36.

13. Morgan, M., *op.cit.*, p. 110

14. *Ibid.*, p. 19.

15. Tuohy, D., Cairns, P., *Youth 2K: Threat or Promise to a Religious Culture?* (Dublin: Marino Institute of Education, 2000), p. 113.

16. Monahan, L., *Moving Forward with Students* (Dublin: Irish Association for Pastoral Care in Education, Marino Institute of Education, 1999), p. 7.

17. *Ibid.,* p. 3.

18. Department of Education and Science, *Whole School Evaluation: Report on the 1998/1999 Pilot Project* (Dublin: Stationery Office, 1999), p. 12.

Bereavement Support in Second-Level Schools

A Review of the Rainbows Programme

Evelyn Breen

Introduction

In 1991, during a class on the Resurrection with sixth-year pupils, I noticed that a particular girl seemed to be getting upset. She started to cry. After class, I took her aside and asked if I could help. She told me that she was upset because her father had died two years previously and that there was nobody to whom she could talk about how she felt. Over the next few weeks, it seemed that a large number of pupils were revealing that there was a loss in their lives and that they would like help to explore and come to terms with it. I felt that surely there must be some programme out there that would help them. I started actively looking for such a programme. Fortuitously, around this time, I discovered the Rainbows bereavement support programme, which is:

> A not-for-profit international organisation that offers training and curricula for establishing peer support groups. These curricula are available for children and adults of all ages who are grieving a death, divorce, or any other painful transition in their family. Since it is necessary for emotional healing to take place after significant loss, the purpose of the support group is to provide those grieving with an opportunity to share their feelings in an accepting environment supported by trained compassionate adults. Rainbows aims to furnish the participants with an understanding of their new family unit; to assist in building a stronger sense of self esteem; and to direct them towards a healthy resolution of the changes that have taken place in their personal lives.[1]

This chapter will initially explore the effects of bereavement on adolescents before outlining a quantitative research project that I undertook to examine the effectiveness of the Rainbows bereavement programme among adolescents in a second-level school.

Changes in society
In many ways Irish family life has changed greatly over the past twenty years.

It can no longer be presumed that all children come from a two-parent home. In 2002, 968 judicial separations and 2,591 divorces were granted. Between the years 1996 and 2002, the numbers granted a divorce increased from 9,000 to 35,000. Of the 60,521 births registered in 2002, 31 per cent of total were to unmarried parents. One of the consequences of these changing patterns is that the traditional supports of the extended family are not available to anyone grieving a significant loss. Commenting on similar changes in US society one commentator said that:

> Like it or not, we are witnessing family changes which are an integral part of the wider changes in our society. We are on a wholly new course, one that gives us unprecedented opportunities for creating better relationships and stronger families but one that also brings unprecedented dangers for society, especially for our children.[2]

Many of these changes have had a significant effect on how people, particularly adolescents, deal with grief.

Adolescence and Grief

Because the young person's experience of life is so much shorter than an adult's, her[3] grief to her may seem more severe or life-threatening. It is more likely to leave her submerged in despair. Kubler-Ross recognised the significance of adolescence for grief:

> With an adolescent, things are not much different than with an adult. Naturally, adolescence in itself is a difficult time and the added loss of a parent is often too much for a youngster to endure. They should be listened to and allowed to ventilate their feelings, whether they be guilt, anger or just plain sadness.[4]

For adolescents, the death of a parent can be doubly traumatic as it occurs at the time when the adolescent is plagued by doubts of her own worth. At this stage also, the adolescent is endeavouring to find new structures and boundaries and parameters for her life and become independent of the parent. Some of what the adolescent is trying to achieve will be worked out through rows or ambivalent or aggressive behaviour towards the parent. If the death of a parent occurs at this time, the young person will need to look at the guilt that she may experience and to recognise it as a normal part of the grieving process.

Another complication that may arise in the mind of the adolescent (and cause problems) is the fact that adolescents sometimes look for what is described as an *idealised parent substitute*. If during this time the parent dies, the adolescent's normal feelings of guilt may be strengthened:

> This very healthy and normal developmental search for substitute parents and families however can greatly intensify the guilt of adolescents whose parent dies during this stage.[5]

Children live in a solipsistic world where they believe that events in their world are the consequence of their actions. For example, if a parent dies or leaves the home, shortly after having had a row with the adolescent, the adolescent may feel that the parental action was caused by their behaviour. It is imperative that adolescents get help to put things into context.

Babies are born with an instinctive sense of attachment. At varying stages throughout their lives, children need to sever the attachment to the parent. Cutting the apron strings and detaching themselves emotionally from the parent can cause emotional anxiety and stress. Gaffney describes this process a follows:

> Of all the instincts we are born with, attachment is the most important and pre-eminent guiding force in behaviour throughout infancy and childhood and remains a potent force throughout life. For a child, attachment is the first necessity for survival. When its attachment needs are not met, all other instinctive behaviours – feeding, exploring, play, take second place.[6]

Consequently, it is important to be alert to previous unresolved losses that can complicate the grieving process for an adolescent. S/he may have in their life unresolved grief arising from anxiety and separation stress or a grief for a grandparent or friend who died and whose death has not been properly grieved.

Also it must be borne in mind that grief has no calendar. Sometimes teachers expect their pupils to have 'got over' the death or divorce/separation of a parent because a certain period of time has elapsed. They then expect them to conform to our perceptions or expectations of how long they should grieve and when the grieving process can be expected to be over. In fact, the time it takes to grieve is as individual as the loss experienced.

Ventilation

The adolescent needs to be supported during this traumatic time, not taking sides or judging her, but helping her to understand that the feelings which she has are in themselves neither good nor bad, they just are. We need to be able to help the adolescent towards a continued sense of self-esteem and dignity as a person. Often, if the parents are having a very contentious divorce or separation, the child can feel disloyal by listening to stories of one parent's betrayal of the other. The young person needs help in voicing their own feelings without feeling blamed or disloyal. It may be important for us to help the young person recognise the members of her extended family who may be a means of support for her. Johnston has highlighted that:

> In a *good* divorce, new partners families and friends take a more neutral stance to the break-up of the marriage, and they honour the rights and duties of both parents to continue to care for their children. This is especially important for children who are painfully torn by loyalty conflicts and a sense of loss, as their family, like Humpty Dumpty, seems shattered to pieces.[7]

It is clear that the school chaplain can have a very significant role in accompanying the young person through a loss but also in helping the pupil to recognise who is still around in their family and who they can rely on now.

Sometimes a grieving teenager is so shocked by the death of the parent that she feels that she should be grieving at all times. She needs someone significant whom she trusts to give her permission to stop grieving for a time after she has cried and talked. She needs to be given a sense that life still goes on despite what happened. Kubler-Ross recommended that she could be encouraged to see a film or other entertainment:

> This gives them permission not to grieve all the time and suggests that it is not an act of disloyalty to the deceased parent to enjoy life again and that there is a future without the deceased parent.[8]

One way in which the school can facilitate this is by the chaplain arranging to meet the pupil at the same time each week and thus providing a focus for her grief and allowing her to get on with the rest of her time in school.

The School's Role

Schools are not always the most sympathetic places for those who are bereaved. Teachers and chaplains may be unaware of the grief with which some pupils have to cope. As educators our focus can be on the syllabus and exams, unaware that the pupil may feel isolated and confused. There can be a presumption in schools that each child comes to school every morning from a family where there are two parents who love her and where they have had a good breakfast. There is a real need to have trained staff in every school who can identify the signs of grief and offer support. Kubler-Ross advises that:

> If we tolerate their anger, whether it is directed at us, at the deceased, or at God, we are helping them to take a great step towards acceptance without guilt. If we blame them for daring to ventilate such socially poorly tolerated thoughts, we are blameworthy for prolonging their grief, shame and guilt which often results in physical and emotional ill health.[9]

Once teachers are trained in what to expect, a much better and easier relationship between pupil and teacher can ensue. Some of the myths we have about grief regard it as an event. In fact, it is a process. Because of these myths, we tend to expect that as we move further away from the event of the death, the intense feelings disappear and we are able to think about the person who died without such a great intensity of feeling, merely because the person has been dead for, say, two years. This has been found to be untrue. According to MacDonald the adolescent moves from a time when she thinks about the person all the time to where she thinks of the deceased person sometimes:

The intensity duration and some qualitative aspects of grief probably change over time, but the peaks of emotional intensity, even after several years have passed, may still be quite elevated ... Intense grief can be experienced even several years after the loss.[10]

Consequently, schools need to have ongoing bereavement support available to pupils. Research carried out among guidance counsellors in the USA investigated the grief counselling services of middle and high schools.[11] The findings of this study showed that only 42 per cent of respondents reported that they had grief counselling service available in their school. Of the 42 per cent, 81 per cent of these said that it was an ongoing service, 67 per cent reported that they had implemented it as a result of a sudden death in school and 18 per cent reported that guidance counsellors themselves provided the service. These findings indicate that there are many pupils in schools in the USA that do not have access to an ongoing bereavement counselling service. There is anecdotal evidence to suggest that the situation in Ireland is not much better. The adolescent spends the greatest part of her day either in, travelling to or from school. Therefore, it stands to reason that grief symptoms may be most apparent and most obviously in need of addressing in the school situation.

Because of the remaining parent being themselves in need of care and support, the focus of attention at home may not be on the young person. This is another reason for looking to the school to provide the adolescent with coping skills to help adapt to and accept the loss. Throughout their life, each person is faced with a succession of minor or major events such as childbirth, new job, illness, serious injury or bereavement. These can be perceived as threats not only resulting in emotional distress at the time of the event but there may also be further long-term cumulative effects on both the person's physical and psychological health.[12] Usually the individual does not remain passive in front of these adverse events; she tries to cope with them. Coping is meant to indicate the way used by individuals to adapt themselves to disruptive situations. If we can help the bereaved pupil to cope in a healthy way we will help them to have a greater quality of life in the long term.

Increasingly in Ireland today we find some exceptional loss situations. These include parent on military tour of duty abroad for an extended period, stepfamilies, succession of different partners to the custodial parent, to some of which partners the children get emotionally attached, and refugee children who experience the loss of homeland. The grieving pupil in the school community may seek out the chaplain for help, counselling or to be offered a programme to help her cope with the grieving process. The young person may base her approach towards embracing a healthy adult life on our response. For this reason, understanding the grieving process and knowing how to respond is vital. The aim of the Rainbows programme is to help each adolescent come to terms with the grieving process by acknowledging the pain and working through it. Bowlby warned that:

Sooner or later, some of those who avoid all conscious grieving break down usually with some form of depression.[13]

Consequently, my research examined the Rainbows programme, as used in second-level schools, with a view to answering the question. 'Is the Rainbows programme efficient in helping or handling the healing process?' In the light of the foregoing, the following were the research questions that guided the research project: what is the adolescent experience of bereavement and how does it differ from the adult experience? In the light of the differences, what is the role of the school chaplain? What are the benefits or otherwise of therapeutic interventions like Rainbows?

The Search for Meaning
Research in the USA has shown that people facing the death of a significant person are helped when they can find meaning in life. The research covered 217 people over two years from the death of a significant person in their lives. It was found that over time most people are able to find meaning and put the loss aside and that finding meaning is critical for adjustment and healing. Other conclusions that they drew from this research were that a significant subset did not search for meaning and yet appeared relatively well adjusted to their loss. As well as this, less than half reported not finding any meaning, even after one year. However, those who did find meaning continue to seek for meaning rather than putting the issue aside and carrying on.[14] We can probably conclude from the above research that if the person has belief that there is meaning in life before the event, this will help them to cope with the losses that they will encounter through life.

Batten and Oltjenbruns[15] in studying sibling bereavement showed that the experience served as a catalyst for the adolescent's spiritual development. Their aim was to discover whether belief in the afterlife enhanced bereavement recovery following different types of death including suicide, homicide, accidental and natural causes. The data collected from the respondents illustrate their shifting perceptions of self, others, the sibling relationship, the higher power, death and life. These studies seem to be supported by separate studies carried out concerning belief in the afterlife as a buffer in suicidal and other bereavement by Smith et al.[16]

The above research highlights how important it is for any bereavement support to pupils in our schools must allow for and facilitate their search for meaning. Furthermore, it is vital that the person who facilitates this search is both personally and professionally trained to engage in this type of work. The role of the school chaplain is clear here.

Practical steps
In an earlier chapter in this book Seán O'Driscoll deals very well with how schools can respond practically to death in the school so there is no need for me to deal with this in detail here except to summarise one plan for dealing with death that I have used myself. Firstly, immediate information needs to be

given. Therefore, an accurate account of the circumstances of the pupil's death needs to be conveyed to the class. Pupils should be given time to reflect, write and talk about how they feel. The next step is to elicit feedback from the pupils. Further information should be provided as it becomes available (donation of organs, results of post-mortem, wishes of the family, funeral arrangements). Questions that arise include the following: Are they (the class) to attend the funeral? Be involved in the liturgy? Following the funeral, they may wish to write a letter of goodbye to the deceased, which may be put in book form and given to the parents. Long-term support and counselling may need to be provided for close friends/staff.[17] As Seán points out in his chapter it is essential that a school has a plan in place before the critical incident occurs.

The Research:
Background – The Rainbows Programme Described
This study intends to be a quantitative study of the Rainbows programme. The Rainbows programme deals with ages from 2 years to adult. Each Rainbows programme is age appropriate; all 4-5 year olds work together, all 11-12 years olds, etc. Each group of five to eight people is led by at least one trained facilitator. They meet at the same time and place every week, to provide continuity and security. The programme offers five age-related curricula: *Sunbeams* for pre-school children, *Rainbows* for 4 to 11 year olds, *Spectrum* for 12 to 18 year olds, *Kaleidoscope* (college age/adult series) and *Prism* which is for separated, divorced or widowed adults.

The Rainbows programme for adolescents is a fourteen-week peer support programme running through twelve one-hour weekly sessions and two half days, one at the end of the sixth session and the other at the end of the twelfth session. During the sessions there is always a topic to be discussed (for example, anger, guilt or fear) which will focus with issues which the young person may be attempting to deal with such as *'who can I trust now that my mum/dad has died* (or left the house)?'

Aim of Current Research
The intention of this study was to compare the responses of the twenty post-Rainbows pupils with the non-attendees at Rainbows, looking for significant differences in their ability to cope with grief. In particular, the study wished to pay particular attention to signs of unresolved grief or denial of feelings around the grieving process. The study also wished to investigate if any significant movement towards healing was evident after participation in the Rainbows programme.

Research Sample
The author sought to develop a representative sample of forty pupils who would meet the following requirements: twenty who had been participants in the Rainbows programme, of whom ten should have been bereaved by death and ten by separation or divorce. The other twenty should not have been participants in Rainbows or any equivalent programme. Over the past ten

years, two hundred and seventy-five pupils had participated in the Rainbows programme in my school, eighty of whom were still in the school. Pupils were invited to participate and permission to carry out the study was received from parents and school management. Those who agreed to participate were roughly even in sex, nine boys and eleven girls, and of these twenty pupils, ten had been bereaved by death and ten by separation. The author then sought and found a further twenty pupils who matched these in sex and bereavement details.

Research Design

The Rainbows programme was selected as the basis of this study because the author has been involved with Rainbows as facilitator, coordinator and registered director. This programme is also widely used in schools and parishes in Ireland. My involvement with the programme over ten years would provide access to pupils at various stages in the grieving process and with a broad age spectrum. Working in a second-level school meant that the author would also have access to pupils who had not participated in the Rainbows programme.

This study looked at the question: 'Does the Rainbows programme bring the young people from hurt through healing to hope?' This was done by means of questionnaire survey of a single group of post-primary pupils, aged twelve to eighteen years. The sample was composed of forty pupils, twenty of whom had a bereavement through death or separation and who had participated in the Rainbows Programme. The other twenty pupils though having a similar bereavement had not attended Rainbows or any equivalent programme.

The instrument used for the survey was the *Texas Revised Inventory of Grief*, henceforth known as TRIG[18] (see appendix two). This was judged to cover the required field of measurements, giving a picture of the study group's current situation. It has three different questionnaires – one on past behaviour, one on present feelings and one on related facts. This instrument, while being primarily a measurement of grief after death, was easily adapted to measure grief after separation/divorce by the omission of two of the 'related facts' questions and by replacing the references to death with appropriate phrases for separation or divorce. For example, the word 'died' is replaced by the word 'left'.

TRIG also elicits the following information: Age and sex of respondents, perceived depth of relationship to person died/left and age of the person who died. Since separation is not an age-related phenomenon (while death is) the age of the person who left is not relevant. TRIG is completed by the respondents who score each question in Parts I and II with one of the five scores (a) Completely true (b) Mostly true (c) Neutral (d) Mostly false and (e) Completely false. The questions in Part III are answered True or False.

Research Data

		Frequency	Percent	Valid Percent	Cumulative Percent
Valid	Separation	19	47.5	47.5	47.5
	Death	21	52.5	52.5	100.0
	Total	**40**	**100.0**	**100.0**	

Table 1
Number of Respondents Effected by Death and Separation

Table 1 shows the numbers affected by death and by separation/divorce. As will be seen, the respondents were divided almost equally between both trauma events. The next table, Table 2, shows the relationship between the respondent and the absent person.

		Frequency	Percent	Valid Percent	Cumulative Percent
Valid	Father	25	62.5	62.5	62.5
	Mother	2	5.0	5.0	67.5
	Grandfather	4	10.0	10.0	77.5
	Grandmother	4	10.0	10.0	87.5
	Brother	1	2.5	2.5	90.0
	Sister	2	5.0	5.0	95.0
	Cousin	2	5.0	5.0	100.0
	Total	**40**	**100.0**	**100.0**	

Table 2
Relationship of Dead/Separated Individual to Respondents

It will be seen from the table that fathers are the highest category of absentees. This is probably because the majority of the separations in Ireland involve fathers leaving the family home.[19]

		Frequency	Percent	Valid Percent	Cumulative Percent
Valid	Male	18	45.5	45.0	45.0
	Female	22	55.0	55.0	100.0
	Total	40	100.0	100.0	

Table 3: Sex of Respondents

It was important to ensure that among the respondents neither sex was over-represented. Table 3 shows how the respondents were broken down by sex. This is a relatively even balance among male and female participants. The next table (Table 4) of information about the respondents shows their age breakdown.

		Frequency	Percent	Valid Percent	Cumulative Percent
Valid	13	9	22.5	22.5	22.5
	14	5	12.5	12.5	35.0
	15	8	20.0	20.0	55.0
	16	11	27.5	27.5	82.5
	17	7	17.5	17.5	100.0
	Total	**40**	**100.0**	**100.0**	

Table 4: Ages of Respondents

Table 4 shows that the participants' are fairly evenly divided over the spectrum of second-level school-going ages.

		Frequency	Percent	Valid Percent	Cumulative Percent
Valid	0-3m	1	2.5	2.5	2.5
	3-6m	3	7.5	7.5	10.0
	6-9m	2	5.0	5.0	15.0
	9-12m	2	5.0	5.0	20.0
	1-2y	7	17.5	17.5	37.5
	2-5y	12	30.0	30.0	67.5
	5-10y	11	27.5	27.5	95.0
	10-20y	2	5.0	5.0	100.0
	Total	**40**	**100.0**	**100.0**	

Table 5: Remoteness of the Death/Separation

Table 5 shows how long it has been since the pupils were bereaved. The data from this study was processed using the SPSS package. The main findings are charted below. Not all of these are significant at any reasonable statistical level. However, some are significant and these are noted. The parameter NOWFEEL in these charts is an average of the answers to the total questions in Part II, where the questions are about current feelings.

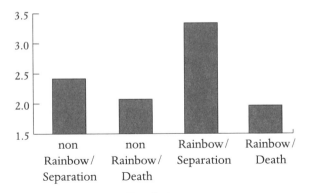

Graph 1
**Current Feelings Shown for Rainbows Participants and Non-Rainbows
Participants for Both Death and Separations**

In Graph 1, the chart explores the current emotional state of four groups of
respondents – (a) respondents who had experienced a death-related
bereavement and had participated in a Rainbows programme (b) respondents
who had experienced a death-related bereavement and had not participated in a
Rainbows programme (c) respondents who had experienced a separation-
related bereavement and had participated in a Rainbows programme and (d)
respondents who had experienced a separation-related bereavement and had
not participated in a Rainbows programme. This set of data contains a
significant result. There is a marked difference in current emotional state of
these respondents who had suffered a separation-related bereavement and who
had participated in a Rainbows programme from those with a similar
bereavement who had not participated in a Rainbows programme. This is a
distinct improvement in well being in terms of how they now feel with regard
to coping with life since the loss of their parent.

In dealing with life after the death of a loved one, there is no significant
difference, on average, between the responses of those who have participated in
a Rainbows programme and those who have not. However individual questions
do show some differences, which will be discussed later. The absence of a
significant result for the death-bereaved may be due to the small size of the
survey or may have some other reason.

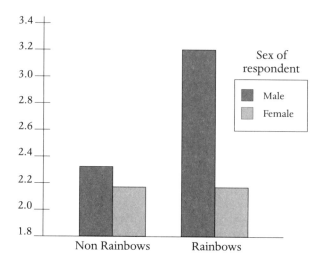

Graph 2: Current feelings Shown for Rainbows Participants and Non-Rainbows Participants Divided by Sex of Respondents

In Graph 2, the respondents who participated in a Rainbows programme and those who did not are separated into groups by sex of respondent. Here, there is a significant distinction evident between the sexes. Boys who had participated in the Rainbows programme were much nearer to acceptance and well-being than those who had not been through the programme.

It would appear that this result does not hold good for girls. Therefore, at first glance, it seems to indicate that Rainbows does not help girls who are suffering from bereavement in the same way as it does boys. However, such a conclusion ignores the documented differences between boys and girls in their responses to bereavement. Research carried out by Judith Wallerstein[20] indicates that response to bereavement must be looked at in both immediate and intermediate time intervals. She found that boys tend to have a very negative immediate response with a more positive intermediate response. Furthermore, her research also found that girls, on the other hand, tend to take on a responsible adult role in the immediate term, but in the intermediate term, when they are in their twenties or late teens, they can run into emotional difficulties. This is a time for commitment to one partner but the victims of childhood bereavement can be haunted by feelings of guilt or uncertainty, which inhibit them from forming and sustaining stable long-term relationships. Wallerstein calls this the *sleeper effect*.

The current research is in accord with Wallerstein's views. Since the survey group are in the immediate phase, no differences between girls is not an unexpected result while, if Rainbows is a successful programme, an improvement may be noted in the boys at this stage. This is, in fact, what the data indicates.

In analysing the answers to questions about present feelings, the analysis shows that respondents who did not participate in a Rainbows programme were nearer to emotional integration than those who did. While this may seem, *prima facie*, that Rainbows is counter-productive, it may also be evidence that the respondents who did not participate in a Rainbows programme may be in denial about their feeling or could have other sources of support – for example, the home.

In relation to questions about being upset (by the absence of the loved one and by their thoughts/memories of this person) when dealing with separation, the analysis showed that respondents who had participated in a Rainbows programme were nearer to healing than those who had not. This would point to a link between a return to wholeness, for both boys and girls, and participation in a Rainbows programme.

It would be interesting to further investigate the other questions in Part II as to why the differences are not significant. It is noteworthy that for no question was there a significant evidence of a greater level of healing for respondents who did not attend a Rainbows programme over those who did. This may indicate that those on the programme were in greater need of support.

When the answers are analysed based on the sex of the respondents, other significant results were evident. In answering questions covering continuity of negative feelings (upset, it is unfair, I can't accept it), the male Rainbows respondents scored significantly higher in terms of emotional integration than those who had not participated.

It can be suggested that the positive responses from Rainbows is due to the programme encouraging the person to explore all their feelings regarding their loss. In doing this, they are able to release them instead of keeping them bottled up and thus achieve integration and healing sooner than their counterparts who may still be in denial about their feelings of loss.

Discussion of Results and Practical Proposals

These findings indicate that Rainbows is effective in building up the self esteem of adolescents who have suffered a bereavement through death or separation, both in helping them to cope through the peer support aspect of Rainbows and also helping them to come to an acceptance of their situation. As stated previously, there is no calendar for grief, so we cannot with any degree of certainty define a 'normal' length for any child to mourn. All we can say is that it takes as long as it takes and it seems to work well if a Rainbows group is in operation.

Death is a fact of life for all families at some point. We certainly have many grieving children in our schools. Separation is also very much on the increase in Ireland as is shown by the statistics mentioned previously. The reality is that many adolescents feel they are going through this alone. Many schools do not provide any bereavement support programme for their pupils. There were 4,032 schools in Ireland in 2001.[21] However, there were only 393 active Rainbows sites in the same year, not all of them in schools. This may be due to curricular constraints or it may be that they rely too heavily on the goodwill of individuals on the staff and prioritise other areas as being in greater need of recognition. Certainly other research has found that bereaved pupils have very mixed experiences of support within their schools.[22] Since the Rainbows programme is seen to be effective, and since there is such an obvious need for some such programme in our schools, it could be well argued that one of the specially funded roles in the school (special duties or assistant principal) could be used to provide for the pastoral care of pupils who have experienced death, loss or significant change. It is essential that the person appointed to such a role has the appropriate personal and professional qualities required to support pupils in this way.

Given that the trauma of bereavement/separation often raises religious and spiritual questions, including the search for meaning and the search for God, obviously there is a role here for the school chaplain. Research on community and comprehensive schools shows that

> Chaplains make a significant contribution to the religious and social dimension of these schools in terms of the support they offer to pupils, parents and other staff.[23]

The same study also shows that one of the areas in which chaplains are most in demand is the provision of counselling and bereavement support. The chaplain provides a listening ear and a non-threatening environment. As well as providing personal support, she could inform the grieving pupil of the existence of Rainbows in the school and encourage the pupil to avail of the service.

In parallel with the child being helped to cope, there is also an urgent need for her parent to come to an understanding of what the child is going through. They can also be helped, as a surviving single parent, to become more effective as a parent. Schools should be encouraged as part of their Home-School-Liaison service to investigate the possibilities of the Prism programme for such parents as a support to the Rainbows programme for children. This would provide an opportunity for greater communication between the adult and child, due to the similarity of the programmes.

A third initiative that a school might consider is that of providing a parenting course at night so that any parent who wishes may avail of it. This would also be a means of support for the grieving parent as well as being a means of providing continuing discipline and support in the pupil's life.

A qualified school chaplain is the ideal person to co-ordinate these initiatives as s/he will have the necessary training to provide a sympathetic listening ear and the expertise to help pupils, parents and staff to search for meaning when faced with grief. The chaplain will also have the training to know when to direct a pupil to a professional counsellor or psychologist where this seems to be indicated.

As well as the parents understanding of what is happening in the lives of their children, the school itself would benefit from such an understanding. Many teachers do not know, apart from a general common understanding, what the psychological effects of bereavement in children are. It is clear that there is a need for a comprehensive in-service training on bereavement, as part of a whole-school plan. This would benefit all pupils. In the short term, there would probably be less anger-related stress for staff as they could empathise with what bereaved pupils were feeling and the pupils would know that they had the support and understanding of the staff. In the longer term, the outlook for the pupils should be positive since pupils do best where they are encouraged most. '*Mol an óige agus tiocfaidh sí*', and we know from experience that children need love most when they deserve it least.

The important thing to note is that death, separation and divorce are facts of life in Ireland. If we can help adolescents cope better then we will alleviate some of the pain associated with loss and will help the pupil reach their full potential as healthy adults, able and willing to take their place responsibly in the Ireland of tomorrow that we have built for them.

Notes

1. Rainbows Ireland Annual Report

2. Wallerstein, J.S., 'Children After Divorce – Wounds That Don't Heal', *New York Times Magazine*, 22 January 1989, p. 42.

3. 'Her' is used as an exemplar.

4. Kubler-Ross, E., *On Death and Dying* (New York: Routledge, 1970).

5. Crenshaw, D. A., '*Bereavement: Counselling the Bereaved Throughout the Life Cycle*' (New York: Continuum, 1990), p. 93.

6. Gaffney, M., 'Knitting the Apron Strings', *The Irish Times Magazine,* 16 December 2000.

7. Johnston, J. K., '*Good Divorce – Bad Divorce*'. Keynote address at the all Ireland Conference 'An eye to the future; accepting the change to family life in the New Millennium', Nov. 25-26 1999.

8. Kubler-Ross, E., *op.cit.*

9. *Ibid.*

10. MacDonald, C.B., 'Loss and Bereavement' in Wicks (ed.), *Clinical Handbook of Pastoral Counselling* (New York: Paulist Press, 1992).

11. Carson, J. F., Warren, B. L., Doty, L., 'An Investigation of the Grief Counseling-Services Available in the Middle Schools and High-Schools in the State of Mississippi', *Omega-Journal of Death and Dying*, 30/3, (1995), pp. 191-204.

12. Paulhan, I., 'The Concept of Coping', *Annee Psychologique*, 92/4, (1992), pp. 545-557.

13. Bowlby J., *Attachment and Loss: Loss, Sadness and Depression*, Vol 3 (New York: Basic Books, 1980).

14. Davis, C. G., Wortman, C. B., Lehman, D.R., Silver, R.C. 'Searching for Meaning in Loss: Are Clinical Assumptions Correct?' *Death Studies*, 24/6, (2000), pp. 497-540.

15. Batten, M., Oltjenbruns, K. A., 'Adolescent Sibling Bereavement as a Catalyst for Spiritual Development: a Model for Understanding', *Death Studies*, 23/6, (1999), pp. 529-546.

16. Smith, P. C., Range, L. M., Ulmer, A., 'Belief in Afterlife as a Buffer in Suicidal and Other Bereavement', *Omega-Journal of Death and Dying*, 24/3 (1992), pp. 217-225.

17. Hynes N., Synnott, M., 'Guidelines for Coping with Grief in the School Situation' in Monahan L. (ed.), *Suicide, Bereavement and Loss – Perspectives and Responses* (Dublin: Irish Association of Pastoral Care in Education 1999).

18. Faschinbauer, T., Zisook, S., De Vaul, R., 'The Texas Revised Inventory of Grief' in Ziscook, S. (ed.), *Biopsycholosocial Aspects of Bereavement* (Washington, D.C.: American Psychiatric Press, 1987), pp. 111-124.

19. Hogan, D., Halpenny, A.M., Greene, S., *Children's Experiences of Parental Separation* (Dublin: The Children's research Centre, Trinity College, 2002), p. 56.

20. Wallerstein, J., Blakeslee, S., *Second Chances: Men, Women and Children a Decade After Divorce* (New York: Bantam Press, 1989).

21. www.education.ie.

22. Hogan, D., Halpenny, A.M., Greene, S., *Children's Experiences of Parental Separation* (Dublin: The Children's research Centre, Trinity College, 2002), p. 83.

23. Norman, J., *Pastoral Care in Second Level Schools: The Chaplain, A Research Report* (Dublin: Mater Dei Institute of Education, Dublin City University).

Religious Education as a State Examination

Implications for the School Chaplain

Paul King

Introduction

Amidst the continuous transformation of Irish culture, where the influence of religion has witnessed a considerable decline, it is not without irony that the place of religious education within schooling should receive renewed attention. Despite the current erosion of the Church's authority in an increasingly pluralist society, an historical account of Irish education reveals the place of religion, in particular Christianity, as a pivotal influence in the past. The symbiotic relationship between the Church and state (which is covered in detail by Marjorie Doyle in an earlier chapter) has historically helped safeguard the place of religion in Irish schools, but the nature of this provision has largely resulted in catechesis rather than religious education. The introduction of the state-sponsored new Junior Certificate Religious Education Syllabus (JCRES) in September 2000 and the new Leaving Certificate Religious Education Syllabus (LCRES) in September 2003 redirects the emphasis on Religious Education as an academic pursuit. A distinction needs to be made between the JCRES and LCRES in terms of curriculum implementation. The majority of second-level schools in Ireland include the religious education syllabus as a core part of the curriculum at junior cycle irrespective of whether it is offered as an examination subject. At senior cycle it is intended to offer the LCRES as an option while simultaneously continuing with non-exam RE as a core subject. Hence the implications, apart from timetabling, are less problematic at senior cycle since schools can offer a parallel approach combining both catechesis and religious education.

At junior cycle the availability of the JCRES has raised a fundamental question for schools: if catechesis was formerly perceived by some as a method of proselytising at the state's expense and at odds with the philosophy of a critical education, does this new curriculum now mean that religious education can be reduced to the level of knowledge and compromise the commitment to the fostering of spiritual values and religious formation among students? Some RE teachers and school chaplains argue that the JCRES will undermine opportunities for the faith formation of pupils in favour of an intellectual framework based on knowledge, understanding, skills and attitudes.

This chapter, focusing mainly on the JCRES, seeks to address the apparent conflict, not as an issue demanding explicit alternatives, but to suggest a possibility for a balanced purpose facilitated by both the chaplain and RE teacher. The place of both the new JCRES and LCRES in the curriculum is educationally justifiable in that both seek to make a contribution to the realisation and provisions of the aims of education as outlined in the White Paper on Education.[1] I wish to argue that the academic, critical approach to religious education as underpinned in the JCRES and the catechetical dimension as expressed in the formative intention to educate young people in the way of being spiritual, are not diametrically opposed. The challenge is to formulate a creative and imaginative response to facilitate a synergy between both. The availability of a full-time chaplain in the school is essential to ensure that the spiritual and pastoral welfare of students is supported and nourished. I will use quotations from interviews I conducted with school chaplains as illustrations throughout the chapter.

In asserting the interdependence of both, this chapter sets out to ascertain how the chaplain and teacher can engage in a mutual process, which respects the dual purpose of religious education. Although the parameters of this response extends to the whole school the syllabus holds particular significance for the teacher and chaplain as key agents in the provision of religious education for pupils. As a curriculum development it raises issues with respect to the implications for the role of the chaplain and the role of the teacher of RE, especially as defined in the context of the syllabus. *Can the chaplain and RE teacher formulate a vision of religious education that is respectful of both dimensions and how are they to engage collaboratively to ensure the retention of balance between both?* It may be that the introduction of both the JCRES and the LCRES will help create the challenge and context for a new vision of religious education that is characterised by a unity of purpose.

Chaplain and Teacher: Clarifying Roles

The reality of RE as an examination subject has shifted the context of debate to a new forum. For the RE teacher there is the issue of role – to teach as a catechist, evangelist, or religious educator with the primary responsibility to remain faithful to the aims and objectives of the syllabus. The teacher, who in the past embraced all or some of these roles, faces a new dilemma – is it possible to co-exist as a catechist and as a teacher of RE within the remit of the syllabus? For the chaplain the issue of role is also pertinent and unique, as he or she may have to contend with the dual mandate of teacher and chaplain. Currently, most chaplains in the community schools and colleges sector have a maximum obligation to teach four hours per week.[2] Formerly, this obligation was more fluid as the chaplain may have used class time as an extension of chaplaincy. The latitude for the chaplain's discretionary use of class time may become minimal if he or she is also required to teach the syllabus. Under these conditions many chaplains express a concern over a conflict in the understanding of their own role and how pupils perceive it. Since many school chaplains are qualified religion teachers, an even greater fear exists that the management of schools may request chaplains to engage in more teaching than required at present. As the following quotation illustrates, some chaplains and RE teachers have expressed unease at the possible demise of the faith and pastoral dimension of religious education.

> I am not sure it [the syllabus] is going to have a great impact. It will be like information, the banking system. It may not have a personal impact, any gospel reflection or attention to feelings or prayer experience. I have class contact with students and if RE becomes an exam subject where will I find time as personal contact? They will lose out on pastoral contact with the chaplain or a good RE teacher.[3]

The Education Act (1998) places an obligation on every school to 'promote the moral, spiritual, social and personal development of students.'[4] While the overall aims of the new JCRES are essentially educational the last aim seeks 'to contribute to the spiritual and moral development of the student.'[5] The RE teacher cannot be reasonably expected to entirely meet the spiritual development of pupils. The teacher under this new syllabus will naturally bring to the subject their own insight, experience and personal faith just as the teacher of any subject on the curriculum conveys a passion for their subject. The classroom is essentially an academic construct and conduit for awareness, exploration and understanding of religion as opposed to an experience of religious faith. Devitt is inclined to call this *extraordinary* teaching where the curriculum is prescribed and taught in the classroom setting.[6] The teacher may also lack the expertise and skill to facilitate appropriately the spiritual development of pupils, particularly with respect to the celebration of ritual and the practice of worship. In addition, pastoral care issues such as bereavement, bullying and illness require a particular kind of skilled intervention. Devitt defines this kind of interaction as *ordinary/immediate* teaching.[7]

Even more crucial is the access of the chaplain to pupils either directly through class contact or indirectly in working with an individual pupil or group of pupils. The Education Act clearly states the right of the pupil to have an education, which embraces the spiritual dimension of the pupil's needs 'in consultation with their parents, having regard to the characteristic spirit of the school.'[8] The classroom does not generally facilitate this aspect of religious formation. A practical illustration of this might be an occasion where pupils come together in an act of prayer and worship to commemorate the memory of a deceased person – a pupil or a member of the pupil's family. To situate such a personal and pastoral issue explicitly in the context of the classroom is to place an unfair burden on the teacher. The experience of bereavement in school would generally elicit the support of the teacher in assisting the chaplain. However, the nature of much of the chaplain's work is confidential and personal and the chaplain may have to withdraw pupils from class for pastoral counselling. This usually happened during the RE class because of the obvious symmetry between RE and chaplaincy. Since the examination focus was absent it was also deemed to cause the minimum of disruption to the pupil's cognitive development and learning. The introduction of an examined syllabus places RE on the same academic par with other subjects and it may be reasonably presumed that teachers will want to maximise the use of class time in order to fulfil the objectives of a demanding syllabus. The possible tensions that may arise are reflected in the views of one chaplain who says:

> As a chaplain you have closer contact with the RE team and you dip in and out of the classes. You withdraw students if you want to work on a particular programme. If these children feel they are going to fall back on a subject or an area being covered there will be a greater reluctance on the part of the teacher to release the students, on the part of parents to encourage the students, or the students themselves, to want to come out because it will mean double work. From a mechanical view having contact to do work that is meaningful to students will be reduced. [9]

This perspective draws attention to one apparent dilemma arising from the syllabus – will the chaplain's use of class time be considered an intrusion in the context where a demanding syllabus requires the optimum use of time? Two issues are central to this question. Firstly, a reading of the syllabus shows that it is possible for the chaplain to function on the level of religious formation even in the academic forum. This tension needs to be carefully facilitated but the chaplain in working with the RE teacher can hold this creative tension. Secondly, there is a need for clarity in order to establish the right of the pupil to religious formation and the responsibility of the school to provide this opportunity. As mentioned earlier, the Education Act clearly states the provision of a holistic education. The second legal basis for the provision of religious formation is enshrined in the Constitution and also reiterated in the High Court judgement of Costello, J. (1996) and further endorsed by the Supreme Court judgement of Barrington, J. (1998). [10]

The 1996 judgement addressed the constitutionality of state payment of salaries to chaplains in community schools, finding in favour of the state. The Supreme Court in 1998, as part of its judgement, restated the salient points presented in the 1996 High Court judgement of Costello, J., which had identified succinctly the key responsibilities of the chaplain. The 1998 judgement is of interest because it reveals an accurate and appreciative understanding of the work of the chaplain in schools, exemplified by the judgement given by Barrington, J., in this extract:

> In Community Schools it is no longer practicable to combine religious and academic education in the way that a religious order might have done in the past. Nevertheless parents have the same right to have religious education provided in the schools which their children attend. They are not obliged to settle merely for religious 'instruction'. [sic] The role of the Chaplain is to help to provide this extra dimension to the religious education of the children. The evidence establishes that, besides looking after the pastoral needs of the children, the Chaplain helps them with counsel and advice about their day-to-day problems. [11]

The Supreme Court, by way of comment, places the chaplain as a pivotal figure in contributing to the ethos of the school where parents have a right not just to the religious instruction but also to the religious formation of their children. Furthermore the pupil has a right, in accordance with the Constitution – Articles 42 and 44 and with law – the Education Act 1998, to an education which extends beyond the academic to include the realm of religious formation.

The official *Guidelines for the Chaplain in a Community School* published by the Department of Education in 1976 set out clearly the role of the chaplain as identified by the Department.[12] This document is of paramount importance for the chaplain particularly in light of the introduction of the syllabus. The purpose in clarifying roles for the RE teacher and the chaplain is that it may serve to lessen the concerns that some teachers and chaplains have over the possible diminution of the religious development of young people. The chaplains whom I have quoted have already expressed some of these concerns. RE teachers share these concerns and if they are to be addressed there is need for the establishment of policy by each school so as to ensure both aspects of religious education are respected. Both the chaplain and the RE teacher need a shared understanding of their respective roles. The ultimate purpose of this clarification is not to protect the identities of the chaplain and teacher but to ensure that the pupil has legitimate access to a religious education that is both *formative* and *informative*. It may be that resistance to this approach may not come from either the RE teacher or the chaplain but from within the broader spectrum of the school. The chaplain has always operated in the wider context of the school, but a natural link existed with the RE department and timetable where flexibility was evident especially in the realm of ritual and worship. While it can be accepted that the formative and academic can be complimentary, nevertheless the practical issue of time and space need a creative response.

The RE Syllabus – An Opportunity for a New Collaboration

The purpose of attempting to clarify both the role of the RE teacher and chaplain is to ensure that both aspects of RE – *formative* and *informative* are mutually respected. The introduction of the syllabus has redefined the term *Religious Education* as traditionally understood in the context of Irish education. The syllabus is justified on educational principles and changes the interplay, which previously existed between the catechetical and critical understanding of religion. The Irish context for the enterprise of RE, at least in community schools and colleges, is unique since provision is now made for an approach that combines both the cognitive encounter with religion as an academic pursuit via the syllabus and explicit provision for the religious and spiritual development of the pupil via the chaplain. The principle challenge arises in the need to reassess how the school can ensure that both aspects are held in harmony. By way of synthesis it is useful to make reference to *The Religious Dimension of Education in a Catholic School* (RDECS) published in 1988 by the Congregation for Catholic Education in Rome.[13]

Although explicitly aimed at Catholic schools the document offers valid educational insights, which shares fundamental common ground with the underlying education philosophy of the RE syllabus. The expectations placed on the teacher to be at one a catechist and a teacher of religious instruction are immense. However, the document is clear that Christian witness is the prerogative of the whole school.[14] It is striking that no reference is made to the presence of a school chaplain. This can be explained by the assumption made in the document that both aspects of religious education are the responsibility of the teacher in the Catholic school. It also reflects the reality that up to the early 1990s, at least in Ireland, chaplains working in community schools and colleges were priests.

I have attempted to construct a valid argument for a teaching of religious education, which embraces the critical understanding of religion and the need to facilitate the process where pupils can mature to growing in the practice and experience of faith. Although the introduction of the syllabus has an educational orientation, the structure of school organisation, principally though not exclusively in the role of the chaplain, has an equally binding commitment to religious formation. By reflecting on the role of the teacher and the chaplain it is possible to envisage a reality where both aspects – education and formation – are mutually inclusive. The Christian story and vision needs the context of a critically reflective forum provided by the syllabus. This helps to engage pupils in a mature and appropriated faith free from indoctrination and fundamentalism. On the other hand, the school can offer a shaping context for pupils to engage in the process of lifelong evolution into faith benefiting from the wisdom, traditions, ritual and symbols that give meaning to the threshold experiences of human life and ultimately engage the soul. Tension arises not only when space and time are limited but also more fundamentally when a dichotomy emerges between the chaplain and teacher where they perceive no connection or harmony in their respective roles. It therefore follows that the primary task of the school, and essentially the chaplain and RE teacher, is to establish the practical philosophical implications of implementing the syllabus. This ought to take account of the particular circumstances of the school, the classroom and the underlying aims and objectives of the syllabus. It must also concern itself with consistency, clarity, and rationale for the work of the chaplain and teacher. Understanding is needed by both partners of the nature of their own specific roles. This enables the possibility for confusion to be minimised and the prospect of a holistic implementation of the syllabus.

The Chaplain's Role in the Introduction of the JCRES

G. Rossiter, in exploring this tension between catechesis and religious education, speaks of the 'creative divorce' necessary to enable both aspects to be more independent of each other.[15] The classroom is the proper context for the intellectual understanding of faith and religion and therefore the primary responsibility of the teacher. The practice of faith via liturgy and worship and the expression of religious experience and meaning requires a different forum and is fundamentally premised on the free response of the participant to the awareness of God. This latter dimension fits more naturally into the role of the school chaplain. However, it is imperative to state that this perspective on the approach to the syllabus does not envisage a complete dichotomy on the role of the teacher and chaplain. There is obvious scope within the syllabus for both the chaplain and teacher to work in harmony while remaining faithful to their respective roles.

It is equally important to call forth the responsibility of whole school involvement in order to adequately comprehend the implications of introducing the syllabus. These include timetabling, allocation of qualified personnel, resources and reflection on the impact for the formative and religious development of pupils. Important issues are raised with respect to the right of the pupil to religious formation as guaranteed under the Constitution and the equal 'right of a child not to attend religious instruction in a school in receipt of public funds.'[16] Previously, most formal religious formation happened in the RE class. Major religious celebrations – opening year liturgy, carol services, graduation ceremonies – generally involved the whole school. Other opportunities for religious activity happened usually in the context of the RE classroom. Thus, in order to ensure the continuation of religious formation and spiritual development of pupils the whole school requires a paradigm shift in attitude since it may be no longer possible or indeed desirable to facilitate catechesis entirely within the classroom. The immediate challenge for the chaplain will be to see the syllabus as an extension of the faith formation and spiritual development of the pupil and to afford the opportunity to engage with their own personal experiences and the lived experience of the Christian tradition. Here the chaplain's role in contributing to the culture and ethos of the school is pivotal so as to ensure that academic formation does not supersede the pupil's right to faith development. For community schools and colleges, the charism and religious philosophy of the trustees deserves special recognition to ensure that it continues as a pivotal shaping influence in the provision of holistic education.

The religious formation of pupils takes place not just inside the classroom but also within the whole school environment, hence the values to which we hope pupils aspire must be modelled by all within our schools but especially by those who have particular responsibility for religious and spiritual development. Pupils are sharp in their perception of the teacher or chaplain who lacks congruence between their 'preaching' and action. Both the teacher and the chaplain have a special duty of care towards pupils, ultimately manifested in the quality of relationship. This care of concern extends to the relationship between the chaplain and the RE department. The prevailing attitude of both to creating a shared vision approach in the implementation of the syllabus will determine the underlying spirit.

Should the Chaplain Teach?

In traditional Church terminology the role of the teacher could be equated to the activities of the external forum and the role of the chaplain more appropriate to the internal forum. Although class contact as a teaching chaplain offers regular and direct contact with pupils, it can be argued that the chaplain's purpose is not necessarily to know each pupil but to be essentially available as a resource, particularly for vulnerable pupils requiring specific pastoral care. Recent developments in education have witnessed practical responses to catering for pupils with special needs. In many instances pupils in this category equally require a specific pastoral response, which attends to their need for personal and spiritual development. They are very often individuals who are disadvantaged educationally and socially which gives rise to a sense of isolation. Often the most valued and appreciated work of the chaplain, especially as a counsellor, is to enable such pupils to have a sense of self-worth and their response is stimulated by the hope and compassion mediated in the person of Christ through the ministry of chaplaincy. J. Norman has acknowledged this in a recent research report:

> [...] the chaplain brings an extra 'faith' perspective to the encounter with the pupil, teacher or parent. It is from this faith perspective that the counselling offered by the school chaplain becomes distinct from the services offered by other professionals.[17]

If the work of the professional chaplain is essentially pastoral it raises a crucial issue about the pivotal role of the chaplain with respect to the teaching element of a chaplain's job description, as defined by the Department's guidelines. Although the guidelines recommend that teaching be limited to four hours weekly some chaplains are teaching well in excess of this recommendation.

As in the case of the RE teacher it appears that the introduction of the syllabus ought to lead to a re-appraisal of the role of the chaplain, especially with respect to the current obligation to teach. It is an issue that deserves consideration not just by the chaplain but also for the entire school and especially the management authority. Are schools faithful to the pupil's right to an education that takes cognisance of the spiritual if they primarily perceive the chaplain as a teacher?

The Syllabus and the Chaplain as a Resource

Having acknowledged the complexities of the chaplain's dual role as a teacher and chaplain, consideration can now be given to how the chaplain can be a specific resource to the teacher with respect to elements of the syllabus where flexibility exists for the exploration of faith and the spiritual development of pupils. It is vital to state once again that spiritual development is not a pseudonym for religious education although there are close connections. It is also tempting to classify the objectives of both as so distinct as to be 'uneasy bedfellows'.[18] This apparent insoluble dilemma calls for the possibility of creative connection between the teacher and the chaplain. It requires systematic planning and organisation to enhance the interdependence between the intellectual and catechetical dimension of religious education.[19] The necessity of forward planning minimises the ad hoc approach to religious formation where the chaplain's informal class contact might be construed as unhelpful or as an interruption to teaching and learning. For example, it may be a noble and worthwhile aspiration in seeking 'to contribute to the spiritual and moral development of the pupil',[20] to organise a liturgy or retreat or establish a peace and justice group, but if the teacher is intending to cover related aspects of the syllabus the timing of the chaplain's intervention holds greater significance.

The Department of Education and Science have issued guidelines to accompany the syllabus and these provide a useful starting point in the planning of creative initiatives between the teacher and chaplain.[21] The introduction to the guidelines offers six possible rationales for the teaching of the syllabus, each offering a plan to cover all the objectives in the course syllabus. The range of possibilities demonstrates a variety of approaches and emphases over the three years of the programme cycle. These guidelines are indispensable in acknowledging that the approach to the syllabus is not constrained by the necessity to utilise a singular definitive structure and other possible plans are feasible.

Where a school has the presence of a chaplain it is vital that preliminary planning takes account of the most desirable approach, which maximises the effective teaching of the syllabus and also serves to facilitate the availability of the chaplain to liase with the RE teacher from the perspective of faith. In attending to the different capacities and development of pupils, these plans take into practical consideration the essential role of the pupils in the learning process. Where a partnership exists between the chaplain and the RE department, reference to these guidelines offers a useful starting point in the building of a combined approach reflecting the academic and formative aspects of religious education. The obvious merit of this advancement allows for the chaplain to connect with the RE teacher, so as to facilitate the celebration of faith and the personal exploration of religious meaning, while simultaneously meeting the aims and objectives of the syllabus. An additional advantage is the incentive to maximise the use of time, particularly where the teacher is concerned to ensure that the syllabus is completed. The crucial element of this approach is recognition that the chaplain and RE teacher are responding to the syllabus using different methods. The teacher's essential concern is to honour the educational philosophy of the syllabus made explicit by the aims and objectives, while the chaplain is committed to ensuring that pupils are facilitated in their search for meaning and an experience of God. D. Smith offers a useful framework to help understand the complexity and flexibility of how spirituality relates to teaching.

> *Procedures* are individual actions in the classroom, *designs* are repeatable patterns in the way teaching takes place, and *approaches* are the background beliefs, orientations and commitments which give rise to one pattern rather than another.[22]

From this framework it is evident that at the level of *approaches* the chaplain and teacher can co-exist with similar purpose. The differentiation occurs in terms of *procedures*, *designs* and assessment. In approaching the syllabus the chaplain and teacher could identify areas of common ground where working together enriches the pupil's spiritual experience and also yields educational benefits in teaching and learning.

Conclusion

The introduction of the syllabus does not necessarily hinder the pupil's opportunity for faith formation and religious development. A synthesis can occur between the formative and catechetical on the one hand, and the investigative and critical on the other. The rationale and educational philosophy of the syllabus, under the direction of the teacher, can serve the affective dimension of religious education, facilitated by the chaplain, in safeguarding against the risk of fundamentalism or naïve piety in the practice of faith. In exploring the possibility for co-existence between religious education and religious instruction a number of other issues has arisen which merit acknowledgement.

Firstly, in adopting the approach suggested in this article the agents involved, the teacher and the chaplain, cannot seek to coerce the pupil to accept the benefits of learning and experience for to do so 'promotes an ethos of power-seeking, overlooks the to-and-fro interplay of teaching and learning, and undermines the very concept of education as partnership.'[23] The initiation and growth in faith is premised on the right of the pupil to embrace or reject the invitation to engagement.

Furthermore, to be effective, the principle of interdependence embraces the distinctive contribution of the teacher and the chaplain and seeks to find common ground where interplay can be manifested, particularly in the syllabus. The transition to a new model of religious education requires the participation of the whole school especially in the effort to protect the faith dimension of the pupil's development. This equally requires imagination in devising ways where a complementarity can occur between the two aims of religious education.

The syllabus has the merit of having a framework with definitive aims and objectives underpinned by an educational rationale. An issue for further discussion might be the need for a similar process within the sphere of catechesis, a process that would acknowledge the impact of the changing culture and the need to become less reliant on the school as the dominant agent of evangelisation. For the chaplain and teacher who wish to remain integral to both facets of religious there is the need to have the support of resources and personnel who can help create the conditions where a combined practical approach is possible.

Another key issue emerging is the need for full-time paid chaplains. Community schools and colleges are fortunate to have this provision and, in the context of the tensions arising from the introduction of the JCRES and the LCRES, are significantly resourced to encompass the dual mandate of religious education, academic and formative. Although denominational schools have an explicit purpose to promote the spiritual and moral in accordance with their ethos, it is regrettable that some such schools do not have access to a full-time chaplain. A number of these schools have recognised the importance of chaplaincy by employing a chaplain paid from private funds. However, where the syllabus is introduced without the presence of a chaplain, such schools may encounter difficulties in preserving the spiritual dimension as an essential attribute of their existence. Since the Constitution and the Supreme Court judgement (1998) acknowledge the right of the pupil to religious instruction, then it is in the interest of justice that these schools have access to a full-time chaplain.

Some perceive the syllabus as an intrusion in the classroom, leading to a reduction in catechesis.[24] Currently, the introduction of the LCRES for senior cycle is under way. As pupils have a larger element of subject choice at this stage of their education the pressure to maintain the faith and spiritual dimension will be greater. In the light of these issues it is crucial that ongoing debate continues and research is carried out to meet the challenges and respond creatively to the unprecedented change in religious education.

In summary, the chaplain's voice within the school as a key contributor to what G.Grace calls 'spiritual capital'[25] will be vital to ensure we learn from the challenges arising from the implementation of the JCRES. With the introduction of the syllabus the spiritual tone of the person and work of the chaplain can shape the dialogue and practice necessary to honour the affective and cognitive dimensions of religious education.

Notes

1. Department of Education and Science, *Charting our Education Future: White Paper on Education* (Dublin: Government Publications, 1995), p. 10.

2. Department of Education & Science/Archdiocese of Dublin, *Official Guidelines for the Chaplain in a Community School* (Dublin: Department of Education & Science, 1976).

3. Qualitative Survey among fifteen school chaplains conducted by the author, November 2001.

4. Department of Education & Science, *Education Act, Part II* (Dublin: Government Publications, 1998) Section 9, paragraph (d).

5. Department of Education & Science, *Junior Certificate Religious Education Syllabus* (Dublin: Government Publications, 2000), p. 5.

6. Devitt, P., *Willingly to School* (Dublin: Veritas, 2000), p. 51.

7. *Ibid.*, p. 51.

8. Department of Education & Science, *Education Act, Part II* (Dublin: Government Publications, 1998) Section 9, paragraph (d).

9. Qualitative Survey of School Chaplains, November 2001.

10. J. Barrington, 'Campaign to Separate Church and State v. Minister of Education, Attorney General and Others: Supreme Court 1998', *Irish Reports 3* (1998), pp. 321-367.

11. *Ibid.*, p. 367.

12. Department of Education & Science/Archdiocese of Dublin, *Official Guidelines for the Chaplain in a Community School* (Dublin: Department of Education & Science, 1976).

13. Sacred Congregation for Catholic Education, *The Religious Dimension of Education in a Catholic School* (Rome: 1988).

14. *Ibid.*, par. 26, 51 and 58.

15. Rossiter, G., ' The Need for a "Creative Divorce" between Catechesis and Religious Education in Catholic Schools', *Religious Education 77* (1982), pp. 21-40.

16. Keane, J., 'Campaign to Separate Church and State v. Minister of Education, Attorney General and Others: Supreme Court 1998', p. 354.

17. Norman, J., *Pastoral Care in Second Level Schools: The Chaplain, A Research Report* (Dublin: Mater Dei Institute of Education, Dublin City University), p. 10.

18. Smith, D., 'Spirituality and Teaching Methods: Uneasy Bedfellows?' in R. Best (ed.), *Education for Spiritual, Moral, Social and Cultural Development* (London and New York: Continuum, 2000), p. 52.

19. Department of Education & Science, *Junior Certificate Religious Education Syllabus* (Dublin: Government Publications, 2000), p. 3.

20. *Ibid.*, p. 5.

21. Department of Education & Science, *Religious Education – Junior Certificate: Guidelines for Teachers* (Dublin: Government Publications, 2000).

22. Smith, D., *'Spirituality and Teaching Methods: Uneasy Bedfellows?'* (London and New York: Continuum, 2000), p. 57.

23. Hogan, P., 'Power, Partiality, And The Purposes Of Learning' in P. Hogan (ed.), *Partnership and the Benefits of Learning: Symposium* (Dublin: ESAI, 1995), p. 118.

24. See Deenihan, T., 'Religious Education and Religious Instruction', *The Furrow*, 53 (Maynooth, 2002), pp. 75-83.

25. G. Grace, *Catholic Schools: Mission, Markets and Morality* (London: Routledge Falmer, 2002), pp. 236-240.

Overcoming Barriers to Effective Learning in Second-Level Schools

Terry O'Brien

Introduction

Schools are a positive social force and are generally valued by most people as being safe, accessible and supportive places where they are able to learn. However they can also be perceived as being intimidating, inhospitable, regulatory and complex places which create difficulties and problems for those seeking to learn. This is heightened if pupils have prior self-doubt or uncertainty or if they have had previous problematical experiences with school, learning or authority. In this chapter I will look at the role of schools in creating barriers to effective learning for pupils. Secondly, I will examine the potential role of schools in providing meaningful learning support. In other words, identifying their pupils learning needs and asking what schools can do to overcome these problems thus making the learning experience more engaging and enriching.

Typical pupils in second-level schools are often perceived as teenagers who are studying full-time, can read or write, are computer literate and as having some idea of what they want to do when they leave school. This only captures part of the picture. There are a plethora of other pupil types or groups such as those who, as well as attending school, hold full-time and part-time jobs, which belong to an ethnic minority and possibly do not have access to computers. Diverse as these groups are, they do share one common characteristic, they can often experience types of anxieties, barriers and difficulties in learning. This is not because they have any specific special needs but because they are teenagers who have feelings of inadequacy, reservation, self-doubt, of being overwhelmed at the prospect of sitting examinations and making future life choices. The way teachers and administrators approach learning in schools can sometimes make this worse.

Learning Anxiety

There is a significant canon of literature on the concept of learning anxiety and how it can negatively affect pupils, their study habits and the whole learning experience. Learning anxiety occurs when pupils feel such a level of anxiety as to be unable to effectively study or use associated resources such as the school library and ICT. This can manifest as an *avoidance* behaviour – non-attendance or poor attendance at school; *insecurity or self-doubt* – feeling unable to make good use of school supports because of a lack of perceived ability or knowledge; or *social* anxiety – fear of the school building, having to socially interact or participate in an unfamiliar environment, adult interaction. Learning anxiety can be a major barrier to effective learning. Schools and the school environment, whether inadvertently or subconsciously, can contribute to this sense of anxiety in many students.

There is a strong correlation between study habits and academic performance; those pupils who are successful in their academic performance generally have what one can term 'good study habits'. Many pupils frequently have feelings of self-doubt, possibly fear, which manifests as anxiety. The school is often a common setting for this anxiety. This anxiety can be said to be counter-productive to the formation of good study habits. In other words, there is a strong relationship between learning and anxiety. If one is not comfortable or has notions of inadequacy, it is likely that they will not use the school facilities effectively or in a way that engenders good study habits. Practically all pupils have had anxieties of some sort. There would appear to be some evidence from the literature that these problems are more pertinent in young males, but changing student profiles in those arriving into higher education and personal experience would indicate to me that it is neither gender nor age specific and, if anything, those studying part-time, by distance, or those returning to study after an absence, such as mature students, are *as* likely to suffer from this type of anxiety. Schools play a very significant part in pupils' study behaviour. Therefore it is critical that schools play a role in both overcoming potential barriers to learning and in cultivating and creating an atmosphere conducive to good study habits.

Barriers to Effective Learning

Although learning anxiety in itself can be a significant impediment, there are numerous other barriers that deter users from getting the most out of their school experience and hence becoming mature, critical and effective learners. The following list is a broad outline of some of the barriers that pupils may potentially experience:

- Language
- Physical
- Bureaucratic
- Psychological and personal
- Socio-economic
- Technological
- Cultural

Language

Like any other profession, teachers have their own language code and conventions that can sometimes fail to connect with some of their pupils. This is further compounded in inner-city areas when we consider that the majority of teachers come from a middle-class background. If a pupil already has difficulty in using or working in a school environment, overly complex or unnecessary use of language will only exacerbate these anxieties. We often use terms of reference and concepts in the assumption not only that the pupil will be aware of them but also that it will in some way help them! This is not to suggest that schools dumb-down or that we underestimate what pupils actually know, but we should never assume, particularly with certain categories of pupils. This also applies to language and terminology used in a school's promotional material such as handbooks, journals, websites and signage. The language of learning can be a major turn-off if it is unfamiliar or if pupils have had previous difficulties. Overly complex language or terminology can be patronising and unhelpful, creating a barrier between teacher and pupil.

Physical
Further barriers can come in physical form and not just for pupils with mobility needs. Schools are often large and intimidating buildings. A typical second-level school may have 1,000 pupils, with class-rooms of perhaps up to thirty pupils. This can be a daunting and often overpowering experience for some pupils, especially those in first year. A visible staff presence is essential in surmounting this. Pupils need points of contact, accessible reference points where they can come for help and support, such as the staff-room, general office or chaplain's room. The irony of this is that help often comes from around a half-opened door at the staff-room, which although perhaps unavoidable, does further create an obstacle and the impression of distance – them and us. The location of some kind of help-desk for new pupils and a hospitable welcome may well go a long way towards counteracting these types of fears.

Bureaucratic
Although the societal experience of schools is generally positive, second-level schools for some pupils are often seen as extremely formal places, with overly regulatory or even stifling environments. This is in part based on tradition, on stereotype, on history and in part based on perception. Traditionally, schools have insisted on rules and regulations: people being quiet, working in isolation and without adverse impact on other pupils. This taken in context is unsurprising, but the role and business of the modern school is very different to that of thirty years ago. But, as the saying goes, it can be very hard to shake a reputation and it is not surprising that schools are frequently still seen in these terms. The reality may be different, but as with any business with a high service component, perceptions are extremely important. New pupils may be coming from a background of what Sargant[1] has called 'unhappy experiences', be this with school, teachers or previous attempts at formal learning. The role the school plays here is critical. If schools add to this sense of an unhappy experience by being overbearing or introducing copious rules and regulations before a pupil even begins to feel comfortable, that pupil may well be lost to the school and further, it may negatively colour their experience of learning and study forever. Rather than telling people what they may or may not do, what the

rules and procedures are, better to create a feeling of 'can-do', of what you can achieve, of the opportunities, services and support that are available to pupils in the school. Advances in school building design have undoubtedly helped in this regard in recent years, with new buildings incorporating many pupil-centred features such as group study areas, dedicated quiet spaces, specific computer areas, consultation rooms, even coffee shops and open spaces. This contributes to making schools more humane, social places. These features also allow for the many different learning styles to be accommodated and go some way to helping schools lose their reputation, whether unfounded or not, of being study halls or simple learning repositories that do not allow interaction. The modern school should be a multi-faceted place that contains elements of quiet, of interaction (both human and technological), that should encourage creativity and social exchange, and above all that should make the user feel comfortable and secure.

Probably the most common way of overcoming this potential anxiety is good orientation and induction. Even before the start of the school year many schools are now involved in induction process, by offering tours and welcoming parents and new pupils at open evenings. This can be a very effective intervention in overcoming potential anxieties at early stage. The emphasis should be on welcoming and on breaking down possible barriers to pupils using the school, rather than on rules and policies. Pupils will learn about these in due course anyway. Further to this, induction – whether in the guise of school tours, information sessions or meetings should not be the preserve of just every September. Flexibility and availability throughout the year, even if at pre-designated times would recognise the year-round need for schools to provide support and be responsiveness to the needs of its pupils.

Psychological and Personal
This is often very much about self-perception, self-image and prior experiences. Pupils entering second-level schools may not have much experience in institutional learning environments and may perceive that they do not belong or that they are viewed differently compared with their experience in primary school. This may manifest as a negative attitude towards authority, teachers and even specific subjects which could affect them later in life. For example, a pupil may have a negative experience with mathematics as a youth and decide to pursue something humanities based such as politics, only to discover that statistics plays a small but important role in this discipline. Perceived inadequacies or lack of a family tradition in traditional or formal learning settings also tends to deter some pupils. Those whose parents are without recent formal learning experiences, or who are from minority ethnic groups, are unemployed or are economically disadvantaged, are particularly at risk.

Other potential psychological or personal barriers might relate to self-image or body image and the strong influence peer groups can have on how students feel they should behave or should look. Further, recent research at third level suggest that up to 15 per cent of students may have some form of dyslexia or learning difficulties. For primary and second-level schools, early detection and support is crucial. The psychological and social difficulties this may create if not identified can be irrevocably damaging to students. Speech difficulties, stammering and poor communication skills can potentially create hurdles for many pupils. It is important that these pupils receive the support and the attention they may require, but in a way that empowers and confers self-esteem, not that draws attention or creates a perception of abnormality.

Whilst schools and teachers on their own cannot overcome all these barriers, it is important to be able to recognise them and to offset their potential difficulties by treating pupils with empathy, as individuals with specific needs rather than with a one-size-fits-all approach.

Socio-economic

When considering socio-economic barriers we generally talk about widening access and participation and this has been reflected with some success in recent years through some government policy initiatives. However, there can be a sense of leading the horses to water only to take a step back. Is it enough to widen access only to ignore underlying issues relating to the access in the first place? For example, a pupil may have a number of reasons for not attending school – financial, family or self-doubt. Enabling this person to access second-level-education perhaps through some financial instrument, is of course encouraging, but this does not help overcome their other existing barriers, and these are often the reason why pupils do not go on to complete their full course of study. This is notwithstanding some excellent work done at local level by schools that have introduced breakfast and homework clubs, for example.

Some social barriers are psychological in nature, with pupils seeing learning as a very formal or conventional process, and as a consequence failing to see the social opportunities it may present in terms of leisure, self-actualisation, friendships, and personal growth. Other social barriers relate to gender: in particular young women who leave school early due to the burden of childcare responsibility. Socio-economic reasons in the form of family background and expectation, finance, childcare and family responsibilities have traditionally been powerful barriers and continue to present major difficulties for many pupils from varying socio-economic backgrounds.

Technological

Schools have begun to embrace technology and information communication technologies (ICT) in a more vigorous and concentrated way, seeing the potential of ICT and educational technology. Technology can provide indisputable benefits for pupils in a range of ways. However, despite increasing levels of computer usage and societal computer awareness, technology is still a source of disquiet and sometimes apprehension for many pupils. In this regard, it can be said to be a very significant barrier. Furthermore, lack of experience of technology can be extremely off-putting and 'techno-fear', or fear of computers, is still very common amongst particular pupils. The recent OECD international report on the use of computers in teaching and learning in schools placed Ireland among the lowest for pupil access and use of computers.[2]

In addition, there appears to be an assumption that all young people are extremely comfortable with technology and computers and although often described as the PlayStation or Net Generation, this is not necessarily the case. In fact, this assumption may often work against pupils. By neglecting or assuming we know their needs they are often left behind, and a barrier that we assumed not to exist is actually fed. Not everybody has a computer at home and according to the OECD it seems that not every school is able to give access to all its pupils.

Schools can and do play a prominent role in attempting to overcome this type of barrier by offering pupils education or learning support in using technology and access tools. Schools need to be as constructive in supporting practical and effective use of technology as they have been in embracing their usage. Many schools have developed programmes for their pupils which have linked them with other schools in Ireland and abroad and in doing so have opened up the classroom experience. In Canada, often through school libraries, programmes on information literacy and information skills have been developed and are proving successful. The public library network in Ireland has gone a long way towards increasing access to the internet for children in an appropriate environment. Some years ago the concept of the 'classroom without walls' or the virtual school was advocated. Whilst technology has enabled a much more interactive learning environment, it continues to struggle to replicate the social and human aspects that are inherent in the education process.

Cultural Issues

As Ireland continues to become more multi-cultural, it is important to recognise the potential cultural difficulties that may exist for ethnic or pupils whose mother tongue is not necessarily English. In recent times, the exchange student was the typical non-national presence in our schools. These pupils were generally middle-class, had good language skills and have a convention of having used schools, and as such would be broadly familiar with school environments. With the advent of an enlarged European Union schools are becoming much more culturally diverse places. Many of these pupils have come from very different backgrounds with different social norms; some may have poor language or communication skills. None of this is unique or unusual. A pupil from Ireland may well have similar difficulties; but these are surely heightened for non-national pupils when confronted with similar barriers – institutional, psychological, and socio-economic. They may not have the same supports in terms of family, peers or financial security and may well lack confidence. Critically, their learning styles and needs may be very different. Although many second-level schools have begun to recognise the potential that such diversity can give and seem to be reacting accordingly in terms of supports, some schools are slower than others in adapting and this will therefore surely augment existing barriers unless addressed. Practical assistance such as liaison with the refugee support groups, signage and guides in multiple languages, designated-staff members, encouraging basic language-learning skills in staff are all small but feasible ways in which schools can make the school environment more secure, welcoming and beneficial to non-national pupils.

Marinetti and Dunn[3] have pointed out that learning is not passive and is strongly influenced by culture. Therefore, there is an amount of cultural adaptation required. It is neither appropriate, nor will it work, if we simply attempt to transfer or apply our value system to others. This will result in what they have termed 'cultural distance'. Appling this thinking to schools and the services they provide, we surely need to show greater levels of cultural awareness in order to overcome any 'cultural distance'.

Implications

Equally important are good customer service and relations, to borrow a business phrase. Whilst schools may not have what business might term a traditional customer-client relationship, nevertheless, the ethos of the school should be one that fits in with treating its users with fairness, equality and respect. Again, how staff personally interact with pupils is crucial. Hackneyed as it sounds, first impressions (in fact all impressions) are important. You do want your pupils to come back and make good use of the school and its facilities. There is no such thing as a typical pupil – pupils today come form every conceivable background, culture and demographic. Each pupil category has their own set of issues and needs; what schools need is an increased awareness of these. The value of personal contact and ongoing interaction between staff and pupil should enhance this.

Information Excess Equals Intellectual Distress[4]

> 'The problem usually wasn't getting access to information.
> It was to stave off drowning in it.'[5]

One of the other key barriers to effective learning for many pupils is the availability of an abundance of information in schools today. Having perhaps got past many of the barriers we have spoken about in terms of institution, psychological or social obstacles, pupils are confronted with so much potential information in school that it is no wonder the whole process becomes an uncritical search for just getting the essay or project done. Pupils may already lack the experience and context knowledge to make appropriate study choices or follow particular research methods or strategies. Bodi[6] identifies three 'troublesome' areas for students in higher education in doing research or project work that are helpful when considering second-level pupils:

- Choosing and narrowing a topic;

- Selecting a subject heading search method;

- Evaluating sources, in particular websites.

Add these difficulties to what is increasingly an overloaded curriculum and it is no wonder that pupils devise a 'coping strategy not an information-seeking strategy.'⁷ Do schools add to these problems or counteract them? The reality is probably a combination of both. Schools have some strengths in managing and categorising information and making it accessible and user-friendly to pupils. However, sometimes in a genuine effort to give pupils as much information as possible, it becomes an overly complex array of resources that simply adds to a feeling of distress, confusion and apathy.

Information Overload

It is a truism to state that we live in the age of information. Commentators have variously described the end of the twentieth century and the start of the twenty-first century as the Information Society, the Electronic Age, the Digital Age or even the Silicon Age. Throughout the Western world, we are literally bombarded with information and images through television and radio, mobile phones, text messaging, computers and music, movies, print, magazines, and books. Tapscott[8] described this impact of the information society as a 'paradigm shift'. The internet has become all-pervasive, a panacea for all our learning and information needs. We are told the world is a global village, a world in which information is accessible, available, immediate, instantaneous – a mouse-click or the touch of a button away. No one would doubt the undeniable power and value of modern mass communication and information tools like the internet. Since Al Gore was famously attributed with describing the internet as the 'information superhighway' in the mid-1980s, growth and usage of the internet and computer technologies has been exponential. Even the most fervent Luddite would acknowledge that the internet and computer technologies such as the worldwide web have proved to be massively important and culturally significant forces. That this force has been a combination of both positive and negative influence is also undeniable.

The amount or rather the availability and accessibility of information presents a huge range of concerns for anyone interested in education and learning. How do we assess and evaluate this information? What gives it value, credibility and authority? This is particularly the case with information that is available to young people online.[9] How do we know what we are using is accurate, relevant and above all reliable? How does this effect how pupils as individuals learn, what does this mean to those uncomfortable or unfamiliar with technology – will they become the dispossessed, the information have-nots? What role, if any, can traditional learning and study environments such as schools play? The Information Society and information overload presents us with a series of very real problems and anxieties. These problems range from issues of decision-making, choice, evaluation, quantity and quality to difficulties in terms of barriers, access and psychology.

Final Comments

Schools play a central and essential role in the second level education and the learning process. This is borne out by the amount of time the average pupil spends in school, the services it offers and the supports and infrastructure it provides. Schools can play a pivotal role in providing learning supports to all types of pupils. A good school can be a flexible, welcoming environment that provides a setting that both enables and supports pupils to overcome barriers to effective learning. In addition it should foster both creativity and critical thinking skills. This is even more imperative in a culture that seems to be on the road to mirroring the UK-experience of what some commentators have called a culture of PowerPoint, tick-box education or bullet-point obsession, valuing labour market skills and employability over independent thought, analytical ability and knowledge creation.

Where schools either create or add to the many barriers that exist for pupils, it is important that they assess their role, overcome these and recognise the needs of individual pupils. A firm pupil-centred ethos will ensure that the needs of pupils may be met. In this context, schools can overcome learning and other anxieties, attract reluctant learners and even contribute towards retaining and preventing early school leaving. Schools themselves are sometimes one of a number of reasons or causes of 'drop-out' or failure amongst pupils. Schools can potentially play a constructive role in addressing these problems. That said, schools can only do so much, any response must be part of an integrated approach, 'while practical obstacles to learning may be overcome with relative ease, more deep rooted psychological barriers may be prove more problematic.'[10] In the long-term, more strategic interventions are required at the level of policy and decision makers. Perhaps most importantly, schools need to ensure that early encounters, whether casual or targeted, are both welcoming and positive in terms of learning experience. The role of schools in this regard can be said to be pastoral or complimentary to the pastoral function.

Notes

1. Sargant, N., *The Learning Divide Revisited: A Report of the Findings of a UK-wide Survey on Adult Participation in Education and Learning* (Leicester: NIACE, 2000).

2. OECD Report on ICT in Schools as reported in the *Irish Independent* (4 February 2004).

3. Marinetti, A., Dunn, P., 'The challenge of cultural adaptation – a question of approach', *Training Journal* (Nov. 2002), pp. 20-24.

4. Oberman, C., 'Avoiding the Cereal Syndrome, or Critical Thinking in the Electronic Environment', *Library Trends*, 39, (Winter, 1991), pp. 189-202.

5. Quotation from '*Earth*' by David Brin (New York: Bantam Dell, 1990).

6. Bodi, S., 'How do we bridge the gap between what we teach and what they do? Some thoughts on the place of questions in the process of research', *The Journal of Academic Librarianship*, Volume 28, no. 3 (2002), pp. 109-114.

7. *Ibid.*

8. Tapscott, D., *Rise of the Net Generation* (Columba, Ohio: McGraw-Hill, 1999).

9. There is broad agreement on the criteria for evaluating websites, namely authority, currency, accuracy, coverage, and objectivity. The question is will pupils (or indeed teachers) take the time to apply these criteria? Expediency for pupils in particular, is a common characteristic.

10. McNicol, Sarah, 'Learning in libraries: lessons for staff', *New Library World*, Volume 103, issues 7/8, 2002, pp. 251-258.

Embracing Life at its Fullest

The Spirituality of Religious Educators and School Chaplains

Gareth Byrne

Introduction

> 'Spirituality for me is a simple walk, saying a prayer, listening to a piece of music.'
> 'My spirituality is linked very much to the sea. I feel God's presence when I'm at the sea – gentle and quiet at times, powerful and moving, angry sometimes, ever present.'
> 'Your word is a lamp for my step and a light for my path (Ps 119:105): Jesus is my guiding light, directing me toward fulfilment.'

The spirituality of religious educators and school chaplains can be looked at from a variety of perspectives. This article begins with an examination of what is meant by spirituality and its relationship with religion. Christian spirituality is considered and life lived in authentic relationship with others and with 'the Other' explored as a basis for nourishment and completion. An integrated spirituality of the human person, grasping and responding to the challenges offered in life, is suggested. In the second half of the article the actual religious education and chaplaincy activities, entered into with their students and with others in the school context, is proposed as a rich theatre of experience within which these professionals are invited to engage with life at its fullest. Three examples to support this argument are offered from school life.

In Touch with the Heart of Our Being

Defining spirituality is not an easy project. 'Spirituality is a mysterious and tender thing, about which we can speak only with difficulty',[1] says Karl Rahner. As Michael Downey points out, the terminology in this area of theology is not always clear.[2] Theological and secular writing often employ the term *'spirituality'* to convey a variety of different meanings. Spirituality, however, is generally understood as a consciousness at the core of each individual's being, affecting the way a person lives life. A close relationship exists between this lived-awareness and the religious dimension of life, that dimension which supports and gives expression to what is experienced as ultimate, discovered both within and beyond self.[3] We may propose, then, with von Balthasar an understanding of spirituality allowing for many varieties of spirituality:

> Spirituality may be approximately defined as that basic practical or existential attitude of man which is the consequence and expression of the way in which he understands his religious – or more generally, his ethically committed – existence; the way in which he acts and reacts habitually throughout his life according to his objective and ultimate insights and decisions.[4]

Whatever a person's spirituality, when it comes down to it, she or he interprets themselves according to that spiritual vision: 'man sees and defines himself in the light of his spiritual quality, and not of his material, bodily or instinctive aspects.'[5] It is a person's spirit that defines the totality of his or her being, characterising who they are and what they believe in. Men and women live their lives according to a basic understanding of themselves related to others and to their world, engaged by a vision of that which is greater than self. As Hay and Nye put it: 'Spirituality by definition is always concerned with self-transcendence.'[6] Moreover, spirituality cannot be limited simply to one part of an individual's reality, affecting them only in that dimension. Nor is it something extra, above and beyond their ordinary selves. 'Spirituality is not something added to our humanity, it is of the very essence of what it means to be human.'[7]

Surprisingly perhaps, the term 'spirituality' is a modern one, occurring neither in the tradition of religious philosophy nor in that of biblical theology. It was in seventeenth-century France that the word 'spiritualité' was first used in a technical sense, indicating the personal relation of human persons with God.[8] The use of the term 'spirituality' rather then the more traditional expression, 'the spiritual life', was only generally accepted in the twentieth century and popularised at the time of, and in the years after, the Second Vatican Council. Although its origin is Judeo-Christian[9] and its tradition Roman Catholic, the term spirituality as it is widely used today need not refer as such to a Christian or even a religious way of life. It has been borrowed to describe the attitude of life associated with diverse religions and lifestyles, such as 'Buddhist spirituality', 'New Age spirituality' and 'Green spirituality'. Furthermore, a person's spirituality, no matter what religious or non-religious interpretation of life they live, is open to being rooted consciously or less consciously in selfishness, denial, anger or materialism, for example, rather than wonder, gratitude, responsibility and joy, and requires therefore ongoing reflection and refinement. Marian de Souza in her chapter in this book highlights the risk of living obsessed with self and somehow disconnected from the interests and desires of others as an indication perhaps of flawed or immature spirituality.[10]

The Essence of Christian Spirituality

While others might like to reflect on the contribution of various forms of spirituality in the broad sense indicated above, we will focus here on the impact of Christian spirituality for religious educators and school chaplains of that tradition. Christian spirituality is essentially a way of life in which a personal, interiorised relationship with God in His transcendent and immanent reality is fully recognised and cultivated in the intimate embrace of Jesus Christ through the power of the Holy Spirit. The Christian believes that in Jesus Christ both the fullness of God and the fullness of human possibility are revealed. By the continuing extravagance of the Holy Spirit this revelation is made known to each new generation and is witnessed to by that human community of faith called Church. Christians gather as a community around the Crucified and Risen Lord in praise, thanksgiving and intercession, seeking forgiveness and reconciliation, experiencing union with God and with each other. Over the centuries they have responded to Christ, recognised as the incarnation of God's love, from within the reality of their own situation and the limits of their time, according to their own abilities and influenced by the dominant philosophies and forces of their day. Day-to-day life, friendship, marriage, commitment to a faith community or to religious life, the birth of a child, adolescent and other transitions, the death of a loved one, all of life is celebrated and even its darker moments are lived trusting in God's love. Prayer becomes an ongoing conversation with God about all of life. For many religious educators and school chaplains in Ireland today their spirituality is inspired by Jesus Christ, built on relationship with him and experienced in living his exhortation to love God and love your neighbour (Lk 10:27). Despite whatever inadequacies they might confess, their spirituality challenges them to reach out with Christ to those in need, to offer forgiveness, reconciliation and healing, to seek justice and peace, to carry joy and hope and love in their hearts: 'We will find healing and wholeness by touching the body of Christ and, as members of the body of Christ, we are called upon to dispense God's healing and wholeness by touching others.'[11]

A survey of the various influences dominant within Christian spirituality, something it is not necessary to undertake here, would examine among other themes the New Testament and Early Church approach to life in Christ, the development of monasticism, and the divisions that gradually evolved between clergy and laity and between East and West. It would also present the progress and evolution of the spiritual life in the Middle Ages, the influence of the Reformation and Counter-Reformation, of the Enlightenment and of the Modern Age, allowing us to situate various approaches to Christian living within what many call a post-modern age. The richness of people's personal journeys, the development of movements in the Church and the challenge provided by reforms at different levels have continually given rise under inspirational figures to a variety of religious ways of life whose spirituality continue to impact on the Church and in the lives of individuals and society. One has only to begin a list – Benedictine, Franciscan, Carmelite, Jesuit, Vincentian, Salesian, Focolare, Sant'Egidio and so many more[12] – to become aware of the wellsprings from which the religious educator, the school chaplain and indeed all people are invited to draw refreshment and experience the challenge of Jesus' all-embracing love: 'God in his many-faced face, has become as visible, as the nearest water-tap. That is the why of the Incarnation.'[13]

Christian Spirituality in the World

The spirituality of religious educators and school chaplains as such may also be considered in the context of their role in society and within a particular school community. Within the Christian family over the last two hundred years there have been significant developments in the understanding of the spiritual life, of the spirituality of the laity in particular and of the relationship between faith and life lived fully as a religious or as a layperson. In the eighteenth and nineteenth centuries a renewed emphasis was placed on the active Christian life. The founding of numerous religious institutes concerned with helping the poor, particularly in caring for the homeless, the hungry, people with intellectual or physical disability, in making education more widely available, and in the provision of hospital and hospice care gave practical effect to the concept of Christian charity. Social and scientific developments at the end of the nineteenth and in the early twentieth centuries saw the development of a new awareness of the identity of the lay person in the Church and of the role he or she could play. Technology, industrialisation, mass employment and the development of huge modern cities, led to the cultivation of the social spirituality taught in a series of papal encyclicals beginning with Leo XIII's *Rerum Novarum*.[14] The popes of the twentieth century have provided, in response, a corpus of social teaching that has been constantly renewed and updated.[15] The meaning of work, the situation of workers and their rights and responsibilities, the role of government and of the people, the social order, and peace and justice have been dealt with in a way that leaves no doubt as to the importance of everyday issues in the mature understanding of the Christian spiritual life. An overview of men and women's needs, the requirement to seek the human development of all peoples, and the appropriateness of solidarity between those who have and those who have not has been emphasised as central to Christian living. Pope John Paul II leaves us with no doubt as to the need for all Christians to be actively involved in overcoming any world order that is unjust:

> Therefore political leaders, and citizens of rich countries considered as individuals, especially if they are Christians, have *the moral obligation,* according to the degree of each one's responsibility, to *take into consideration,* in personal decisions and decisions of government, this relationship of universality, this interdependence which exists between their conduct and the poverty and underdevelopment of so many millions of people.[16]

Among others, Yves Congar's book *Jalons pour une theologie du laïcat,* published in 1953 and later revised and reissued in English in 1985, was a milestone in the renewal of the theology of the laity. The necessary foundation according to Congar, in overcoming any separation between lay people and clergy, is an ecclesiology focused on the 'People of God': 'All do not take part in the laying of the foundations and in directing the building, but all share in the dignity of the whole, in the functions that compose it and in the activities of its life.'[17] In a later book, *Ministères et communion ecclésiale*, Congar argued further that ministry in the Church extends far beyond that reserved to the ordained. He finds a remedy to clericalism in a return to the New Testament perspective that speaks of a variety of ministries, all situated within the community. Priests, religious and laypeople all working together according to their role, abilities and energy foster the local community of faith and encourage each other to live consciously in God's love. All ministries, while admitting their differences, build on the common Christian reality shared by all, under the impulse of Christ and guided by the Spirit.[18]

Contemporary Christian Spirituality

The deliberations of the Second Vatican Council (1962-65) were of singular importance in the ongoing development of Christian spirituality giving rise to a renewed vision of Christian life. It can justifiably be argued that the Second Vatican Council both legitimised the efforts earlier in the twentieth century for a renewal of the understanding of Christian spiritual life and gave a new impetus to that renewal by returning Christianity to the fundamentals of the Early Church. Three aspects of the work of Vatican II are particularly important for an understanding of contemporary Christian spirituality as perceived today; the renewal of the liturgy, the rediscovery of the concept 'People of God' and the overcoming of the spirit/world duality.

Enabling Christians to participate knowingly, actively and fruitfully in the liturgy (*SC* 11) was confirmed by Council members as the first step in drawing people into an authentic religious experience, leading to conscious participation in the mysteries of Christ's life, ministry, death and resurrection. The liturgical renewal embarked upon set up expectations of welcome, understanding, participation and belonging. Action has not always been as strong as words, however, and the result has often been disaffection on the part of the young and not so young.[19] Secondly, taking account of the ecclesiological renewal in the pre-Vatican II years, particularly the work of Congar, the Council returned to the use of the image of the Church as the People of God (*LG* 9). Derek Worlock, one of the participants at the Council, stresses, that *Lumen Gentium*: 'lifted the concept of the lay person out of the negative status of "non-priest" and set him positively among the faithful People of God, sharing fully in the salvific mission of the Church.'[20] Thirdly, the Pastoral Constitution on the Church in the Modern World, *Gaudium et Spes*, clarifies the relationship between the Church and the world, confessing that the Church, that is all its members, could learn from the world and its peoples and should be receptively reading 'the signs of the times' in the light of the Gospel (*GS* 11). The Church's mission is always religious but this mission can provide light and energy to the political, economic and social spheres of society by speaking of the dignity and rights of all people, strengthening the seams of society and imbuing the everyday activities of men and women with a deeper meaning and sense of importance (*GS* 40-41).

The search for a complete understanding of lay membership in the Church has become, then, one of the trademarks of the post-Vatican II era. To be Church means to live as a community in the world and at the service of the world. The salvation in Jesus Christ proposed by Pope John Paul II is a salvation that is offered within human relationships and conflicts, within the concrete historical reality of men and women's lives.[21] It suggests an integrated approach to spirituality taking into account the unity of all that goes to make up human truth, and by so doing remains true both to humankind and to Christ.

> There cannot be two parallel lives in their existence: on the one hand, the so-called 'spiritual' life, with its values and demands; and on the other, the so-called 'secular' life, that is, life in a family, at work, in social relationships, in the responsibilities of public life and in culture.[22]

The diversity of issues highlighted within Christian spirituality today is vast. Such richness offers the religious educator and school chaplain a wonderful variety of influences within which to shape their authentic selves. An inability to face real questions or to respond to them in life-giving ways can, conversely, have a negative, limiting or even deforming effect. Together with the spirituality of religious life in all its various manifestations, lay spirituality, popular spirituality, the spirituality of movements and groups in the Church and ecumenical spirituality have been given consideration.[23] Certain issues are also seen to suggest a specialised approach, for example, socio-political spirituality and the spirituality of the poor,[24] spirituality and the arts[25] and the spirituality of healing.[26] Other issues highlighted by contemporary writers and thinkers include the need for an awareness that lived spirituality resides in a particular context and culture, in Europe or the Middle East, in Asia or Africa, in North or South America. In an increasingly industrialised, consumer-oriented and globalised world, threatened by nuclear weapons and international terrorism of one kind or another, the relationship between members of the human race[27] and their relationship with the earth have become central to the way Christians live their spirituality.[28] Concern for those individuals and groups on the margins of society, and of the Church, has also led to new awareness. In particular greater attention to the place of women's experience in the Church and in society has been one of the most notable characteristics of spirituality in our age.[29] Adolescence as a time of transition in the life of the young person and as a phenomenon in society today has also been highlighted as never before. The young person's struggle to come to terms with their own developing self-identity and grow into an authentic person able to relate intimately and appropriately with others raises faith and religious identity issues for them and also for their parents.[30] At the beginning of the twenty-first century fragility within the Church as it navigates its way through a chaotic world should not be discounted either as a powerful source of spiritual reflection. Christian spirituality today must deal with the experience of polarisation between fundamentalist forces and secularising tendencies within the People of God, of insecurity and sinfulness, of financial and sexual scandals among its members, and in particular with an inability on the part of so many to respond adequately to those who have suffered sexual abuse as children. What new light and life, one asks longingly, might come out of darkness and distress?[31]

Religious Education as a Context for Spiritual Development

Thus far we have been considering the influence of a developed personal spirituality supported by family, culture, faith community and religious tradition, taking Christian spirituality as our example. We have become aware of the implications of their own spiritual journey for the religious educator and the school chaplain. 'We teach who we are', says Parker Palmer.[32] Another approach, however, would highlight concrete religious education and chaplaincy activities themselves as possible contexts for spiritual development. Their work, as well as impacting on their pupils, has at least the potential to upset, challenge and renew not only the knowledge and attitudes of these professionals but at a deep level their spiritual connection with self, others and with God.

James Michael Lee has considered this question with particular reference to religious educators. He focuses 'on the religious educator's spirituality in terms of that educator's own religious education ministry rather than in terms of that individual's own personal spiritual development per se.'[33] For Lee spirituality is intimately connected with the concrete reality of a person's life. It is not something otherworldly, separate, a pocket of prayer detached from the rest of a person's life. 'A person's spirituality is suffusively part and parcel of the individual's here-and-now concrete life.'[34] Spirituality, Lee says, is specifically and directly linked with its demonstration in one's life. He argues that the quantity and quality of time spent by any person in lifework activities, associated with their career or occupation, indicates the power these activities can have in contributing to growth at a whole series of levels, intellectual, emotional, moral and spiritual. Lee believes this to be true for everyone at some level whatever their occupation; office manager, coffee shop waitress, nurse or gardener. Moreover, the individual usually invests a great deal of their very self in their lifework. Limiting factors may be present but a person's self-concept, personal needs and perception of personal development are intimately bound up with their initial selection, engagement, change (if necessary), and ongoing commitment to a particular lifework.[35]

Having argued the link between lifework generally and spirituality, Lee considers specifically the process undertaken by the religious educator in her or his teaching work and its bearing on spiritual development. He highlights what he calls the substantive content (subject matter) and the structural content (teaching process) central to the lifework of the religious educator.[36] Since the substantive content associated with religious education is, Lee argues, 'lived religion', concentration is maintained in one way or another on religious, spiritual and moral life experience. The dialogue between religion and science for example, or an investigation of the meaning of faith encourages the religious educator into deep reflection on life. Engagement with students, focused on this content, cannot leave the religious educator untouched or unmoved. Secondly, the structuring of the lesson for religious learning influences not only *how* something is learned by students but contributes also to *what* is learned. Choices made in the preparation of lessons, in the type of interaction with students and in assessment of learning are not neutral. They contribute to what students pick up and they effect appreciably how and what the educator herself learns in the process. The detail involved in structuring specific behaviours to facilitate desired learning outcomes becomes significant for all participants in the dialogue. The way a person goes about teaching-learning activities reflects something of how they see themselves and their role. 'The concept of lifework spirituality implies that the quality and the texture of pedagogical practice itself contributes significantly to the shaping and the forming of the religious educator's spiritual life.'[37] The religious educator gives a great deal of himself or herself to their students in orchestrating the pedagogical act. Being at the service of students is the heart of all teaching activity. Working with young people as they grow into life-questions keeps the conversation very real indeed. In the process, Lee suggests, the religious educator receives as much as she or he offers.

Implications for the Religious Educator, the School Chaplain and the School Community

The spirituality of the religious educator, James Michael Lee argues, is coloured by their religious education engagement with students. If this is so, all those who engage in helping others to question the meaning of life, to awaken their religious and moral imagination, to find the language necessary to express their spirituality, assisting them at an appropriate level to become involved in religious exploration and undertake a journey toward religious discovery, are in turn opening themselves to all the spiritual and religious questions they help others pose. How they do this also contributes to their learning experience. Parents, grandparents and wider family, priests and parishioners, those who give expression to spiritual and religious questions in various media and cultural forums, all find themselves drawn into this process according to their willingness to become openly involved in the exchange.

For the purposes of this reflection focused on professional religious educators and school chaplains, three examples within the school context will serve to help us realise the importance of Lee's assertion. The introduction of the Junior Certificate Religious Education Syllabus and the Leaving Certificate Religious Education Syllabus allows for state assessment and certification of pupil learning in the subject Religious Education for the first time in the Republic of Ireland.[38] These syllabuses in common with other subjects across the curriculum are built on an holistic vision of the human person. Operating within the characteristic spirit of a school, they hope 'to contribute to the development of all aspects of the individual, including aesthetic, creative, critical, cultural, emotional, intellectual, moral, physical, political, social and spiritual development.'[39] They focus on the human search for meaning, its expression in religion, the contribution of religious traditions, particularly Christianity, to the culture in which the students live, the development of an appreciation of the richness of religious traditions and non-religious interpretations of life and seek also to contribute to the spiritual and moral development of the student.[40] The religious educator's role sees them assisting their students encounter and engage with religious traditions in Ireland and elsewhere, while encouraging and supporting them in reflecting on their own experience and commitment to a particular religious tradition and/or search for meaning. The role also envisages helping students, within a spirit of respect for the values of all, to dialogue with the Christian tradition in Ireland and its denominational expressions, acknowledging the unique role of Christianity in Irish life and culture.[41] If such is the work of religious educators then it seems very clear that their lifework will immerse them in all these questions. The subject matter itself and the teaching procedures adopted to enhance pupil learning will test the knowledge, understanding, skills and attitudes of the religious educators themselves as laid out by the syllabuses. The requirement of an open and respectful approach to all religious traditions and to those of no religious tradition, for example, implies not just intellectual assent by the teacher but the development of a reflective way of life, a spirituality that willingly embraces such hospitality. The Irish Catholic Bishops comment positively concerning both the legitimacy and the impact of such an approach:

> Honest and respectful study of Christian and non-Christian religion, secularist and atheistic philosophies and the beliefs of those who do not espouse any religious or philosophical affiliation will ensure an openness and respect for humankind as commanded by Christ in the Gospels.[42]

A second example might consider the role of the school chaplain who 'animates the spiritual life of the school community.'[43] The chaplain's is a relational role accompanying both students and staff on their journey through life. Schools chaplains in Ireland report their main activities as one-to-one counselling, providing liturgical celebrations, supporting other staff, bereavement support, addressing the causes of student indiscipline, meeting with and visiting parents and hospital visitation.[44] Day-by-day the chaplain interacts with students concerning ordinary adolescent realities such as self-esteem, friendship, growing spiritual awareness, stress, peer pressure and family relations. They also find themselves invited to engage with students at a deeply personal level when something vital in life takes centre stage such as illness, broken relationships, violence, death and suicide. The chaplain responds to and supports individuals and the school community, helping them to come to terms with their personal, emotional and spiritual needs. By being present to students and staff, encouraging them to tell their story, confirming when appropriate their need for silence and space, providing symbolic, ritual and prayerful support and at times reconnecting them with others and with their community, the chaplain touches people in their deepest reality. Such work puts the school chaplain, whether a layperson, a religious or a priest, in direct contact personally with ultimate questions. Standing in solidarity with others affects who the chaplain is and who they become.

A third example invites all those involved in a school community focused on student learning to consider how their participation with students in school life affects them personally. Board members, school principals and leadership teams, teachers generally and other staff, parents and representatives of local faith communities associate themselves with the characteristic spirit of a school and involve themselves in supporting and developing that spirit. In so doing their own spirit is engaged in a conversation about things that really matter to individuals and to the school, a dialogue searching the depths of what is held to be of value. Academic learning is recognised as interconnected with other areas of knowledge and an inclusive environment open to the education needs for life of all is created. Issues such as school identity, school leadership, teamwork within the school, partnership with parents and with local faith communities, ecumenical and inter-faith dialogue, and the impact of all these matters on the full human development of pupils ask profound questions not only of a particular system but also of self. A renewed professionalism within the school community, it has been suggested, demands integrity, empathy, vision and adaptability.[45] It is difficult to envisage members of the school community and those associated with it becoming involved in an ongoing and genuine exchange of ideas and expression of passion in relation to ethos issues without finding themselves continually reviewing and renewing their own awareness, decisions and way of life.

A Place of Revelation, A Space in Which to Grow

In conclusion, understanding their own developing spirituality, learning to love and dialogue with their religious tradition, coming to apprehend who they are in relation to others, the world and God, opens the religious educator and the school chaplain to experience life at its fullest. The integrated approach suggested above encourages them to reflect on the connection between the intellectual, social, cultural, moral, religious and spiritual dimensions of life. The religious educator and the school chaplain find themselves working together[46] and working with others in the school community in promoting this integrated approach to life. Working collectively, the opportunities not only to inspire their students but for personal self-reflection and growth are multiplied. The work to which they give so much of themselves contributes in no small way to their own experience of life lived openly, generously and compassionately. A person's lifework should never, of course, be allowed to master or control them. Instead, the lifework of the religious educator and school chaplain may be understood as an arena adapted and prepared for spiritual enrichment. Through their interaction with students and with each other their everyday working environment can become a privileged place of revelation. The school community, with all its ups and downs and with new things happening all around, even if at times they find themselves over-burdened, offers itself as a space in which to grow. When there is enough courage to embrace life with all its remarkable questions and to embrace each other with all our dreams and imperfections, the religious educator, the school chaplain and so many others, find themselves held, engaged, in touch with power and creativity:

> True religious education and genuine spirituality will have to foster the kind of artistic, creative power that is not only in the mind but sedimented in bodily practice as a lasting song in the marrow bone of contemporary life.[47]

Notes

1. Rahner, K., 'The Spirituality of the Church of the Future' in K. Rahner, *Theological Investigations* 20, (London: Darton, Longman & Todd, 1981), p. 143.

2. See Downey, M., 'Understanding Christian Spirituality: Dress Rehearsal for a Method', *Spirituality Today* 43(1991)3, pp. 271-272. For a full introduction to issues central to Christian spirituality, see M. Downey (ed.), *The New Dictionary of Catholic Spirituality* (Collegeville, Minnesota: The Liturgical Press, 1993).

3. For an overview of the variety of beliefs, activities and customs commonly designated as religious see P. Barnes, *World Religions, Into the Classroom Series* (Dublin: Veritas, 2003).

4. von Balthasar, H.U., 'The Gospel as Norm and Test of All Spirituality in the Church', *Concilium* 1(1965)9, p. 5.

5. von Balthasar, H. U., 'The Gospel', p. 5.

6. Hay, D., with Nye, R., *The Spirit of the Child* (London: Fount Publications, 1998), p. 172.

7. Treston, K., *Paths and Stories: Spirituality for Teachers and Catechists* (Dublin: Veritas, 1991), p. 10.

8. See Sudbrack, J., 'Spirituality' in K. Rahner (ed.), *Sacramentum Mundi: An Encyclopedia of Theology* 6 (New York: Herder and Herder, 1968), p. 148. For a history of the term 'spirituality', see Sheldrake, P., *Spirituality and History* (London: SPCK, 1991), pp. 34-36.

9. For a concise overview of the emergence and meaning of words such as, 'ruach', 'pneuma' and 'spirit' in the Hebrew tradition, in Greek thought and in New Testament theology see Noffke, S., 'Soul' in M. Downey (ed.), *The New Dictionary of Catholic Spirituality*, pp. 908-910.

10. See de Souza, M., 'The Role of the School and Educational Programs in Nurturing the Spirituality of Young People' in this publication.

11. Rolheiser, R., *Seeking Spirituality: Guidelines for a Christian Spirituality for the Twenty-First Century* (London: Hodder & Stoughton, 1998), p. 82.

12. See, for example, Lanly, T. M., (ed.), *As Leaven in the World: Catholic Perspectives on Faith, Vocation and the Intellectual Life* (Franklin, Wisconsin: Sheed & Ward, 2001).

13. Rolheiser, R., *Seeking Spirituality*, p. 74.

14. Leo XIII, *Rerum Novarum, Acta Leonis XIII* 11(1892), pp. 97-144.

15. See Pius XI, *Quadragesimo Anno, AAS* 23(1931), pp. 177-228; John XXIII, *Mater et Magistra, AAS* 53(1961), pp. 401-464; Paul VI, *Octogesima Adveniens, AAS* 63(1971), pp. 401-441; John Paul II, *Laborem Exercens, AAS* 73(1981), pp. 577-647; John Paul II, *Centesimus Annus, AAS* 83(1991)2, pp. 793-867.

16. John Paul II, *Sollicitudo Rei Socialis* 9, *AAS* 80(1988)1, pp. 513-586.

17. Congar, Y., *Lay People in the Church: A Study for a Theology of Laity* (London: Geoffrey Chapman, 1985), p. 453.

18. See Congar, Y., *Ministères et communion ecclésiale* (Paris : Cerf, 1971), pp. 9-49.

19. See Conn, J. W. , 'Spirituality' in J. Komonchak, M. Collins, and D.A. Lane (eds), *The New Dictionary of Theology* (Dublin: Gill and Macmillan, 1990), p. 979.

20. Worlock, D.J., 'Toil in the Lord: The Laity in Vatican II' in A. Stacpoole (ed.) *Vatican II by Those Who Were There* (London: Geoffrey Chapman, 1986), p. 240.

21. See John Paul II, *Redemptor Hominis* 13; 15-17, *AAS* 71(1979)1, pp. 257-324; John Paul II, *Dives In Misericordia* 10-12, *AAS* 72(1980)2, pp. 1177-1232.

22. See John Paul II, *Christifideles Laici* 59, *AAS* 81(1989)1, pp. 393-525.

23. For a variety of ways to enter into key issues being addressed in Church today see the Vatican website available from: www.vatican.va; also Churches Today in Britain and Ireland (CTBI) available from www.ctbi.org.uk

24. See Reiser, W., *To Know God's Word, Listen to the World: The Liberation of Spirituality* (New York/Mahwah: Paulist Press, 1997); Coleman, B., and Coleman, P., *Discovering the Spirit in the Poor: Whispers of Revelation* (Mystic, Connecticut: Twenty-Third Publications, 1992).

25. See Murphy, A.M. Cassidy, E.G., (eds) *Neglected Wells: Spirituality and the Arts* (Dublin : Four Courts Press, 1997); *Aspects of Religious Education* 28(1982).

26. See Kearney, T., (ed.), *A Prophetic Cry: Stories of Spirituality and Healing Inspired by L'Arche* (Dublin: Veritas, 2000).

27. See Donders, J.G., 'Ministering in a Globalizing World: The Challenge of a Cross-Cultural Spirituality' in R.J. Wicks (ed.), *Handbook of Spirituality for Ministers* 1 (New York/Mahwah: Paulist Press, 1995), pp. 174-190.

28. Edwards, D., *Earth Revealing – Earth Healing: Ecology and Christian Theology* (Collegeville, Minnesota: The Liturgical Press, 2001).

29. See Loades, A., (ed.), *Feminist Theology: A Reader* (London: SPCK, 1990); Ruethers, R., 'Feminist Theology' in J. Komonchak, M. Collins and D.A. Lane (eds), *The New Dictionary of Theology* (Dublin: Gill and Macmillan, 1987); Schneiders, S.M., 'Feminist Spirituality' in M. Downey (ed.) *The New Dictionary of Catholic Spirituality*, pp. 394-406.

30. See Tuohy D., Cairns, P., *Youth 2K: Threat or Promise to a Religious Culture* (Dublin: Marino Institute of Education, 2000); Byrne, G., 'Factors That Influence Religious Belief and Practice in the Life of the Adolescent' *LOGOS* (Mater Dei Institute of Education, 2001) [online]. Available from: www.materdei.ie/logos/D1; Carotto, M., *Sometimes We Dance Sometimes We Wrestle: Embracing the Spirituality of Adolescents* (Orlando: Harcourt Religion Publishers, 2002).

31. See Arbuckle, G. A., 'Letting Go in Hope: A Spirituality for a Chaotic World' in R.J. Wicks, *Handbook of Spirituality for Ministry, Volume 2: Perspectives for the Twenty-First Century* (New York/Mahwah: Paulist Press, 2000), pp. 121-133.

32. Palmer, P.J., *The Courage to Teach* (San Francisco: Jossey-Bass, 1998), p. 2. See also Barry, C., 'Spirituality and the Educator: Cherishing and Challenging the Spirituality of the Educator' in N. Prendergast and L. Monahan, *Reimagining the Catholic School* (Dublin: Veritas, 2003), p. 46-55.

33. Lee, J.M., (ed.), *The Spirituality of the Religious Educator* (Birmingham, Alabama: Religious Education Press, 1985), p. 1.

34. Lee, J.M., 'Spirituality and the Religious Educator' in J.M. Lee (ed.), *The Spirituality of the Religious Educator*, p. 7.

35. Lee, J.M., 'Lifework Spirituality', p. 17.

36. See Lee, J. M., 'Lifework Spirituality', p. 19-42.

37. Lee, J.M., 'Lifework Spirituality', p. 40.

38. See Department of Education and Science, *Junior Certificate: Religious Education Syllabus* (Dublin: Government Publications, 2000); *Leaving Certificate Religious Education Syllabus* (Dublin: Government Publications, 2003).

39. National Council for Curriculum and Assessment definition of the general aim of education, *JCRES*, inside cover.

40. See *JCRES*, p. 5.

41. *JCRES*, p. 4.

42. Irish Catholic Bishops' Conference, *Guidelines for the Faith Formation and Development of Catholic Students* (Dublin: Veritas, 1999), pp. 8-9.

43. Monahan, L., Renehan, C., *The Chaplain: A Faith Presence in the School Community* (Dublin: Columba, 1998), p. 20. See also Feheny J.M. (ed.), *Beyond the Race for Points: Aspects of Pastoral Care in a Catholic School Today* (Dublin: Veritas, 1999).

44. See Norman, J., *Pastoral Care in Second-Level Schools: The Chaplain* (Dublin: Centre for Research in Religion and Education, Mater Dei Institute of Education, 2002).

45. See Norman, J., *Ethos and Education in Ireland Today,* Irish Studies 7 (New York: Peter Lang, 2003), pp. 65-81.

46. For a discussion of contemporary issues related to religious educators and school chaplains working together, see P. King, 'Religious Education as a State Examination: Implications for the School Chaplain' in this publication.

47. Harris, M., *Proclaim Jubilee! A Spirituality for the Twenty-First Century* (Louisville, Kentucky: Westminster, John Knox Press, 1996), p. 16.

A Study of Pupils' Perceptions and Experiences of School Chaplaincy

Siobhán Murphy

Introduction

This study was undertaken to determine how second-level pupils who have a full-time chaplain present in their school, understand and encounter the role of the chaplain. Although chaplains are present to serve all involved in the school community – pupils, staff and parents – the focus was specifically on the relationship between the chaplain and the pupils.

A selective view of the literature attested to the fact that the chaplain's role embraces a number of tenets. Factors identified included the chaplain as a faith presence, a spiritual guide, a community builder and a 'counsellor'. The centrality of spirituality and counselling in the chaplain's daily work was also clear.[1] Consequently, the role of school chaplain can be said to be far-reaching, embracing a multitude of elements. However, much of the literature to date has not dealt with the experience of pupils and so whether pupils actually experience these aspects of the role warranted attention. Hence, the study was centred on the beliefs, values, opinions and attitudes of those who encounter and experience first hand the work of the chaplain. It sought the views of those who are best in a position to judge the role – the pupils – and it examined their understanding of the work of the chaplain.

In addition, the research set out to understand if there is a difference in the role of the ordained and the non-ordained chaplain. While the presence of both is tentatively acknowledged in the literature, whether there are any variations between how pupils encounter the ordained and the non-ordained chaplain also merited review.

The Research Design

The study was conducted in two schools, a small rural community school, and a larger suburban one. The first was selected because it had a lay chaplain, and the second because it had an ordained chaplain. Both chaplains were male, approximately the same age, and both were established in their roles for a number of years. The researcher considered these factors to be important, insofar as part of the study included making comparisons between pupils' perceptions of the role of ordained and lay chaplains. The pupils did not know the researcher and this was felt to be important in minimising bias. A qualitative approach was used to determine and describe how pupils viewed their chaplain. Qualitative studies primarily involve the use of in-depth interviews as they facilitate the process of exploration. In effect, they enable the generation of rich, insightful, contextualised data.[2]

A central concern of the researcher was the selection of participants insofar as the design was guided by the need for pupils who could yield sufficient quality data. The inclusion criteria used for this study were that participants should:

- Be in 5th year (The chaplain may be very involved with 4th years (transition year) while 6th years were approaching their state examinations. Hence, greater contact could occur with the chaplain during these stages possibly influencing findings).
- Not be using the chaplaincy service on an ongoing or long-term basis, thus avoiding inherent bias.
- Be both male and female to avoid a gender imbalance

Of the final pupils selected, half had previous personal experience with their chaplain while the other half had never sought assistance.

During the interviews, while the researcher used a topic guide to provide direction, open questions were used. The emphasis during the interview was on encouraging respondents to describe experiences, that is, to tell their own story, in their own terms.

A modified version of Colaizzi's framework was used to help with analysis.[3] Each transcript was read several times in order to gain complete familiarity with the data. Then, significant or relevant meanings that provided descriptions or highlights of experiences and encounters were noted. These were coded. Following this process categories were formed by grouping similar codes together. Discrepancies, contradictions and relationships between respondents' descriptions were sought. From these categories major themes were identified, which described and encapsulated pupils' experiences with their chaplain.

Research Findings

The findings illustrate the encounters and experiences second-level pupils had with their chaplains. Analysis revealed that findings could be divided into four main themes. These included the chaplain as counsellor; the promotion of faith, liturgy and prayer; accompaniment of pupils in their life journeys; and the somewhat unique interactions respondents experienced with their chaplains. Interwoven throughout the fabric of all the narratives, was the understanding that the chaplain contributed to the pupils' personal and faith development, because of key qualities previously highlighted. Of significance was the level of consensus that emerged in relation to the multidimensional nature of the role and the unique way that the chaplain achieved this.

It is worth noting that respondents A1, A2, A3 and A4 had recourse to the ordained chaplain while respondents B1, B2, B3 and B4 had access to the lay chaplain. Also the researcher was conscious of remaining faithful to the pupils' stories, consequently the findings include primary data.

Furthermore some limitations are identified which merit attention when interpreting findings. Firstly, it is difficult to draw any conclusions on the extent to which these findings are representative of pupils' experiences elsewhere. The experience described is the reality for those individuals who participated in the study. In addition, only eight pupils were interviewed, which suggests that data saturation was not reached. Though, it should also be acknowledged that each school has its own unique culture that may have an influence on pupils' perceptions and experiences, the respondents' accounts in this study ultimately attest to the similarity in the range and performance of both chaplains' roles. Furthermore, similar themes have emerged in other studies, which enhances the credibility of these findings.[4]

The Chaplain as Counsellor

The most significant theme to emerge in all the interviews was the chaplain's role as counsellor. Pupils identified not only the types of problems they would seek help with, but their narratives revealed how the chaplain facilitated a therapeutic process. The chaplain as counsellor is discussed under a number of sub-themes.

These accounts attest to the fact that respondents readily identified the counselling aspect of the chaplain's role:

A3: If there is anything wrong with anybody, he would usually be like a counsellor to those people. There was a boy from around here who died and a couple of people knew him here so he [the chaplain] was like, kinda counselling all of them.

B3: He is the person you come and talk to if you are in trouble or if you have a problem or something – he is the guy you will talk to, to get it sorted. That's his main job.

A2: He is the only one I would consider coming to with a problem.

Interestingly, in acknowledging the chaplain's role as a counsellor, the pupils clearly identified the tenets of that role. Ultimately, they experienced the chaplain as willing to listen, available and approachable, which helped the therapeutic process. Several of the respondents expressed similar views:

A1: It's just that he listens, you know, he doesn't say what is right or wrong straight away, he listens first.

B4: With the chaplain it's about you and he convinces you that you can deal with whatever it is that is going on. He helps people to deal with their problems. He listens, he lets them talk and gives them advice. People can cope better by going to him.

In relation to availability the pupils were consistently clear that the chaplain was there for them:

B1: If he is in the staff room and you have a problem, he'd come out and talk to you and give up his own lunchtime for you. He will make time for you all the time.

In addition, respondents perceived the approachability of the chaplain as an important aspect. In fact, even those who had not used the chaplain expressed the opinion that because of his approachable nature they would go to the chaplain should the need arise:

B1: If you have a problem, he would be the first one you'd go to really, because he is the most approachable teacher in the school by far.

B4: Even though I've never gone to him, I know I could if I needed to. He makes that clear.

For pupils, an important aspect of the chaplain's counselling service is that it remains confidential. Six of the eight specifically refer to this, expressing similar views:

B4: You know if you talked to him, it would be an anonymous conversation.

B2: You know he's not going to take it any further.

Moreover the confidentiality aspect influenced the pupil's decision to use the chaplain.

B1: You can talk to him and there is no problem or anything… there is no panic that you're going to say something and he is going to use it against you later, or tell someone else or something like that.

A4: We all know it's confidential, we always know when talking to him that he wouldn't go and say anything unless he really had to, he's not the type. Say someone came in here now and said 'I'm taking these drugs', he wouldn't be running to the principal's office.

Remarkably, three respondents realised there may be circumstances so serious that the chaplain may be forced to involve parents. However, they intimated that this would in no way preclude them from seeking advice from the him. Of significance was that the pupils were aware that they would be informed if parents had to be consulted.

B2: If you have a problem it stays between you and him and that's important unless of course he absolutely has to tell someone, like maybe your parents, but he'll tell you if this has to happen.

In terms of the counselling role, respondents identified that the chaplain deals with a wide variety of problems. The range includes:

Bullying:

I suppose he deals with bullying a lot, because you can just slide a note under his door or come up to him and he doesn't make a big fuss about it, you know, he does it quietly and sorts things out without getting a lot of people involved or drawing too much attention to you. I guess you could say he is subtle. (**B1**)

Bullying was an issue identified by most respondents.

Drugs/Solvent Abuse:

A3: Well, my friend got kicked out of school and when he came back he came down about twice a week to the chaplain for about four weeks or something like that. He was kicked out because the principal said he was doing drugs.

A4: I know a few people who came to him about a petrol situation at one stage, so that was deadly dangerous. Some of the lads came in all right, because they were getting too into it like, every day after school they couldn't wait for it. They didn't know who else to go to, other than the chaplain, and I'm sure he was part of the reason that they managed to stop.

Family situations:

A4: I'd say people who have problems at home come to him and he'd listen and then ask questions about what's going on and then he'd bring out these leaflets for you to read and all these management skills of what you could do.

SM: Why do you think he asks the questions?

A4: So he can get a deeper understanding of what is actually happening in the house, you know, and so he can give more accurate solutions, and so that you can go away and say, 'I'm going to do this now and it will work for me'.

Self esteem:

A1: If you have any problems you just go to him and he makes you feel better and he helps you make sense of things. Last year my self-esteem was about that size [makes a gesture to suggest very low], but since talking to him, I feel a lot better about my self.

SM: And how did he make you feel like that?

A1: I don't know, just by convincing me that I wasn't what I was thinking I was, that I wasn't how I felt. He put me in touch with myself and I saw that I was better than I thought, um.. he told me I was good.

A sentiment expressed in different ways by the respondents is their belief that the chaplain, as a counsellor, is competent in what he does. Some refer specifically to his training:

A3: I probably would come here for help [gestures around the chaplain's office] because he is trained in it anyway. He seems to be very good at all that stuff.

B4: Pupils could discuss anything with him really and I'd say there are not too many other people like him who can move from one level to another and adapt to all these. I'd say he deals with a wide range of things, but he is able to deal with anything that comes his way. I think he has done some kind of counselling course.

These two respondents felt that in addition to specific training, competence was enhanced by the chaplain's own varied life experiences.

A3: He's been a big help. He knows what he is talking about. He knows about the really important things in life.

B4: Well he has twenty years experience and so he has dealt, I'd say, with most of the issues before and so he is more experienced. He has seen life, he has lots of examples himself, friends and stuff. He relates everything back to real life and it's easier to understand then, because it's more real, it's not just talk.

The Promotion of Faith, Liturgy and Prayer

The pupils perceived the chaplains as a religious presence in the school, whether lay or ordained. Respondents were in agreement that they created a religious atmosphere. Of special importance seems to be the celebration of the main liturgical events in the Church calendar, with many pupils mentioning specific occasions. Respondents cited Advent, Christmas, Ash Wednesday, Lent, Easter and a May Service as marked by the chaplain. Moreover, they also recalled other times celebrated with liturgy such as a mass to open the school year, or prior to exams. The chaplain as faith presence is threaded throughout many of the narratives, with some pupils overtly discussing this aspect of his role. Respondents from both schools recounted time and time again that the chaplain was fundamentally concerned with promoting the liturgical year. This is aptly illustrated in the following extracts:

A4   At the beginning of the mass itself the first thing he'd state is that we're having Mass because it's Advent. He'd say these are the candles, these are their jobs, there will be one lit every week, three purples isn't it and a pink one?

B1   At the start of Lent we had Mass for Ash Wednesday and you could receive ashes if you wanted. For the ashes part he himself did each year group individually, as a prayer group, so it wasn't completely crowded and meant more.

Although not articulated by all pupils, some testified that the celebration of the Eucharist made a lasting impression on them. A few, like respondent A4, expressed what effect the mass had on her:

A4   You'd feel yourself more in touch with God. You'd come out of Mass then, all holy for a week or so.

SM   So you think it impacts on your life, even after the Mass?

A4   Yeah, it really does. You definitely would be thinking about what the chaplain said in the Mass, and about what Jesus did during his life, it is always there subconsciously.

Furthermore, the chaplain also facilitated prayer and it was evident from the narratives that pupils benefited from such experiences:

B1   We say a prayer at the beginning of every class and that reminds me of God.

Two other respondents shared similar views on meditation, for example respondent B2 states:

B2   We had mediation in there. First we listened to soft music and relaxed and chilled out. It was cool. It wasn't talking or discussing or learning or nothing, the chaplain just said prayers when we were relaxed and then he'd stop and we'd listen to the music again and think about what we had heard. It was nice, it gave us time to think, you know.

Having a specific place to pray/meditate or go to, was also identified as important. One respondent credited the chaplain with securing the prayer room:

B1   E11 is our prayer room. It was built there with the last extension because we felt there was nowhere that pupils could go for time apart, or just to relax and think about things. I think the chaplain was responsible for getting that up and running.

It was evident from the majority of pupils that a fundamental aspect of the chaplain's role in relation to liturgy was the facilitation of participation. Respondents described how at times they were actively involved in the preparation or delivery of religious ceremonies. They articulated that it was the chaplain's knowledge of them, as individuals, which promoted participation insofar as they were encouraged to use their specific talents. They all suggested that getting involved was an aspect they enjoyed and benefited from:

A4   He knows who'd get involved in the readings, he knows who'd be good at playing music, he knows who'd be good at setting up the altar, and he gets people to do the jobs, even things like making the brochure.

A1   You feel you are not just sitting there like at ordinary Mass. You know more about what's going on and you listen, there is a feeling there you're involved.

A3   It's nice being able to go out in front of the school and show others what you are good at. It's nice to be able to take time out of classes and focus on the bigger picture, on life outside of school.

B3   I did a sketch last year at the Mass. It was the Good Samaritan. We put it on up at the altar, instead of the Gospel. In fact we did a modern adaptation of the Good Samaritan story, it was way more interesting for the pupils. By seeing the sketch, you can understand it better and see how it can happen in today's society. It was great.

Respondents explained how the chaplain's teaching role was advantageous. Pupils from both schools highlighted how class was used to reinforce the theology behind the religious services:

A4   The chaplain in religion class always tells us when things are going on, outside ordinary time, like if it's Lent, he'd be saying how this started and the history about it and why it is important. I wouldn't know that stuff really because it's not talked about.

When talking about religion class, some respondents outlined how they liked discussing the life of Jesus in a concrete way, insofar as it helped them relate to him. It seemed that they felt comfortable in class with the structured discussions and activities that the chaplain orchestrated. Occasionally, such discussions triggered further inquiry in pupils, and they felt free to approach the chaplain to continue the conversation:

B1   He is very good, he explains things very well in religion class, you can ask him any question and he'll explain it completely to you, and you'd be satisfied with his answers. Every few days he'd read a story from the Bible and then he'd give an example of something that is happening at the moment that relates to it in some way and this explains it a bit better and helps us make more sense of it. It's better than just reading it out and having to accept what was on the page or thinking it was just for those times. The chaplain shows us how to understand it for what's going on now.

B4   As well as that you can talk to him out of class about things he mentions in class – I did that one day and he was a world of knowledge.

While several respondents identified the chaplain as the religious person in the school, a few referred specifically to the chaplain's faith. Although no respondent mentioned spirituality per se, the presence of the chaplain as a spiritual or faith being was acknowledged. Some pupils intimated that the chaplain's *own being* provided a living witness to God. In effect they felt God through him. Respondent number B4 vividly captures this:

B4   It's very obvious to see that he has strong faith, and that he is discussing all these points in relation to his own beliefs.

When questioned further he described the impact this can have:

SM   So you think his faith comes through?

B4   Oh yeah, you see it all the time.

SM   How?

SM   Well he says religious things all the time, and at first we thought it was a bit corny, but now we know that he absolutely believes in what he says and you'd believe him better then, because what he says, his beliefs, he backs up with facts, so he gets it through to people. If you listen, you'd totally believe him. And he is a happy person, so it obviously works for him and pupils might feel they might get something like that by believing too.

In recognising the chaplain as a faith presence, another pupil identified that when questions arise in relation to personal faith, the chaplain may be approached:

B1   I know someone who had a problem in another religion class with what the teacher said. She wanted it to be discussed more, and because it was a religious thing she just came straight away to the chaplain and he set her straight on it. I think it was actually some question she had in relation to the Bible, so he told her a story to explain things and she could relate to the story he told then, no problem, and she got a connection that way.

Accompanying Pupils on their Way

While the presence of all staff members in the school is ultimately for the pupils, they themselves feel the chaplain is there for them in a particular way. The notion of the chaplain's constant availability was evident in the accounts of his physical presence:

B3 Really, it's hard not to find him. He's very easy to find

A4 He is always up and down the corridors, constantly like. If you really want to make an appointment with him, you just go up to him there and say it to him. If he is not on the corridors then you just give his office a quick knock and nine out of ten times he will be there. He is always dead easy to find. You see him every day at least once, but often loads more. If you see him you can just approach him, hassle free like.

B3 We would be down in the 'C' corridor and we'd be talking away, during the breaks and he'd walk down and start interacting by saying, 'How's it going?' and he'd start talking then to us, about music and stuff, all that kind of thing, things we're interested in. My friends are in a band and he'd always be talking to them about the band, see he is trying to get them to play Neil Young or Rory Gallagher or something like that and the lads be having none of it [laughs].

His arranging of or engagement in many school activities reinforces the chaplain's physical presence. The range of activities is extensive and included sporting events, activities that promote personal development including drama and debating and working with community or Church organisations, such as the Simon Community and the St Vincent De Paul Society. Respondents described how these contributed to their physical, mental and social well-being. Furthermore engagement in such activities gave the pupils self-confidence, which they both recognised and appreciated:

A3: Well, when I was on the pupils' council he said how best to get things done, he taught us how to approach people properly. If there are meetings, he shows us how to run these properly. I don't know, it's kind of difficult to explain, but I feel more part of the school now.

B1: I don't think I would have had the confidence to do things without his encouragement. He really helped me to do things and get involved. He's great really.

Pupils from both schools recounted how the chaplain went the 'extra mile' for them. His encouragement and involvement was warmly received:

B4: Through these things people get to know him and soon find out they can go to him. He has a load of degrees, I don't think it necessarily says anywhere that he has to do these things, like get involved, but he's not the type to just sit there. He is a nice guy who gets involved and this helps people trust him and see him as approachable.

Emotional Support

For many pupils it was the continuing emotional support, on a day-to-day basis, with everyday life events, that was perceived as the important variable. This emotional support identified by the pupils is best summed up by the term 'acceptance' and was implicit in many of the narratives. Pupils explained how they shared personal thoughts and feelings with the chaplain that they felt unable to share with others. Interestingly, many referred to the fact that they discussed things they could not mention to their parents. The underlying rationale provided was that the chaplain was non-judgemental and therefore particularly easy to be open and frank with:

A4: The pupil actually feels happy that they can talk to someone who is not their parents, their parents wouldn't understand, and wouldn't look on them with as much respect as they did. I can come in and say these are my problems and he doesn't hold it against you. He wouldn't look at you differently as a person, he wouldn't mind, you know, he just listens. This is a good aspect of his job

Respondent A4 further states:

A4: Whatever type of problem you are going through, you know you can at least *talk* to the chaplain about it, and once you talk to him about it, you are going to feel better straight away anyway and cope with it better too – so that will help you set your life back on track then, you know.

B2: He helps you think about things and maybe helps you to be more mature and responsible – and you don't talk to your parents about stuff like that. You can't really, so it's good to have an adult to talk to – it's easier to talk to someone who doesn't know all your family, your past or your background, if you know what I mean. He won't judge and won't be disappointed in you if you tell him something.

Surprisingly, three pupils inferred that accompaniment encompassed more than participating in overt activities. They suggested that the chaplain somehow facilitated them in their everyday life by creating a safe place. His room is always open to them.

A4: His office, well, you wouldn't even call it part of the school. It's a different place from everywhere else, where you can get away from everything in the school here.

B1:   Well this is the nicest room in the school I think. You come in and it seems very quiet compared to everywhere else and you feel safe here. There is no problem; you can talk away in here. His office is open all the time so if there is no one else here you can come in, no problem at all and wait for him if you needed to talk to him.

B2:   You'd come in here [chaplain's office] and talk. I mean it's a small room, but it's nice and bright, and at least it's only him that's here anyway, there is never any other teacher.

What Sets the Chaplain Apart
There was unanimous agreement between respondents that their everyday encounters with the chaplain were fundamentally different to those they had with other staff members in the school. In essence, they explained that they experienced his role differently. Pupils spoke glowingly of relationships built up over time, nurtured and fostered, which contributed to their sense of belonging.

A2:   He's different really, because he is the one person that really listens to you. He seems to have time for you. It's hard to explain, but the other teachers are always rushing, whereas the chaplain isn't like that.

A4:   He treats you as a person, unlike the rest of the teachers. All they are worried about is getting the school-work done and getting their homework done, and I suppose I can understand that, but because he is not exactly a teacher, he is different I suppose, so friendly like.

Through the narratives, it is evident that pupils experienced the chaplain's role in a unique way. They highlighted the various aspects that made the relationship between them special. Frequently discussed were tenets such as genuineness, authenticity and affability.

A4:   He is always positive, he is never ever negative, do you know what I mean? He's always, I don't know, whatever they taught him when he was learning to do this job (laughs)! He is very genuine, you know he means what he says and he's always happy.

B4:   He's what I think a proper teacher should be, there are no levels here, we are all equal to him, he treats us all the same. A lot of teachers would be slower to be like that, but he has such respect for everyone. I suppose that's what makes him the chaplain and the others teachers; and so, pupils chose to come to him before anyone else in the school. They can relax around him.

B2:   If I saw him, I'd always say 'Hi', and he'd be like 'Hi, how are you?' He is funny, outgoing and easy to talk to. I get on with him, because I have had him as a teacher since first year and I have done lots of things in school with him. I really couldn't say a bad thing about him, he's just brilliant really.

The pupils not only spoke of the respect the chaplain had for them, but they recounted the respect they in turn had for him. Acknowledging the fact that he was an authority figure many of the respondents suggested that the chaplain was also a friend:

B4: He does a lot of tours to Prague. He has also brought a group to Barcelona, and once you go on a big trip like that with him, you are friends for life. He is a big organiser. As I said, he could control pupils too, which is a big thing, because lots of teachers if they were that friendly with pupils would have no control, but he is different. You'd respect him and look up to him.

A4: Pupils respect him – as a priest and also as kind of a friend. Yeah, you could say friend, you know it's hard to explain. We know he's a priest, but he's really dead on.

Another factor identified by pupils as being distinctive, in relation to the chaplain's role, is the emphasis he places on creating a sense of community within the school. Pupils recounted that this began in first year and continued right through their school life experience:

B2: In first year he interviews everyone and he just asks, 'Are you enjoying your new school and first year, or are you getting on with people?' I mean, he kind of makes you think how you are interacting with people and he just makes it easier, he talks about it and you know then you are aware of it, and if you were feeling kind of left out he would get you involved in things.

B1: He is actually gone on a retreat today, with the transition years. He organised one for us as well last year and it was very good. Last year when I was in T.Y.1 class groups stayed together, but this year there are going to be mixed groups from the different classes and one of the ideas is that you'd get to know people you didn't know before.

In fact the interviews were full of examples, both spiritual and secular, of how the chaplain facilitated and built this sense of community.

B4: He tries his best to get people together. Like at the retreat he really went out of his way to bring us together as a group and he talked to us. He kind of unites everyone like this and in his discussions and debates and even though we'd be arguing – messing like – there is a sense that everyone is involved.

A3: Well Meitheal is an organisation that's all about helping other people within the school, so it's team based and we basically do good acts around the school and we try and help out with various aspects. We raised funds; we got the benches outside, that kind of stuff. We just try to improve the life of the pupils within the school and the chaplain is our co-ordinator for that.

In addition to creating a sense of community within the school, respondents also spoke of how the chaplain made them think about the local or global community. He brought contemporary issues into their lives, creating an awareness of these thus helping them reflect on broader concerns:

B3: He opened a lot of our eyes to the inequalities between us and the people in the Third World and how the companies in the middle are making all the real money. While the other religion teachers covered these topics too, with the chaplain it's different. He has a knack of making you think about things, things you normally wouldn't think of. He makes religion into things that are really happening in the world.

Ordained Chaplain or Lay Chaplain – Is There a Difference?

In order to fully explicate the role of the chaplain the researcher sought also to ascertain whether there were variations between the roles of ordained or lay chaplains. Insofar as respondents either experienced a lay or an ordained chaplain, the researcher was not in a position to directly ask whether they perceived any differences. However, in terms of the experienced role, no discernible variations emerged. In fact, what was clearly evident was the overwhelming consensus in respect of the purpose, function and performance of the responsibilities of both chaplains. In effect, respondents from the two schools:

- Described similar roles for the chaplains.
- Explained how they achieved these in a comparable way.
- Agreed that the chaplain was a positive force in their lives.

Respondents who had an ordained chaplain recognised and respected that he was also a priest. Moreover, while they felt that this might have enhanced his role, from their perspective it was his ministry as chaplain that was of prime importance and which they held in esteem.

A3: He is his own person I think. I don't think that's just because he is a priest – that's important I know, but he's just dead on as a chaplain.

Those that encountered the lay chaplain daily in school, while aware of his marital status, regarded him as the main religious presence in the school. They equally held him in high regard:

B4: I'd say he went into the job to instil the Catholic faith in us, but I think he basically wants to know that all the pupils are OK and I think maybe he wants them to turn to religion if they are in trouble.

Conclusions

This study contributes to the body of knowledge that already exists on the role of the chaplain. The focus was on hearing the views, opinions and voices of pupils on how they encountered the chaplain's role. What is interesting about the findings is the depth of respect and genuine feeling exhibited by pupils towards their chaplain. Moreover, they clearly delineated the various aspects of the role in surprisingly specific detail. Pupils' views in both schools were consistent and these largely concurred with the role of the chaplain as outlined in various literature.

One of the single and possibly most important themes that pupils identified is that chaplains have a specific, if not unique role, in terms of the quality of relationships established with pupils. Because these relationships are underpinned by nurturance (emotional, social, mental and spiritual) the chaplain effectively achieves his role, that is, the holistic well-being of pupils. While suggested in the literature, it was captured vividly in the in-depth accounts provided by pupils.

However, this author suggests that ultimately the findings indicate that the chaplain may be a pivotal force in the personal development of pupils. Implicit in many of the accounts was that the chaplain appeared to fill a void or a vacuum that is filled by no other. This has only been tentatively suggested in the literature to date. These conclusions are based on the pupils' personal revelations of the interactions they experienced and encountered. For example the interviews were replete with stories of how time and time again pupils felt they could open up and be true and honest with their real issues and concerns. In effect, with either ordinary or extraordinary events, when pupils needed to reach out, it was usually the chaplain they sought.

Furthermore, one surprising new finding emerged as a sub-theme; in addition to respecting and liking the chaplain's personal attributes, the respondent also believed the chaplain was well qualified for the role. They described him as having an advanced level of educational, pastoral and theological training and suggested that, collectively, these enabled him to function effectively. In essence such preparation and training underpinned the respondents confidence and trust in the chaplain's ability.

In congruence with the literature, the chaplain was perceived as a faith presence. This was evident when pupils spoke about the chaplain's own faith, and the impact or impression this made on them. At times, pupils overtly identified this as a real and tangible force. However, it was very much there when pupils spoke about the ordinary everyday interactions they experienced. Possibly this is why pupils spoke about such encounters as different, yet important.

Overall the findings suggest that there is a need to re-evaluate the role of the chaplain in second-level schools, as currently the only established guidelines in Ireland are those agreed on by the Department of Education with the Archdiocese of Dublin in 1976. The study highlights that it may be time to modify these guidelines in light of changing society and the current needs of pupils.

Perhaps, considering these findings, the whole question of whether all second-level pupils should have access to a chaplain merits serious attention.

Notes

1. Norman, J., *Pastoral Care in Second-Level Schools: The Chaplain, A Research Report* (Dublin: Mater Dei Institute of Education, Dublin City University, 2002) p.9.

2. Robson, C., *Real World Research: A Resource for Social Scientists and Research Practitioners* (Oxford: Blackwell, 2002).

3. Colaizzi, P., 'Psychological Research as the Phenomenologist Views It' in Valle, R. and King, M. (eds) *Existential Phenomenological Alternatives for Psychology* (New York: Oxford University Press, 1978) pp. 78-105.

4. See Norman, J., *Pastoral Care in Second-Level Schools: The Chaplain, A Research Report* (Dublin: Mater Dei Institute of Education, Dublin City University, 2002), Bryk, A., Holland P.B., Lee, V.E., *Catholic Schools and the Common Good* (Cambridge: Harvard University Press, 1996), Grace, G. *Catholic Schools: Mission, Markets and Morality* (London: Routledge Falmer, 2002).

The School Chaplain as Professional

Some Theological Reflections

John Murray

Introduction

Some people are rather uncomfortable with the idea of the school chaplain as a 'professional'. The term suggests high pay and status, neither of which, alas, is associated with the reality of being a school chaplain. More seriously, the term often implies a cold, detached expertise that simply does not describe the essentially pastoral and spiritual character of what a school chaplain is and does. A widely accepted definition of the school chaplain sees him or her as 'a faith presence committed to the values of Christ, [who], on behalf of the school and Church communities, accompanies the students on their journey through life'.[1] This may seem a million miles away from being a 'professional'; in fact, it might seem to be the opposite of what that term implies. Instead, chaplaincy is often seen as a spiritual *vocation* in which one is called to serve people in a very personal way. In this paper, I propose to look at how theological reflection can support the description of the school chaplain as a 'professional', in spite of its negative connotations, in a way that harmonises fully with the notion of chaplaincy as a vocation. I will do so by offering insights from the faith tradition that illuminate and support entirely *positive* definitions of a professional.

Positive Definitions of Professionalism

Such definitions can be found in several recent sociological and philosophical treatments of the concept of 'professional'.[2] Several typical characteristics of a professional are indicated. A synthesis of these includes the following: the attainment of specialised knowledge and skills through education or training and the use of this knowledge and skill to serve others; 'a high degree of self-control of behavior through codes of ethics internalised in the process of work socialisation and through voluntary associations organised and operated by the work specialists themselves';[3] 'autonomy of judgement and authority restrained by responsibility in using their knowledge and skill';[4] and personal commitment to a calling or vocation to serve others.[5]

Obviously, this is a more attractive concept of professionalism than the pejorative concept I mentioned first; it is one that we would be happy to apply to the school chaplain. It portrays an understanding of the professional as one with a particular commitment or calling to serve the needs of others by using one's special knowledge and skill, both individually and in the context of a community of service, in a thoroughly responsible way. Is this concept of professional supported by theology? In this paper, I will focus on moral theology in particular, developing an introduction to a Christian ethics of chaplaincy.

The Value of Being Specific

Stepping back for a moment from individual elements of analysis and interpretation, however, it is worth remarking that the issue of what is meant by 'theology' itself raises interesting questions concerning professionalism in chaplaincy. It could be said that chaplains are understood at times to be concerned with merely a rather vague, non-specific 'spirituality'. Of course, a choice not to identify oneself with a particular denominational tradition could be motivated by an admirable intention to avoid alienating or seeming to exclude anyone on the basis of differences of specific faith commitments. Identifying the chaplain with a particular faith tradition might seem to be overly narrow and so risky or even dangerous. It would be even more clearly perceived as a risk or danger in the context of an increasingly pluralistic school population in Ireland. On the other hand, a vague concept of faith could be taken as an indication that the chaplain has a rather nebulous role, and that the identity of the chaplain is unclear. If this happens, then it can be difficult for chaplains and others to grasp the difference between what a chaplain does and what, for example, a counsellor or social worker does. Surely if the chaplain is a 'professional', he or she will be clear about the nature and value of the role and identity and will confidently communicate this to others in various ways, particularly in the way he or she carries out the tasks of ministry, whilst always respecting the freedom and sincere convictions of others.

To be a professional is *to stand for something*. Note the root, 'profess'. Think of the 'Profession of Faith' prayed at Mass each Sunday, for example, or the profession of vows taken by a religious.[6] You cannot stand for something if you are confused, or unclear, or diffident about your commitment. This applies as much to a writer as to a chaplain. If you are unclear about what you stand for, what you profess, this will not help you to be focused and professional in what you do. Nor will it help others to understand what the 'service' is that you, as a professional, offer. It should be clear who and what you are in your professional role. Honesty demands it; so too does a concern to effectively serve others.

A Faith Perspective: Specific *and* Inclusive

The theological reflections in this paper come from within the Catholic tradition, my own tradition. It is a specific, defined faith tradition, but not an exclusive one. It acknowledges that God's truth and grace can be found in the other Christian traditions, and indeed other religious traditions too.[7] Much of what I have to say, therefore, will find an echo, I hope, in the heart of all concerned with ethical professional chaplaincy.

There is little value anyway in professing an interest in a vague 'spirituality' or a commitment to a woolly 'faith'. The concept of 'professional' highlights the values of precision, clarity and honesty in one's commitment and work for others. This is not to deny that the faith dimension of chaplaincy involves an essential element of mystery that defies narrow definition and is always both within and yet beyond our grasp. Mystery is of the essence in God's self-revelation, to which faith is our free response in grace. Nor does an emphasis on clarity and definiteness promote an understanding of professionalism in chaplaincy that ignores the constant necessity for chaplains to exercise sensitivity and demonstrate respect for freedom and conscience in carrying out their role. One carries out one's chaplaincy *for others* and this means that one must never treat others manipulatively or aggressively or impose one's convictions on them, even for the best of motives. I hope in what follows to indicate, albeit briefly, that a firm commitment to a specific faith tradition and the truth it teaches can support and guide a professional approach to chaplaincy that is secure in its identity, clear in its role, but always suitably flexible and competent in its application to varied circumstances and in its aim to serve the needs of each and every person with respect for his or her human dignity.

The Theological Theme of Creation
This mention of the concept of human dignity shared by all leads nicely to the first theological heading or theme I wish to reflect on: Creation.[8] Our focus here is especially on the beginning of the Bible, the first chapters of Genesis. These describe the prologue for the story of salvation. They also provide a foundation for morality and ministry. The human person is created in the image of God (see Gen 1:26-27 and 2:7). This foundational text of the scripture indicates that each human person has an inherent dignity and worth because he or she is created by God in his image. All God's creation is 'good' (see Gen 1:31). The human person is given a task by God. In the first chapter of Genesis this is expressed by the command to 'fill the earth and subdue it' (Gen 1:28);[9] the second chapter sees it in terms of cultivating and caring for the garden (see Gen 2:15). It is worth emphasising the fact that the human person is described in essentially social terms in these chapters (see Gen 1:27 and 2:18).[10] We also notice the situation of freedom: the human person is free to eat the fruit of any tree, but not 'the tree of the knowledge of good and evil' (Gen 1:17).

These texts can speak God's word to the chaplain about his or her own self and the selves of those to be served. Indeed, we can approach *all* aspects of these theological reflections on chaplaincy with this dual focus: what we learn about ourselves as persons and chaplains on the one hand, and what we learn about those we serve in our ministry on the other. Quite often what we learn about the chaplain will be a reflection of what is learned about the one served by the chaplain, and vice versa. In other words, you, as chaplain, must love your neighbour *as yourself*. The biblical message is that all human persons are sacred in our human dignity, in our free will, and in our God-given vocation to care for our world and develop it. How we treat people should reflect the truth. It is because of this truth that there are limits beyond which we should not go, just as the Man in Genesis 2 was warned not to eat of the forbidden tree. The human condition is one that has built-in boundaries, so to speak, and we must not transgress them.[11] To do so results in a loss of happiness and harmony, symbolised in the Adam and Eve story by their shame, their lies, their hiding from God, their blaming of others for their sin and ultimately their expulsion from the paradise that God intended as their home. These opening chapters of the Bible express an inspiring, but sobering view of humanity – we have tremendous value and potential, but we can abuse our freedom terribly and do great damage. Applying this to chaplaincy is not difficult. We are called to treat others with respect always, as equals in dignity, no matter what their status or age or popularity or wealth. We are never to treat another human person merely as a means, but always as an end in himself or herself. In addition, we are called to be stewards of God's creation, appreciating and using the various skills and talents we have been gifted with for others in our chaplaincy.

God's Word in Creation: Natural Law

The creation accounts in Genesis suggest another related ethical theme: Natural Law.[12] This is a vast subject, so I will confine myself to mentioning only a couple of ideas. The classical definition of natural law in the theological tradition is in the *Summa Theologiae*, I-II, question 91, article 4: 'the rational creature's participation in the eternal law'.[13] Briefly, this means that, by means of our natural human reasoning about what it is to be a human being (in community with others), we can come to know what is right or wrong. Morality, in other words, is grounded in our very humanity, a humanity that we share with all other human beings. For school chaplains, this indicates that it is the shared humanity of their pupils and themselves that *creates* the ethical requirements of chaplaincy; these requirements are not imposed by external authority or law. There is a basic human equality between the chaplain and the pupil that forbids any treatment of the latter by the former that is manipulative or condescending or harmful in any way. To abuse the confidence of a pupil, for example, by gossiping about personal details learned in counselling, would be to sin not only against a professional code of ethics, whether written or implied, but against one's own humanity as a chaplain and the humanity of the pupil too. Ultimately, it would be to sin against God, the creator of humanity, and to act contrary to his wise and loving plan for our happiness. (This is what God's 'eternal law' in Aquinas' terminology means). All that a chaplain does should be done for the happiness of the pupils he or she serves, the happiness God has created each of us to enjoy and share. The happiness referred to here is not an emotion, as such, but human fulfilment.[14] To be happy is to be a *good* human person, to be the person you were created to be. The chaplain's role is to help the pupil to pursue this goal of happiness, that is, of goodness.

Participation Matters

The concept of *participation* is central to natural law thinking as championed by Aquinas in the thirteenth century and developed by many others since. It is interesting to note that the concept of participation has been central to the liturgical renewal since Vatican II and is an important aim in education too. Natural law refers to the natural *ethical* participation of the reasonable human person in God's loving and wise providential plan for the happiness of his creation. What might this suggest for chaplaincy? One idea it suggests, in my opinion, is related to *empowerment*. The chaplain is called (by the nature of the humanity of the pupil he or she serves) to treat the pupil as a *participant*, not an object or a passive receiver of attention. The pupil, as human, is a person endowed with reason and will, with potential for thinking and choosing, and this must always be respected. One must not minister to a pupil, therefore, in ways that reinforce dependency or passivity. Rather, one ought to be concerned to empower the pupil to choose to pursue happiness reasonably. We must be concerned with the individuality of the pupil, his or her personal human dignity, though not in a merely individualistic sense. We are persons in community always. Our freedom and responsibility is always a shared freedom and responsibility. Nevertheless, one's own participation is one's own task and privilege. Remember, the school chaplain is dealing with pupils at a very important phase of their development. They are leaving childhood and entering adulthood. The challenge of participating maturely and well in all the various spheres of existence – family, school, parish, nation, church, and so on – is a challenge to be faced by all teenagers as they grow up. It is a difficult challenge, and it often presents formidable obstacles. No pupil should have to face this challenge alone. The school chaplain is one of the people who can accompany the pupil, informed by the faith tradition, on the journey to ever greater participation in all that is good. Every pupil, whether those of a religious tradition or those of none, can have access to the natural truth about how to be happy, or in other words how to be good; nevertheless, the light of God's Revelation that the chaplain shares in through the gift of supernatural faith can enable the chaplain to facilitate each and every pupil, whether in an explicitly religious fashion or in a more implicitly religious fashion, (as appropriate to the particular situation and person), in searching for and finding happiness, in finding the good.[15]

The Theological Theme of Covenant
The Creation theme in the Bible is followed by the Covenant theme:[16]

> God also spoke to Moses and said to him: 'I am the Lord. I appeared to Abraham, Isaac, and Jacob as God Almighty, but by my name 'The Lord' I did not make myself known to them. I also established my covenant with them, to give them the land of Canaan, the land in which they resided as aliens. I have also heard the groaning of the Israelites whom the Egyptians are holding as slaves, and I have remembered my covenant. Say therefore to the Israelites, 'I am the Lord, and I will free you from the burdens of the Egyptians and deliver you from slavery to them. I will redeem you with an outstretched arm and with mighty acts of judgment. I will take you as my people, and I will be your God. You shall know that I am the Lord your God, who has freed you from the burdens of the

Egyptians. I will bring you into the land that I swore to give to Abraham, Isaac, and Jacob; I will give it to you for a possession. I am the Lord'(Exodus 6:2-7).

What might this suggest to the chaplain? Again, with such a rich theme, I must be content to outline only a couple of ideas. Though all people are related to each other and to God by nature, as we have just been exploring, there is a more specific relationship created by God by means of the *Covenant*. At first, God called a particular people and gave them a particular land. (Later, as we shall examine below, he widened this call in the New Covenant.) He promised the Jewish people to be their God and to protect them. He called them to live in a thoroughly ethical way by the Ten Commandments given to Moses on Mount Sinai (as well as by the other laws contained in the Old Testament and oral Jewish tradition). We may be tempted today to look upon the Commandments as mere rules or regulations. By seeing them in their proper context, as part of the Covenant, we can gain a more accurate and more positive understanding. They 'spelled out for the people the nature and content of their loving response to God's all-merciful and faithful love *(hesed)*, which characterised his covenant with them.'[17] Also, when we remember that they were given in the context of God's liberating act, which saved his people from slavery in Egypt, we can link the following of specific commandments to the privilege and challenge of being free. The Decalogue 'warned the recently liberated people of forms of slavery infinitely more subtle and pernicious than those experienced in Egypt.'[18] God's rules were given, in other words, to help his people to avoid becoming slaves to sin and to help them to be a truly free people, a community of faith and peace.[19]

Covenant Informs a New Appreciation of Discipline

This suggests a particular way of understanding discipline and ethics in school chaplaincy.[20] The requirements of a relationship need to be specified in definite guidelines or rules so that one can be freely faithful to the relationship. Good rules are not an imposition on one's creativity or one's individuality, but a protection of them. This applies to both the code of ethics guiding the ministry of the chaplain as professional and the code of discipline of any school. It offers to the chaplain a way of appreciating the ethical requirements of his or her own ministry as the way a relationship necessarily shapes one's freedom, rather than as a mere formality or as authority arbitrarily telling one what to do. It also offers the chaplain a way of integrating his own faith into an appreciation of the exigencies of school discipline. This can be very important for chaplains. Even if they are not expected to be an official part of the discipline structure of a school, they will sometimes have to deal with issues arising out of problems in the area of school discipline, and will need to do so in a way that is faithful to the school and to the pupil. The positive understanding of commandment outlined above can help here.

Covenant Is Not Mere Contract

The notion of *covenant*, including particularly its focus on relationship as the central dynamic of one's identity, offers a useful reminder that ministry is more than mere *contract*.[21] Although it includes specific duties that may be listed in a contract or a code, professional ministry is better understood as a personal task or set of tasks carried out in the service of others to whom one is connected by *a relationship of trust*. God's election of his people is a sign of his trust in them; it calls for a response of fidelity. Covenant as *agreement* embodies trust and invites fidelity. Much of the Old Testament is taken up with God calling his people back to the covenant (which they frequently broke), especially through the prophets. In Hosea, for example, the covenant relationship between God and his people is seen as a marriage, which the people have betrayed by their infidelity, and to which God implores and warns them to return (see Hosea 3:1-5, 9:1). The role of chaplain in a school is one that is characterised by trust; therefore, it calls for fidelity. A chaplain ought never to take advantage of the vulnerability of those he or she ministers to. God's care for his people in the Covenant and his ethical requirements of this relationship included a particular focus on the needs of the most needy and vulnerable – the widow, the orphan, and the stranger (see Exodus 22:21-22; Deut. 14:27-29). God calls his people to act like he does and to care for the needy. A strong concern with respecting the trust placed in us by the vulnerable and our attempts to meet their needs are not just matters of legality; they are a matters of faithfulness to one's identity as chaplain, as one called to a covenant relationship with one's pupils, a covenant relationship that requires high ethical standards, professional standards.

Covenant and Professionalism

The link between covenant and professionalism has been a major focus of the work of William F. May,[22] (though not mainly from an explicitly theological perspective). The following quote from a recent work of his illustrates some of what this link implies:

> The professional's covenant, in my judgment, opens out in three directions that help distinguish professionals from careerists: the professional professes something (a body of knowledge and experience); on behalf of someone (or some institution); and in the setting of colleagues. This summary definition highlights three distinguishing marks: *intellectual* (what one professes), *moral* (on behalf of whom one professes), and *organizational* (with whom one professes). These distinguishing marks call for three correlative virtues – practical wisdom, fidelity, and public spiritedness. Professionals need these virtues to be fully themselves...[23]

This description echoes some of the characteristics of a professional noted at the beginning of this paper, but takes them further. It is interesting that May sees the *moral mark* of the professional in terms of faithfulness to a *personal* relationship, rather than fidelity to an impersonal code or law or ethics. This is one of the implications of viewing one's role as a minister through the lens of the covenant theme. We are reminded that morality, whether *private* or *professional*, is a matter of our response to a personal link between God and ourselves (and our pupils), shaping the requirements of our particular duties and responsibilities. It is also interesting that May sees virtue as integral to the idea of professional, virtue being understood as those personal abilities or dispositions that make it possible to be fully what one is called to be in and for the covenant relationship.[24]

The Theological Theme of New Covenant

This central idea of relationship, of right relationship to be more precise, is developed in the New Testament where the covenant theme becomes the New Covenant theme. Christian faith leads us to believe that 'the covenant between God and the Chosen People was but the preparation for the new and definitive covenant to be made between God and humankind in and through the redemptive work of his only begotten Son, Jesus Christ.'[25] Again, I must ask the reader's understanding and patience as I can focus here on only one or two main points of this rich theological theme.[26]

With reference to the three *marks* of the professional described above, we could say that the distinctive Revelation of God's love in the Gospel provides the theological truth of God's love to be professed by the chaplain (the intellectual mark), the ethical values and wisdom of Christ to guide the chaplain's work (the moral mark), and the Church community that believes and celebrates and lives the Gospel (the organisational mark). Or, referring further back to the characteristics of a professional mentioned at the beginning of this chaprter, we could say that the Gospel Revelation of God's love is at the heart of the specialised knowledge the school chaplain professes to have learned (however necessarily limited that knowledge of God's mystery will be). In addition, the Gospel shapes the ethical code of chaplaincy as a life lived *in Christ* for others (who are also *in Christ*). Finally, the Gospel as it is historically mediated provides the chaplain with a communal matrix, the Church, calling the chaplain to a vocation to share in its mission to complete Christ's work on earth, thus shaping the identity of the chaplain as a minister-among-ministers.

Two Commandments of Love Compared

To unpack all that would require a book in itself. Let's simplify matters by focusing on two well-known Gospel *love-commandments*. The first is Jesus' summary of the Decalogue, at least insofar as it refers to our treatment of each other: '*Love your neighbour as yourself*' (Mt 22:39). The second is his new commandment given to his disciples at the Last Supper to 'love one another just as I have loved you' (John 15:12).

The first can be seen as an expression of the Creation theme, of the natural law. We are called, personally and professionally, to treat our neighbour as we would like to be treated. This is expresssed in the Golden Rule taught by Christ (Mt 7:12), which is found in other religious traditions too, as it expresses a moral principle of the natural law accessible to all. Note the phrase in the commandment, 'as yourself'. This implies a focus on the truth that we are all equally human, created in God's image as persons of great innate dignity, with the universal gifts of conscience and free will. This focus on equality should highlight for the chaplain the necessity of treating all pupils with respect and sensitivity. Though firmly informed by the Christian Gospel, this love-commandment is one that can shape a chaplaincy that reaches out to all pupils, no matter what their faith, to help them discover the goodness of their humanity and their dignity.

We are all called in some way to be part of God's Chosen People, though this call was first limited to the Jews before Christ's time. This first *love-commandment* summarises the Old Testament Decalogue, the heart of the Covenant for which we have been created and to which we are called. Our creation and call find their fulfilment in Christ and the New Covenant.

As part of this New Covenant, Christ gives us a new commandment: 'I give you a new commandment, that you love one another. Just as I have loved you, you also should love one another. By this everyone will know that you are my disciples, if you have love for one another' (John 13:34-35). The call to love is common to the two love-commandments: love grounds the ethical requirements of our personal and professional lives. What is *new* in the second commandment examined here, however, is the phrase 'as I have loved you'. What does this mean? What does it mean for the school chaplain?

The New Commandment: How Is It *New*?

The phrase 'as I have loved you' specifies morality as *Christian* by focusing attention on the source of morality – the love of God. This was revealed primarily in Christ's life, death and resurrection.[27] John 3:16 puts it this way: 'For God so loved the world that he gave his only Son, so that everyone who believes in him may not perish but may have eternal life.' The whole Bible, in fact, can be seen as the revelation of God's great love for us, a love that reached its greatest epiphany in Christ's salvific death. This revelation of divine love is shared with the whole world and carried forward through history by the Church's tradition: its teachings, liturgy, martyrs and saints, and everything that makes up the living faith of the Pilgrim People of God. The essential point for ethics, including professional ethics, is that God's love provides the basis for our response of love. This is summed up in another rich Bible verse: 'We love because he first loved us' (1 John 4:9). What the chaplain is and what the chaplain does (and how he or she carries out this role in character) are thoroughly theological whilst being thoroughly professional: both aspects of chaplaincy are founded on the truth of God's love calling us to respond with love.

The chaplain's Christian faith enables his or her acceptance of the Good News of this divine love and so shapes the *content* of the service the chaplain offers the pupils and grounds the ethics that guides the *process*. Another way of putting this is to say that as chaplain, you receive your identity from your standing for Christ and all that Christ himself stands for. The chaplain professes Christ and his values. This is the faith dimension that informs all that the school chaplain symbolises and does in a school. It might be better, therefore, to revise the definition mentioned at the beginning of this paper[28] to state that the chaplain is 'a faith presence committed to Christ and his values' instead of 'a faith presence committed to the values of Christ'. The former clarifies the commitment as a *personal* relationship. Christianity is not a philosophy, but a relationship. We are called to live *in Christ*. And relationships of love are at the heart of pastoral care and, indeed, all education in schools.[29]

Growing in the Knowledge of Christ

These theological reflections are far from comprehensive[30] and certainly too short to do justice to the mystery to the love of God, but I hope that they have introduced you to some areas for further study and prayer (or, at least, reminded you of what you already knew). On-going development of one's knowledge is a central feature of professionalism.[31] For chaplains this means a daily effort to grow in the knowledge of Christ, who is the norm for our ministry and the hope that we profess. With this in mind, we can understand that being professional as a chaplain implies a dedication to spirituality and all the elements of Christian living that nourish and express one's vocation as a follower of Christ.

Postscript: The Busy Parish Curate Chaplain

Some school chaplains are not full-time, but are priests with many duties in their parishes. What I have written above applies to them too, even though they may not think of themselves as professional school chaplains, and may not, unfortunately, be seen by others as such either. Their ministry in school is shaped by the same theology outlined here. It is incumbent on such priests to use their limited time well, however, and this would suggest the importance of meeting with the pastoral care team in one's school at the start of the school year (or perhaps every term if possible) to focus on the precise needs of the school and how best to use the time available. Even limited time can be very valuable and I know, having taught in secondary school for many years myself, that the work of chaplain priests (especially the busy ones) is much appreciated by catechists and other staff. The story of the Disciples on the Road to Emmaus (Luke 24:13-35) suggests a few final theological reflections appropriate for such chaplains.

I hope it will not be too fanciful to guess that it was helpful to the disciples on the road that the Risen Jesus joined them at first as a stranger. This allowed them to share honestly their doubts, fears and disappointments. Their religious experience seemed to them to be a total letdown; this mirrors the situation of many young people today. The curate chaplain may appear as a kind of stranger to these pupils, but maybe this is not always a bad thing, though it may appear so to many curate chaplains. The fact that the curate chaplain is not very well known to them, and, in addition, is not identified with the school institution and its procedures, may help to put pupils at their ease in talking with the chaplain about their honest concerns. (This may well be of prime importance in the school's organisation of the Sacrament of Penance, for example, where pupils often express greater comfort in confessing to a 'stranger' than to a priest they know.)

The Risen Christ was able to explain the scriptures to the disciples, enlightening their minds and helping them to make sense of the puzzling events of the previous few days. The priest's study of theology, and subsequent knowledge of its mysteries, is a gift and a responsibility. Pupils can gain from this knowledge and should be encouraged to ask questions and expect answers.

Finally, the Risen Lord was revealed to the disciples in the breaking of bread. So, too, the curate enables the Mass to be celebrated in school and makes communion with Christ possible. Even the very presence of a curate in the school is a reminder to staff and pupils and parents of the wider context within which schooling occurs and is an invaluable symbol of the love of God that puts all our work, including exam work and all that goes with it, into proper perspective.

Notes

1. Monahan, L., Renehan, C., *The School Chaplain: A Faith Presence in the School* (Dublin: Columba Press, 1998), p. 13.

2. See Ashley, B., O'Rourke, K., *Health Care Ethics: A Theological Analysis*, 4th edition (Washington, D.C.: Georgetown University Press, 1997), pp. 69-73 and Gula, R., *Ethics in Pastoral Ministry* (New York/ Mahwah, N.J.: Paulist Press, 1996), pp. 1-14 and the literature cited therein. The former volume is applicable to school chaplaincy although it specifically focuses on professionalism in health care; the latter deals with ministry in a general sense, including chaplaincy.

3. *Health Care Ethics*, p. 72, citing B. Barber.

4. *Health Care Ethics*, p. 72, citing W. Moore and G. Rosenblum.

5. See *Health Care Ethics*, p. 72. Gula is particularly good on the relationship between vocation and profession; see his *Ethics in Pastoral Ministry*, pp. 10-14. There is an interesting section on whether teachers are professionals in J. Norman, *Ethos and Education In Ireland*, Irish Studies, Vol. 7 (New York: Peter Lang, 2003), pp. 67-73, much of which is easily applicable to school chaplains.

6. See Gula, *Ethics in Pastoral Ministry*, p. 12.

7. See Vatican Council II, 'Lumen Gentium', nos. 13, 15-16. This document, also known by its English title 'The Dogmatic Constitution on the Church', was first promulgated in 1964. It is available on the official Vatican web site at http://www.vatican.va/archive/hist_councils/ii_vatican_council/documents/vat-ii_const_19641121_lumen-gentium_en.html [accessed 5th Dec 2003].

8. I will draw on Gula's first chapter in my choice of three major theological themes: creation, covenant and discipleship. I have changed his ordering of the themes, however, to emphasise the creation theme and to invite a more narrative approach to synthesising these themes. Gula emphasises the covenant theme more than the creation theme, giving it more space and treating it first. I believe the creation theme allows for a more inclusive approach to pupils, particularly those who might seem to have little or no faith.

9. All biblical quotations are from the The New Revised Standard Version (NRSV).

10. The sacred and social nature of the human person in Genesis is dealt with in *Ethics in Pastoral Ministry*, pp. 21-25.

11. Gula deals in detail with the practicalities of respecting boundaries in one's ministry in chapters 4, 5 and 6 of *Ethics in Pastoral Ministry*.

12. This theme is only briefly mentioned in Gula's *Ethics in Pastoral Ministry* (on page 23). His treatment of the theme in an earlier, well-known introduction to moral theology, *Reason Informed By Faith* (Mahweh, NJ: Paulist, 1989) is interesting but, in my opinion, seriously weakened by an unnecessary bifurcation between natural law as biology and natural law as reason. A more accurate, though intellectually rather demanding, treatment of the topic is found in William E. May, *An Introduction to Moral Theology*, second edition (Huntington, IN: Our Sunday Visitor, 2003), pp. 71-140.

13. The most accessible edition of the *Summa* is found online. Though it is the English Fathers' translation from the 1920s, and difficult in places, for reasons of both the old-fashioned translation and sheer intellectual challenge, it is worth at least a look! It is available at http://www.newadvent.org/summa/ [accessed 2nd Dec 03].

14. This means, for example, that the chaplain should not expect pupils to always feel happy; nor should a chaplain evaluate his or her ministry by how good the pupils feel. It can be appropriate for a person to mourn in times of bereavement and a chaplain will rightly aim to sympathise in such a situation rather than feel obliged to constantly 'cheer up' the pupil. A feeling of guilt, to take one more example, is appropriate and can be helpful after sin, if it leads one to repent and accept God's forgiveness.

15. Rice, C., *50 Questions on the Natural Law: What it is and Why we need it*, revised edition (San Francisco: Ignatius, 1999), pp. 175ff., details how the light of faith can and must illuminate our natural knowledge of morality.

16. Gula, *Ethics in Pastoral Ministry*, pp. 14-21, deals in some detail with the ethical implications of this theme. Indeed, it is a central theme in the whole book. May, *An Introduction to Moral Theology*, pp. 32-37, provides a concise discussion of the place of 'covenant' in moral thinking. A recent treatment of covenant in the OT can be found in Hegarty, B., *The Bible: Literature and Sacred Text* (Dublin: Veritas, 2003), pp. 41-53. This is one of the 'Into the Classroom' series for teachers of the new Leaving Cert. RE syllabus.

17. Bohr, D., *Catholic Moral Tradition*, revised edition (Huntington, Indiana: Our Sunday Visitor, 1998), p. 46.

18. *Catholic Moral Tradition*, p. 46.

19. This linkage of law and freedom is developed in depth in Pope John Paul II, *Veritatis Splendor*, nos 35-53.

20. See also on this *Ethos and Education in Ireland*, pp. 91-94.

21. See *Ethics in Pastoral Ministry*, pp. 14-16, 21.

22. Not to be confused with William E. May, to whom I refer elsewhere in this work.

23. May, W.F., *Beleaguered Rulers: The Public Obligations of the Professional* (Louisville/London/Leiden: Westminster John Knox Press, 2001), p. 7.

24. The area of virtue and its importance for ministry is treated in the second chapter of *Ethics in Pastoral Ministry*.

25. *An Introduction to Moral Theology*, p. 35.

26. Gula develops this theme under the heading of 'discipleship' (see *Ethics in Pastoral Ministry*, pp. 25-30). I intend to take a different, though complimentary, approach following William E.

May's work on the distinctiveness of Christian ethics, a dominant issue in modern Christian ethical debate (see *An Introduction to Moral Theology*, chapter 6).

27. My comparison of the two love-commandments is indebted to Germain Grisez's work; see *The Way of the Lord Jesus, volume two: Living a Christian Life* (Quincy, Illinois: Franciscan Press, 1993), pp. 306-317.

28. See note 1 above. I should mention that my point here about personal commitment to Christ is implied in how the authors understand their own definition, but I think my revision is more explicit. See *The Chaplain: A Faith Presence*, p. 14: 'the chaplain recognises that the most effective way to follow Christ is in the effort to *live* the values of Christ' (original emphasis).

29. See *Ethos and Education in Ireland*, p. 102: 'From the *Declaration on Christian Education* (1965) up to the latest document on education, *The Catholic School on the Threshold of the Third Millennium* (1998), the Catholic Church has recognised that young people are above all educated through relationships.'

30. Due to limited space, I have not mentioned, for example, one of the most important areas in need of accurate theological understanding by chaplains and teachers: sin and reconciliation. Nor have I developed the area of ecclesiology, which is an important aspect of vocation and professionalism as the Church in its different levels forms the religious community context for school chaplaincy. These topics are addressed in various ways in the literature I have mentioned, particularly that of Gula, and deserve attention and further study.

31. See *Ethics in Pastoral Ministry*, pp. 51-56.

Collective Worship in Schools

Community Building

Jennie Clifford

Introduction

Worship derives its *raison d'être* from the 'awareness that there is something other, something greater than the course of everyday events.'[1] As has been highlighted by Gareth Byrne and Marian de Souza elsewhere in this book, we are spiritual beings who pursue 'the quest for meaning in life, for truth and ultimate values.'[2] Through worship we give expression to 'the inner world, the indefinable, the ineffable, the intangible, the mystical.'[3] Interest in spirituality is widespread in modern society, but it is to a large extent privatised and is thus robbed of its potential to build community. When this happens, 'the fabric of relationships becomes very thin, and as a result there are fewer and fewer constraints on the excesses of individualism.'[4] According to Mark Searle, modern Western society has forgotten some of the most basic truths about society. 'One such truth is that the community is prior to the individual, that each individual is a social product, that the idea of the autonomous self is a delusion.'[5] Community is essential to collective worship. It is necessary that those taking part in collective worship already experience themselves as a community. Collective worship, in turn, strengthens the bonds of the worshipping community. It is only in so far as the school is a community that authentic collective worship can take place there and that worship contributes to the building up of that community.

Competition versus Community in Second-Level Schools

In the educational system, second-level schools are situated between the feeder-primary schools from which their pupils are drawn and the third-level colleges and workplaces to which those pupils will go. Parents' choice of school is often determined by the school's record in securing places in third-level education and in the workplace. Since such places are limited, competition is an unavoidable aspect of life in second-level schools. But education involves much more than academic achievement. The formation of character and personality is essential to the educational process. Moreover, the Education Act (1998) obliges schools to offer pupils a holistic education, which promotes 'the moral, spiritual and personal development of pupils.'[6] The whole school curriculum shares the responsibility for this objective. 'The curriculum which is supposed to be shot through with concern for spiritual development is the same curriculum which is supposed to achieve the required standards through the application of the right methods.'[7] Since every teacher is a spiritual being no teaching method may be regarded as neutral. According to David Smith, there is a 'relationship between spirituality and the ways in which we go about trying to secure learning outcomes.'[8]

A school is not a gathering of individuals each pursuing his/her own goals but, ideally, a community of people who communicate with each other, identify with each other, work together, help, support and encourage each other. The challenge to the school is to create an environment in which personal achievement and community are held in a creative tension. Strong leadership; excellence in teaching; solidarity among the staff and pupils; commitment on the part of staff and pupils to the values enshrined in the school's mission statement; high standards of discipline and achievement in all fields of endeavour; support for school teams in sporting, debating and other events; pride in the motto, uniform and flag; the use of school chants and songs contribute to this end. Most important is the teachers' ability to 'weave a complex web of connections among themselves, their subjects, and their pupils.'[9] Through collective worship the school expresses and consolidates its awareness of itself as a community. 'There can be no group cohesion without ritual, as there can be no ritual without a group to maintain it.'[10]

Worship is Directed to God

The building of community may be an outcome of collective worship but it is not its primary aim. Worship is primarily concerned with communication with God. Through worship we acknowledge ourselves as created by God and dependent on God. In worship we express praise and thanks; we look for forgiveness and make intercession. While this chapter is written from a Catholic perspective it recognises that pupils of other Christian denominations and of other religions and none attend second-level schools in Ireland at the present time. It is necessary that the school takes account of this in its arrangements for worship. Otherwise, worship itself may become a divisive element in the school community.

An Integrated Approach to Religion and Worship

The fact that, in many schools, Religious Education is now an examination subject in the Junior and Leaving Certificates creates an urgency to ensure that collective worship is maintained as an element of moral and spiritual formation in its own right. A well-organised, progressive programme of worship built into the curriculum will help to allay the reservations being expressed against the new examination system. 'Clifford Geertz [...] sees ritual as central to religion because it is there that religionists are exposed most directly to their symbol system.'[11] Worship enables us to 'know our God in a way that lessons and classroom work can never match.'[12] On the other hand, worship requires religious education. For example, as a result of many influences, pupils often have 'vague notions of God which, even before the question of worship arises, agree little or not at all with the Christian faith.'[13] Through religious education pupils are made aware that Christians worship a personal Trinitarian God. They are taught the theological meaning of Mass and the Sacraments and given an understanding of the Bible. These are basic foundations for meaningful worship. An integrated approach to the teaching of the Religious Education syllabus and a programme of worship will ensure that they complement each other in promoting the religious formation of the pupils.

Forms of Worship

Worship in second-level schools includes the liturgy of the Church, in particular, Mass, the Sacrament of Reconciliation, and the Prayer of the Church. It also includes prayer services called para-liturgies, indicating that they are not isolated acts of worship, but the building blocks of the liturgy which 'is the summit toward which the activity of the Church is directed; it is also the fount from which all her power flows.'[14] It is important that pupils experience worship as a unified whole.

Liturgy is the work of the people. It is 'something done, not merely something said; and even its verbal elements are ... ways of doing things, not merely communication of information. To participate in ritual then is to *do* something.'[15] Liturgies and para-liturgies are enacted through patterns of ritual that are learned through repetition. Taking part in the ritual of liturgy bonds the pupils to each other:

> The participants in ritual separate themselves from the ordinary in some way. ... There is a sense of comradeship and communion which normal social structures often inhibit, a loss of self and ego-boundaries, a powerful sense of at-oneness, an awakening of the transcendent dimension through myth and symbol.[16]

The school year provides many opportunities for collective worship. Daily prayers are the foundation for liturgies and para-liturgies. The beginning and end of the school year, graduations, the seasons of the liturgical year, feasts of Our Lady, St Brigid, St Patrick, the school patron, and remembrance of the dead are occasions to be celebrated through worship. The form of worship must suit the occasion. The Mass as the 'the high point of the work that in Christ his Son we offer to the Father'[17] is appropriate on some occasions. However, it is important for teachers and chaplains to remember that by celebrating Mass on occasions for which it is not suitable 'we actually empty it of meaning and diminish its value. ... It becomes commonplace, boring and tedious.'[18] On other occasions, para-liturgies, designed by the combination of readings from Scripture and other sources, hymns, prayers, reflections, gestures, movements and symbols, may be used.

Adolescence is a time of rapid transformations. The form of worship offered must always take into consideration the stage of development of the pupils. The same pupils who enthusiastically embrace worship in first year are the same pupils who may not be willing to participate in third year, but who may seek to do so at a later stage. In the process of establishing his/her own identity, the adolescent may reject the norms and values of the community:

> It is as though a strength has been established which can now 'push away from the dock' of that which has been sure moorage to move out into the deep waters of exploring for oneself what is true and trustworthy.[19]

A community that is not too rigidly defined will allow the young person the space in which to grow during this period. The programme of worship must also be sufficiently flexible to accommodate the changes taking place in the lives of the pupils.

Whole Staff Approach to Collective Worship

The chaplain, with the religion teachers, class tutors and year heads, is usually responsible for the organisation of collective worship in second-level schools. Other teachers, because of their particular expertise in music, art, drama and dance will be invited to assist. Teachers may request a celebration of an aspect of their subject area. For example, a science teacher may request a celebration of the cosmos. The co-operation and support of all teachers is necessary if worship is to be accepted as an integral element of school life.

> The development of faith is a communal process dependent not only upon the capacities and yearnings of the self, but also upon teachers, mentors, colleagues and neighbours who together form the social context that nourishes and enhances or diminishes and blocks the cultivation of the life of faith.[20]

In terms of building community in a school, it is important that when a teacher accompanies pupils to worship it is preferable that he/she participates in the worship rather than appear as an outsider or as the person responsible for discipline, otherwise pupils' experience of community may be undermined.

Furthermore, the increase in the number of subjects in the curriculum has resulted in a reduction in the time allocated to each subject. Teachers are under pressure to cover the syllabus. Agreement is needed at staff level regarding the frequency and times of worship so that teachers may plan accordingly.

Full, Active, Conscious Participation

Children receive First Holy Communion, make their first Confession and receive the sacrament of Confirmation in primary school. They also take part in the prayer services of the 'Alive-O programme'. The aim in second-level school is to bring the pupils to a deeper level of celebration. Since Vatican II, the Church has emphasised the importance of full, active, conscious participation in the liturgy:

> The Church, therefore, earnestly desires that Christ's faithful, when present at this mystery of faith, should not be there as strangers or silent

spectators. On the contrary, through a good understanding of the rites and prayers they should take part in the sacred action, conscious of what they are doing, with devotion and full collaboration. They should be instructed in God's word, and nourished at the table of the Lord's Body.[21]

It is not sufficient to give pupils an opportunity to participate in worship, they should also be involved in the process of preparation and reflection. 'The process of celebration is at its formative best when it happens in three distinct and separate stages: preparation, celebration and reflection.'[22]

Preparation
Worship requires careful preparation. The preparation of para-liturgies includes the planning of the ritual. In the case of the Eucharistic liturgy the ritual is a given, therefore no such planning is required. However, there are decisions to be made in relation to options within the rites. Ideally everyone taking part in worship should be involved in its preparation. This is possible when the worship involves a single class. When a year group or the whole school worships an *ad hoc* committee, consisting of representatives of each class, should be set up. The task of this committee is to ensure that each person's ideas are valued and respected even if they are not incorporated in the final ritual.

> At this point we must ask to what extent young persons have any opportunity of building up within the liturgy a fruitful relationship with themselves, to what extent their thoughts and sensitivities are taken seriously, and to what extent the emphases specific to their age ever get affirmed and they themselves can bring the totality of themselves into the celebration.[23]

The selection of those who will perform the various ministries is a sensitive issue. Those who have special functions in the worship should have the required abilities. 'Pupils should not be called to ministry simply because it's their turn or because they need or deserve public recognition.'[24] Readers, cantors, musicians, or those who take part in processions or dance should be trained to do so. The readers of the sacred scriptures carry the privilege and responsibility of proclaiming God's message to the assembly. They should endeavour to 'capture the inner form of the written words, making it their own and re-embodying it in the outer words they speak.'[25] Through religious education classes they are taught to understand the world and language of the Bible and to see the passage in its biblical context.

> But if we fail, in catechesis and in liturgy, to lead young people into the biblical message, then the already existing far-reaching alienation of young people from the Bible must inevitably bring with it alienation from one of the most important parts of the liturgy and so from the liturgy altogether.[26]

Music is essential for every occasion of worship. It should be possible for all present to contribute to the music either by singing or by playing an instrument.

> Human society has long recognised the power of music to reach to the depth of our being and to bond people together. The music of our liturgy carries the truths of our faith to the core of our being. Joining our voices in liturgical song can, like the rousing chorus of a national anthem or even a drinking song, create instant camaraderie and unity.[27]

It is possible to join in the singing only if one knows the hymns/songs. The musical repertoire of the pupils in the school should be clearly established. This may be limited initially, but it can be built up gradually. 'Planning the repertoire ensures that music will be used often enough for comfort, while allowing for the growth that will lend variety when necessary.'[28] The use of folders for the school's musical repertoire makes it possible to add or withdraw material as necessary. Pupils should be encouraged to learn the words so that folders or handouts do not become a distraction at the time of worship. Instrumental music enhances the celebration and pupils who have the ability to play should be encouraged to do so. The use of percussion instruments may be considered as they afford many pupils an opportunity to play and create a heightened awareness within the group.

Processions and other movements and gestures must also be rehearsed. Movements and gestures develop a reverent attitude in prayer and are a means of expressing it outwardly. Occasionally, it will be appropriate on include sacred dance as a form of prayer. 'One may dance as a prayer only if one prays as a dancer!'[29] Rehearsing the dance unifies the dancers. In the worship the whole assembly should be drawn into this unity. The dance should never become a performance for spectators.

The space in which worship takes place is critical to its success in terms of communication with God and the building of community. Some schools have a dedicated prayer room and/or religion room, but in other schools worship takes place in a classroom, library or hall. The size of the space should match the size of the worshipping group. The movement required for meaningful ritual is not be possible if the space is too small, while too large a space is not conducive to community.

> A space that does not match the size of the group militates against the experience of community in worship that matters to young people, because mutual physical proximity, which is not unimportant, cannot be achieved. In addition, a smaller space is more likely to give a feeling of security, manageability, and intimacy.[30]

A space may be converted for worship by removing surplus furniture or draping it with material, preferably, the colour for the liturgical season. Notice boards and blackboards may likewise be concealed. Stained glass plaques attached to the windows and doors and a carpet or cloth on the centre of the floor create the sacred space. Attention must also be given to the light. Lighting that is too bright is not conducive to prayer, nor to the intimate experience of community. The arrangement of the seating is critical to the pupils' perception of themselves as participants or as onlookers. A circular or semi-circular arrangement is recommended. A checklist will ensure that the sacred vessels and symbols required for the worship are available.

Catechesis, by which the elements of ritual are opened up to the understanding of the pupils, should take place before the worship is celebrated. Explanations given throughout the celebration of worship prevents the words, the symbols and the actions from conveying their meaning to the worshippers. The 'actions, words and symbols have an obvious integrity and authenticity about them and an ability to speak to the people assembled.'[31]

While it is necessary to prepare every aspect of worship in order that the celebration itself may occur in a relaxed atmosphere it should not be thought that worship is a difficult and complicated exercise. Michael Carotta's story 'Fishing the River' is relevant to those who prepare worship. In the story, the difficulty experienced by the three very intent anglers who used the correct rods, line and lures in catching fish is contrasted with the ease with which the grandfather and his ten-year-old granddaughter caught the fish with a toy-like fishing rod. Their secret was that they used the eggs of the fish as bait.[32] In worship simplicity is the keynote and the most important resource is the pupils themselves. Through involvement in the preparation and celebration of worship the pupils are enabled to claim the worship as their own.

Celebration

The high point of the process of worship is the celebration itself. In the celebration we praise and thank God. We proclaim the great things that God has done for our salvation in joy and freedom. A genuine welcome at the door acknowledges that each person is a cherished member of the worshipping community. Moreover, all participants should show an attitude of welcome for each other. Pupils will be aware that the assembly is itself symbolic. It is the Body of Christ/the People of God/the Community of Disciples. Pupils coming to worship from class need a few minutes to warm up. This may be done by singing some of the hymns/songs of the worship or by a brief discussion of what is to take place.

As the worship proceeds each person should be fully involved in listening, responding, praying, singing/playing, and in taking part in movement and gestures. Worship is a learning experience in its own right. When the words are spoken, the actions performed, and symbolic objects used with care and reverence they touch people at a deep level.

> Young people are very interested in symbols, and their layers of meaning. Speaking to several layers of meaning for the symbols helps to draw the youth deeper into the religious experience. Fire, water, incense, candles, colour, nails, and barbed wire: All these help young people to delve deeper into their faith.[33]

Taking part in the worship does not guarantee that a person is in communion with God or with the assembly. It is always a matter of the heart. It is necessary have an open attitude and to allow oneself to be transformed by the ritual. In collective worship, a person's lack of faith or inability to pray need not be an obstacle. The praise, the gratitude, the forgiveness, the intercession of the assembly may be claimed by all present. Ultimately, the worship of the Son to the Father becomes ours in the liturgy. 'Ritual bonds the individual to the community, preventing aimless wandering; it helps us to know who we are in relation to others and the world. Membership of the ritual community preserves from the ultimate, radical identity crisis.'[34]

It must be emphasised that everyone present at worship is a celebrant, yet worship requires president: a person who through the warmth of his/her personality has the ability to draw the assembly into the celebration. The president at Eucharist is necessarily a priest. If he not a member of the school staff, he should be invited to be involved in the preparation. Presiding at worship is a strong witness to the faith. Teachers, other than the priest chaplain, may preside at non-Eucharistic celebrations. Pupils, who have the ability, should also be given the opportunity to fulfil this role.

A good celebration has an energy, a flow and a momentum of its own. This can only happen if the pupils are comfortable within the live celebration, if they know the direction it will take, and are confident in what they are doing.

Evaluation and Reflection

In an educational environment the ideal is to learn from experience so that change may take place constructively. Worship lends itself to the pedagogical method generally known as action – reflection. An evaluation should be done, if possible, immediately after the worship. Bernadette Gasslein offers a simple form of evaluation based on two questions: 'What enabled me to praise God?' and 'What hindered my praise?'[35] These questions focus on the purpose of worship, which is to praise God. We do not worship in order to feel good, although this may be an outcome. These questions also help pupils to take responsibility for their own involvement and reactions. If a class is new to the process of evaluation it is best to use the first question only. The second question: 'What hindered my praise?' may be introduced when pupils have gained enough confidence as a group to cope with criticism. All responses should be accepted respectfully and filed for use when preparing the next worship experience. Worship is a skill to be learned. Pupils will find it satisfying when the quality of worship improves from one experience to the next.

Reflection 'helps us to explore the sense of the mystery we have celebrated.'[36] It looks for the deeper meaning of the celebration. Gilbert Ostdiek offers a three-step method of reflection: attending, reflecting and applying.[37] The first step, *attending*, requires that we describe what happened. All experience comes to us through the senses, so we ask the question: What have I seen / heard / smelled / tasted or touched? The second step, *reflecting*, requires that we consider what the experience means to us in terms of our life story. 'We quickly feel the need to name the inner quality of our experience, the feelings and attitudes it evokes in us, the sense of ourselves and relationship with others and to the world around us subtly contained there.'[38] The stories are then shared in small groups. 'What we discover at this point is that our life stories have similar patterns and rhythms. A larger, common version begins to take place around the common stuff of our lives.'[39] This larger story is then looked at in the light of the stories of the Christian tradition, especially of the Gospel stories, in order that we make these stories our own and are challenged by them. The third step, *applying*, requires that we 'take what we have learned and use it to shape our future celebration of the liturgy.'[40] Thus, preparation, celebration and reflection are experienced as a cyclic process. This process increases pupils' ability to learn how the liturgy speaks to them. It heightens their awareness of themselves as a school community and as part of the larger community of the Church.

Community-Building Themes
It must be emphasised that the central theme of every celebration is the praise and glory of God. We do have specific reasons for giving thanks to God and these may give the celebration a special character. Para-liturgies for first years are generally designed with the specific purpose of building community in mind. It is rather awesome for thirteen-year-olds to meet so many strangers during their first days in secondary school. The confidence experienced as the senior pupils in primary schools eludes them now. Self-esteem must be regained and a sense of comfort in the new environment built up.

A prayer service on the theme of harmony and friendship is appropriate at this time. As pupils stand in a circle, each person is requested to call to mind a talent he/she possesses. One pupil is given a ball of primary-coloured wool and asked to announce his/her name and talent and then, holding the end of the thread, cast the wool to another person. This is repeated until all pupils have cast the wool. The web of colour created is a symbol of the giftedness of the entire class and indicates the possibility of building bonds of friendship and support. Spontaneous prayers of gratitude for all the talents in the class and prayers of intercession for the challenge to use them for each other are then said. When reflecting on this prayer service, pupils will recognise that the colours represent the rainbow, a religious symbol of the covenant relationship between God and the people. 'When I gather the clouds over the earth and bow appears in the clouds, I will recall the Covenant between myself and you and every living creature of every kind' (Gen 9:15). This prayer service could be repeated at the end of the year, but with this difference: pupils announce the name and a talent of the person to whom they cast the wool in recognition of that person and his/her talents.

If an unhealthy competitiveness is developing in a class, a drama based on the colours of the rainbow may be used as a basis for prayer. Each 'colour' boasts of its special importance. The 'rain' washes them until they blend together to form a rainbow. The 'colours' realise that their strength lies in their combined giftedness.

Many schools invite the parents of all the first years to the school for an evening during the first term. Worship in which teachers, pupils and parents take part is usually included in this event. The preparation for such worship provides the opportunity to broaden the pupils' vision of community beyond the class to incorporate the entire year group. There are other occasions such as a prayer service before the end-of-year examinations when the entire year group worships together. During the senior cycle class boundaries are less well defined as classes are determined by choices of subjects at any period of the school day. Year-group consciousness increases and worship as such is more appropriate. Year-group consciousness is at its highest at the graduation worship for the Leaving Certificate pupils. On this occasion, memories of the pupils' experiences of life together at school may be recalled with the aid of appropriate symbols.

It is not possible for pupils to get to know all the other pupils in a school population, but they can achieve a sense of solidarity with the members of the whole school. Whole-school assemblies take place for a variety of reasons on numerous occasions throughout the year. Morning assemblies usually include a brief period of worship. The responsibility for preparing such worship may be assigned to each class in turn. Singing hymns and psalms from a limited selection will ensure that everyone can join in and that a sense of identity with the school is created. The idea of including the psalms arises from the intention of preparing pupils to participate in the Morning and Evening Prayer of the Church in adult life.

It is regular practice in many schools that the chaplain conducts a centring prayer at the beginning of staff meetings. He/she may also be requested to organise a prayer service specifically designed for the staff. The preparation, celebration and reflection on this prayer service offers the staff members the opportunity to work together for a common purpose and to minister to each other in very meaningful ways. For example, anointing each other's hands with oil as a blessing is pronounced is a very moving experience, which helps to bond the members to each other.

Enlargement of the Vision of Community from School to Parish

The emotions and tears at graduation ceremonies of the Leaving Certificate year indicate that deep bonds of friendship with each other and an attachment to the school have been created in the pupils over the years. Pupils leave second-level schools to go their separate ways in adult life. They will seek community in the clubs and societies of colleges and of the work-place. In the religious context, it is to be hoped that they will seek and find a faith community wherever they go. This is unlikely if they have not participated in the adult faith community of a parish during their school years. Most Catholic pupils have been baptised as infants in their parish and have received First Holy Communion and Confirmation there. Many of them will have participated in the life of the parish as altar servers, members of choirs and parish youth clubs. Research has shown that such participation falls off dramatically when they enter second-level schools.[41] If this separation persists it is unlikely that they will seek a faith community in any parish in adult life. We need to look at the possibility of extending the sense of community beyond the confines of the school to the parish where the school is located and where possible to the other parishes to which the pupils belong.

We must sympathetically understanding of the difficulties which adolescence experience in relation to the parish. Some may be coerced by parents to attend church while others receive no support or encouragement within the family. They may not find their concerns articulated in the liturgy. If the understanding of the assembly as the symbol of the Body of Christ/the People of God remains only a theological concept and is not given concrete expression through 'mutual exchange among co-worshippers, through the action of the assembly truly felt as a communal experience'[42] young people may feel isolated and as a result decide not to attend.

Through co-operation between school and parish these difficulties can be overcome. If the parish clergy are not already involved in the school, the chaplain should make contact with them and with other members of the parish team to establish if there is a mutual desire to involve the pupils in the parish. The chaplain will need to know what is being done for young people in the parish and what possibilities are open to the pupils. If the structure of parish pastoral council has an inbuilt mechanism whereby some members retire each year and new members are recruited it may be possible for representatives of the senior-cycle pupils of the school to be given a place on the council for a period of one year. Through this experience they will gain very valuable insights regarding parish life to be shared with those they represent. They will also have opportunities to bring items onto the agenda of meetings and have a voice in decision-making.

> Unless young people ... are given a voice and power to participate in the formation of Church life, the Church itself is in danger of cultivating exactly the passivity that it may criticise in the surrounding culture. It is not enough to foster 'reproduction of religious meaning'; each generation needs to forge an 'original production' of the Christian vision.[43]

The parish may be willing to share items needed for worship with the school. This will give pupils opportunities to become familiar with the places where these items are stored and to begin to find their way around the church property. The items borrowed, such as sacred vessels, candelabra, thuribles, vestments and cloths enhance the worship of the school. The school, in turn, may have items which the parish may wish to borrow. There may be aspects of the church, such as its stained glass windows, statues, Stations of the Cross, and symbolic displays for liturgical seasons, which may be used for worship *in situ*. The church may be a suitable venue on some occasions for whole-school worship. For smaller groups, such as year groups, it may be possible to move pews to create a worship space or to use an oratory or the sanctuary. Most importantly, the pupils meet and get to know the members of the parish team, who may be invited to participate in school worship occasionally.

Pupils may be initiated into the ministries of the parish liturgy, not to replace the adults, but to share the ministries with them. This will give pupils a sense of belonging and a purpose in attending parish liturgy. This is proving successful where parish and school are co-operating with each other. We must continue to search for new and more effective ways of doing this.

Conclusion

Here we have considered the school as a place where pupils experience community and where that community celebrates its life through its programme of worship. At the present time, both the notion of community and the notion of celebration are difficult concepts in our society. Increased urbanisation has led to increased alienation and isolation to the extent that the family, as the basic unit in society, is threatened. Industrialisation is strongly rooted in a work ethic which regards play and recreation as necessary only as a means of greater productivity. Drugs and alcohol are seen as ways of escaping from the realities of life. Songs of social discontent and songs about the failure of society are common. People tend to be onlookers in the arts and in sports.

School, therefore, has a prophetic role in society both in relation to community and to celebration. Collective worship is not merely added on but the very goal of education. It is the result of an educational process which gives the pupils the capacity to rejoice in God and to celebrate the fullness of life as a community.

Notes

1. Hay, D., Nye, R., *The Spirit of the Child* (London, Fount Paperbacks, 1998) p. 54.
2. Best, R., 'Introduction' in R. Best (ed.) *Education for Spiritual, Moral, Social and Cultural Development* (London and New York, Continuum, 2000) p. 10.
3. Smith, D.,'Spirituality and teaching methods: uneasy bedfellows' in R. Best, (ed.) *Education for Spiritual, Moral, Social and Cultural Development*, p. 55.
4. Hay, D., Nye, R., *The Spirit of the Child*, p. 36.
5. Searle, M., 'Ritual and Music', *Pastoral Music* 3 (1987), p. 13.
6. Education Act (1998), 9d.
7. Smith, D., 'Spirituality and teaching methods: uneasy bedfellows', R. Best, (ed.) *Education for Spiritual, Moral, Social and Cultural Development*, p. 52.
8. *Ibid.* p. 56.
9. Palmer, P.J., *The Courage to Teach: Exploring the Inner Landscape of a Teacher's Life* (1998), in D. Smith, 'Spirituality and teaching methods: uneasy bedfellows' in R. Best, (ed.) *Education for Spiritual, Moral, Social and Cultural Development*, pp. 63-4.
10. Searle, M., 'Ritual and Music', *Pastoral Music* 3 (1987), p. 15.
11. *Ibid.* p. 15.
12. Bick, M., *Preparing to Celebrate in Schools* (Ottawa: Novalis, The Liturgical Press, 1996). p. 12.
13. Klöckener, M., 'The Estranged Relationship between Young People and Liturgy' in *Studia Liturgica* 20 (1990) p. 141.
14. Flannery, A., (ed.) 'The Constitution on the Sacred Liturgy, # 10' in *Vatican Council II, The Conciliar and Post Conciliar Documents* (Dublin: Dominican Publications, 1996) p. 6.

15. Searle, M., 'Ritual and Music' in *Pastoral Music* 3 (1987), p. 13.

16. Drumm, M., *Passage to Pasch: Revisiting the Catholic Sacraments* (Dublin: Columba Press, 1998) p. 22.

17. 'General Instruction of the Roman Missal, No. 1' in *The Liturgy Documents Volume One: A Parish Resource*, p. 49.

18. Bick, M., *Preparing to Celebrate in Schools*, p. 7.

19. Parks, S., *The Critical Years: The Young Adult Search for a Faith to Live By* (San Fransico: Harper and Row, 1986) p. 55.

20. *Ibid.* p. 69.

21. Flannery, A., (ed.) *The Constitution on the Sacred Liturgy*, No. 48 in *Vatican Council II, The Conciliar and Post Conciliar Documents*, p. 17.

22. Bick, M., *Preparing to Celebrate in Schools*, p. 16.

23. Klöckener, M., Tripp, D., tr. 'The Estranged Relationship between Young People and Liturgy' in *Studia Liturgica* 20 (1990), p. 143.

24. Bick, M., *Preparing to Celebrate in Schools*, p. 36.

25. Ostdiek, G., *Catechesis for Liturgy* (Portland: Pastoral Press, 1986) p. 63.

26. Klöckener, M., Tripp, D., tr. 'The Estranged Relationship between Young People and Liturgy' in *Studia Liturgica* 20 (1990) p. 141.

27. Bick, M., *Preparing to Celebrate in Schools*, p. 32.

28. *Ibid.* p. 33.

29. Weyman, G., Deiss, L., 'Movement and Dance as Prayer' in *Liturgical Ministry* 2 (1993), pp. 72-3.

30. Klöckener,M., Tripp, D., tr. 'The Estranged Relationship between Young People and Liturgy' in *Studia Liturgica* 20 (1990) p. 153.

31. Ostdiek, G., *Catechesis for Liturgy*, p. 9.

32. Carotta, M., *Sometimes We Dance, Sometimes We Wrestle*, pp. 10-13.

33. Elliott, K., 'Adolescent Spirituality: Razzle Dazzle or Rock Solid', *Liturgical Ministry* 1 (1992), pp. 65-6.

34. Fleming, A., *Preparing for Liturgy: A Theology and Spirituality* (Washington: Pastoral Press: 1985) p. 14.

35. Gasslein, B., *Preparing and Evaluating Liturgy* (Ottawa: Novalis, The Liturgical Press, 1997) p. 41.

36. Gasslein, B., *Preparing and Evaluating Liturgy*, p. 29.

37. Ostdiek,G., *Catechesis for Liturgy*, p. 17.

38. *Ibid.* p. 18.

39. *Ibid.* p. 19.

40. *Ibid.* p. 20.

41. Sheehy, C., *The Differences In Belief And Practice Between First Year And Leaving Certificate Students In A Killarney School* (Dublin City University, Unpublished Thesis) p. 31.

42. Klöckener, M., Tripp, D., tr. 'The Estranged Relationship between Young People and Liturgy' in *Studia Liturgica* 20 (1990) p. 146.

43. Dorr, D., *Divine Energy* (Dublin: Gill and Macmillan, 1996) p. 133.

Finitude: the Final Frontier?

Heidegger and Levinas on Death

Ian Leask

Introduction

Can we talk meaningfully about life beyond death? Can there be any rational discourse about what might be 'beyond-finitude'? More specifically, can contemporary philosophy have anything significant to say about what might be 'beyond-finitude' – particularly given that the massive presence of Martin Heidegger's thought would seem to militate against such a possibility? This chapter seeks to provide a philosophical framework for teachers and school chaplains in addressing these questions by confronting Heidegger's thinking on death with its Levinasian counterpart (or, perhaps, contrary). As we shall see, Levinas's challenge to Heidegger opens up the remarkable possibility of a phenomenology of meaning and significance beyond finitude; as such, Levinas also opens the possibility of refuting the supposed 'primacy' of death.

Before we consider Levinas's specific points, we first need to outline something of how Heidegger's stress on authenticity is, at the same time, a stress on the utter centrality of our mortality. Levinas's critique – and the alternative he offers – needs to be seen against this very particular background.

Heideggerian Finitude

For Heidegger, the human being is that 'entity' for which Being *per se* is, at least sometimes, an issue, a question. Thus, in *Being and Time*[1], his concern is with how this being approaches existence, with how – from the most basic level – humans interpret or understand their being. Heidegger's 'fundamental ontology', his analysis of human beings in their concrete existence, is not about positing a disembodied notion of the 'nature' of humanity; instead, it seeks to provide a description of the phenomena of human existence. Just as Husserl had sought to strip away presuppositions and provide an account of 'the things themselves' (minus unwarranted philosophical assumptions), so Heidegger wants immanently to describe what it is to be a human.

What this fundamental ontology stresses is that the human being is bound up with its environment, and that the human being cannot be understood outside of such a context, or world. Hence the designation *'Dasein'* – 'there-being' (and not simply 'being'). Part of my condition of being human is being – of necessity – worlded: any assumption of a world-less subjectivity is an abstraction that ignores this fundamental. And what is particularly significant about Heidegger's analysis – for our purposes here – is that he goes on to elucidate how being in the world, being-involved, means, necessarily, being in a world of others, being involved with others. No-one is an island: the world I inhabit is, essentially, an inter-personal world. Thus: 'So far as Dasein is at all, it has Being-with-one-another as its kind of Being'.[2] It is not that Dasein first of all exists as alone and self-contained; on the contrary, Dasein is already Mitsein. Dasein is already with Others, before any cognitive exercises (like transcendental constitution) takes place. Dasein is always being-with, being-there-with, other people.

The problem, however, is that being in a world of other people means that – all too often – Dasein gets swamped: I 'lose myself in the crowd'; I get carried along by the herd, the 'They' (das Man); I do and say and 'think' what 'They' do and say and think; my intellectual faculties are reduced to a mere curiosity; instead of having a definite position, I am everywhere and nowhere; instead of communication, I get wrapped up in idle talk, gossip, trivia. In short, so much of everyday being-in-the-world-with-others can be summed up as 'falling', as being 'lost' in the 'They'. And it is not so much that this average, mediocre state is something we occasionally lapse into: on the contrary, this is the predominant 'mode' of Dasein.

In other words, from stressing the ontological primacy of the 'We', in BT s.26, Heidegger then precedes, in s.27, to portray Mitsein as inconspicuous subjection [Botmässigkeit] to Others; as the dissolution of Dasein; as levelling down [Einebnung], glossing over, suppressing.[3] Now we are alerted to the dictatorship [Diktatur] of das Man: Heidegger warns that the Being of Dasein is 'taken away by the Others' and that Dasein is left as an indefinite nobody, as no-one in particular. All of which, for him, amounts to the very essence of fallenness and inauthenticity [Uneigentlichkeit], the 'failure to stand by one's Self' [Unselbständigkeit].[4] Indeed, the they-self, das Man-selbst, is explicitly identified as the antithesis of the authentic Self, which has 'been taken hold of in its own way';[5] consequently, inauthentic Dasein must find itself, must discover the world in its own way, must 'clear away concealments' and 'disclose to itself its own authentic being'.

All of which directs us to the centrality of death. For Heidegger, our awareness of death has the capacity to shake up the averageness, or fallenness, of being merely part of the crowd. Death is mine: it is unique and individual. Dasein is being-towards-death in a way that can serve to underline its individuality. Heidegger may have outlined a quite gloomy view of Dasein as inauthentic (according to which our immersion in the world all too often means being washed along in the world, part of the crowd, the They, the public). Now, however, he is going to suggest that death might provide the focus for an alternative state.[6] And in order to explicate our potentially authentic existence, Heidegger wants to focus upon what he terms the totality of Dasein – the fact that we are always limited by time.

He begins by pointing out that *Dasein* is always what he terms 'ahead of itself'. There is always something that looms in the future, something else to do:

> The 'ahead-of-itself'... tells us unambiguously that in Dasein there is always something *still outstanding*, which... has not yet become 'actual'. It is essential to the basic constitution of Dasein that there is *constantly something still to be settled*. Such a lack of totality signifies that there is something still outstanding in one's potentiality-for-Being.[7]

This structural open-endedness, where there is always something else to be done, only concludes when I cease to be *Dasein* – when I die. My life can only be considered as a totality when I am no longer living: as long as I am living, I am structurally orientated towards the future, the not-yet. Once I start to focus on this, so I might leave the realm of fallenness and inauthenticity.

But must I try to consider *my* life as a totality in order to achieve some Heideggerian authenticity? Might it not be through others – their deaths, their funerals, their wakes – that I encounter finitude? Not as far as Heidegger is concerned. Certainly, he tells us, I can have an experience of someone else's death: I can have an 'objective' understanding of how someone I knew has passed from being to non-being; I can attend funerals, grieve, and so on. But this does not mean that 'therefore' *Dasein* has a proper insight into the totality of its existence: no matter how much I reflect on the other's death, his or her life as a totality, no matter how much I grieve, it is a fundamental error to think that reflection on someone else's death can provide a 'proper' analysis of *Dasein's* totality: someone else's death cannot possibly make sense of my life.

This is an extremely significant point in *Being and Time* (and, negatively, in Levinas's alternative to Heideggerianism). Earlier, Heidegger had stressed how any *Dasein*, lost in the crowd, in the They, can be substituted for any other; *Dasein* – in this situation – is everywhere and nowhere, nothing particular. Now he is suggesting that death is wholly different: with death there cannot be substitution. No-one else can die for me. Someone can sacrifice himself for me, but this does not take away the inevitablity of *my* death:

> Dying is something that every Dasein itself must take upon itself at the time. By its essence, death is in every case mine, in so far as it 'is' at all. And indeed death signifies a peculiar possiblity-of-Being in which the very Being of one's own Dasein is an issue.[8]

Death, in other words, is able to force me into a consideration of 'mine-ness'. In all other respects, it seems, I can be substituted for anyone else (for any other part of the 'They'). But when it comes to thinking in terms of death, there is nobody else who can do this for me:

> [Death] must be conceived as an existential phenomenon of a Dasein which is in each case one's own. In 'ending', and in Dasein's Being-a-

whole, for which such ending is constitutive, there is, by its very essence, no representing. These are the facts of the case existentially; one fails to recognize this when one interposes the expedient of making the dying of Others a susbstitute theme for the analysis of totality.[9]

Death, or coming-to-an-end, is something that is wholly particular and cannot be represented by anyone else. This is the first point Heidegger wants to establish about death – how it underlines the uniqueness of *Dasein*.

More than this, though, he also wants to focus our attention on how death could happen to any of us at any moment, regardless of age or occupation (even if we do not like to dwell on this). And, of course, the suddenness of death means that we are robbed of the possibility which constitutes us:

> With its death, Dasein has indeed 'fulfilled its course'. But in doing so, has it necessarily exhausted its specific possibilities? Rather, are not these precisely what gets taken away from Dasein?... For the most part, Dasein ends in unfulfilment, or else by having disintegrated and been used up.[10]

Death robs us of any *'finishedness'*, any neat and tidy 'ending': there is no sense in which the end of *Dasein* can be compared with other entities' endings – the loaf of bread's, the bad weather's. *Dasein's* ending is different because we are aware of ourselves in terms of 'thrown projection' – in the way no other entity is. Thus death is part of our being; simply talking about 'an ending' fails to appreciate the centrality, within our being, of the possiblity of not-being; death 'enters into' *Dasein* as a possibility of its Being.

Despite the fundamental significance of this 'throwness into eventual death', it is, needless to say, not something we focus on all the time. On the contrary, we are terrified of death, and we do our best not to face up to the fundamental truth that we could die at any moment:

> proximally and for the most part Dasein covers up its ownmost Being-towards-death, fleeing *in the face* of it. Factically, Dasein is dying as long as it exists, but proximally and for the most part, it does so by way of *falling*.[11]

So often, it seems, we flee our own most Being-towards-death. In other words, Heidegger is now placing our inauthenticity in a 'mortal', finite context: falling, our failure to live authentically, is an expression of our fleeing from our own finitude.

So, Heidegger asks, how does death, or being-towards death, express itself in the midst of inauthenticity, everydayness, 'idle talk', they-ness? Death, for 'the public', is a mishap, an event encountered in the everyday world and yet never really grappled with: we see obituaries, pass funerals, walk past graveyards; but we never 'live up to death', so to speak.

> The 'They' has already stowed away an interpretation for this event. It talks of it in a 'fugitive' manner, either expressly or else in way which is most inhibited, as if to say, 'One of these days one will die too, in the end; but right now it has nothing to do with us.'[12]

Death, for the average, everyday, public understanding, is 'indefinite', it is unthreatening. Death is something that happens to *das Man*, the 'They' – in other words, to nobody.[13] We are tempted to avoid confronting the unavoidable; we show 'an evasive concealment in the face of death', a 'tranquillization'. Indeed, for Heidegger, the 'They' actively discourages a proper grappling with the fact of death: 'The "They" does not permit us the courage for anxiety in the face of death'.[14] The fundamentality of death is thus 'neutralized' – and in cultivating this indifference, they-ness alienates *Dasein* from its inner core. The public attitude to death is one of falling – in the extreme.

Nonetheless, even this cultivated indifference still shows how death is a fundamental issue for us: by examining the inauthentic relationship to death, we might make visible what was previously concealed, and so open the possibility of an authentic relationship to death. Thus Heidegger suggests that, although our everyday evasion of death is inauthentic in the extreme, inauthenticity is itself based upon the possibility of authenticity. And what an authentic 'relationship' to death involves, he says, is *Vorlaufen*, facing up to death: accepting as unavoidable my own finitude. That is to say, Heidegger has already outlined an inauthentic response to death – and so he has 'prescribed in a negative way' how we should not react to death. More positively, he now says, we should not seek to evade or to 'cover up' or explain away, in terms of the 'They', this 'own-most, non-relational possibility' (a repeated mantra). In particular, we should give concentrated thought to the possibility of death.

To look at this in slightly more detail, the world of entities is a world of possibilities which I sometimes actualise, but death is not a possibility in this sense: death is a possibility, which, if actualised, would put an end to 'Being-towards-death'. This is a possibility that we are not seeking to actualise – and yet, there is no denying the fact it is coming, sooner or later. So we have to approach this question in the right way: 'Being-towards-death... must be understood *as a possibility* and we must *put up with* it *as a possibility*, in the way we comport ourselves towards it'.[15] The stress must be on the possibility of death, at any moment: not an expectation of death, for expectation is closer to the actual than the possible; more a consideration of how the possibility of not-being is a constant in our being. And, of course, this is not about 'human existence in general'; rather, it is a definite, inescapable fact about *my* existence. There is no substitution here; no-one can have my death for me; it is – inescapably – mine.

Once we meditate upon all this, Heidegger is suggesting, we start to take major steps on the 'road' to authenticity: contemplating death as my possibility lifts me from the realm of anonymity, publicness:

Death is Dasein's *ownmost* possibility. Being towards this possibility discloses to Dasein its *ownmost* potentiality-for-Being, in which its very Being is the issue. Here it can become manifest to Dasein that in this distinctive possibility of its own self, it has been wrenched away from the 'they'.[16]

Death is for me to confront, alone. And in doing so, Heidegger suggests, I become individualised in way which I am not in everyday existence:

Death does not just 'belong' to one's own Dasein in an undifferentiated way; death *lays claim* to it as an *individual* Dasein. The non-relational character of death, as understood in anticipation, individualizes Dasein down to itself.

So, strangely enough, death – properly confronted – can open up a realm of freedom; it can liberate us from so much trivia. Confronted by my death, I might start authentically to choose and understand the various possibilities ahead of me. In thinking of my life as a finite totality, the importance of an authentic individuality becomes more focused: I come to see how I must take hold of my own possibilities, and raise myself from the realm of the they. Now, instead of being surrendered to the 'common-sense ambiguity of publicness', *Dasein* is summoned from lostness in the 'They'. The awareness of my contingency and mortality is thus a way of 'galvanising' my existence. In a sense, I have to 'use' death, I have to face up to it in order to give my life now authenticity and individuality. In doing so, I become 'free': I discover what Heidegger terms 'an impassioned freedom towards death – a freedom with has been released from the Illusions of the "They"'.[17]

In short, authenticity is centrally bound up not just with finitude, but also with solitariness: I rise above the herd, the They, by confronting *my* death. Meditating upon my finite existence allows for the emergence of the lone 'I', sure of itself in its appeal to itself. Anticipatory resoluteness unveils *Dasein's* ultimate, insurmountable [*unüberholbare*] horizon – death – and so the primordial experience of temporality; with the resultant understanding of its own finite existentiality comes Self-Constancy and so 'essential', authentic *Dasein*. Authenticity, in other words, is about the reciprocal relationship between understanding death as the ultimate horizon and doing this despite the Other. As we shall now see, these are the precise points on which the Levinasian reading will differ. Levinas will suggest that the question of death must always presuppose the question of the Other, and that, in turn, this more fundamental issue itself undermines the supposed primacy of finitude.

Levinasian Infinity

Heideggerian being-towards-death is, Levinas suggests, 'a supreme lucidity and hence a supreme virility'. It is *'Dasein's* assumption of the uttermost possibility of existence, which precisely makes possible all other possibilities':[18] in confronting its own death, *Dasein* becomes 'authentic', self-standing, heroic.

Levinasian death, by contrast, means a radical passivity, a 'relationship' with an ungraspable mystery which overwhelms the subject, and which can never be mine. (The crucial difference here is that, for Levinas, death is the 'impossibility of possibility'; for Heidegger, it is the 'possibility of impossibility'.) Death, for Levinas, is not an 'event of freedom', but, rather, 'the end of the subject's virility and heroism';[19] it is the eversion of mastery and self-assurance. As death approaches, we realise that there is no *a priori* vision that can contain it, that it cannot be assumed; when death comes, we are 'no longer *able to be able*'.[20] So death is not something that I can 'make mine' (as the central element of 'making me'). Death is absolutely other, 'something whose very existence is made of alterity',[21] something that shatters autarchy. In other words, Levinasian death introduces a dualism – a plurality, even – into existing; death's alterity is wholly unknowable and can never be subject to adequation, representation, comprehension, *Sinngebung*. With death, we face sheer exteriority.

This radical exteriority is significant, Levinas suggests, for the two related yet distinct aspects it displays: death 'experienced' as an Other, and death 'experienced' through the Other. The former is a kind of outcrop of the latter; more importantly, both combine to emphasise the priority of Otherness – or, rather, the priority of the Other. (As we shall see, the scission in solitude provoked by death gestures toward a more fundamental scission in solitude: that provoked by the face-to-face encounter.) The first of these two cases, death as an Other, refers us to Levinas's *personification* of death. Death, in this case, may well amount to something like the Talmudic *malach hamoves*, or Angel of Death;[22] it is certainly a murderous assailant.[23] Whatever the status of its otherness, it is not nothingness: it is against me, and I fear its violence rather than its void. It is not solitary and impersonal, as it is for Heidegger, but more like 'one of the modalities of the relation with the Other'.[24] Death is a hostile and foreign will, 'more wily, more clever than I'.[25] In other words, my 'relationship' with death presupposes my more fundamental relationship with an Other: death is personal because I 'experience' it in and through the Other – in the dead body without response, through hatred and the desire to murder.[26] Contra Heidegger, the event of death is an aspect, or modality, of the 'wider' event of alterity; 'Death... is present only in the Other'.[27] Thus:

> [T]he death of the other affects me more than my own... It is my receiving the other – and not the anxiety of death awaiting me – that is the reference to death. We encounter death in the face of the other.[28]

Where Heidegger takes it that the autogenous comprehension of my death is fundamental for all meaning, certitude and resolution,[29] Levinas gestures toward what Heideggerian self-identity assumes in its exclusion; Heideggerian finitude is sublated by Levinasian Infinity. And so what was previously accepted as the self's 'solitary resoluteness in the face of death' unfolds as autarchy undone in the face of the face of the Other, in the face of sheer exteriority. We could say that, for Levinas, Heidegger's subject (the lone self) and his predicate (finitude) are reciprocally related misunderstandings.

The nature of these misunderstandings becomes clearer, perhaps, if we focus more upon the significance, for Levinas, of Infinity. In one (now celebrated) respect, Levinas's point is that Descartes' 'Idea of the Infinite' is structurally similar to (or perhaps as one with: the distinction is not always clear) the face-to-face encounter: just as Infinity is an idea not comparable with any other; just as it ruptures any cognitional aim; so too the Other's face overflows any concept I form of it. As Levinas puts it:

> [the relation with the other] is in fact fixed is the situation described by Descartes in which the 'I think' maintains with the Infinite it can nowise contain and from which it is separated a relation called 'idea of infinity'. To be sure, things, mathematical and moral notions are also, according to Descartes, presented to us through their ideas, and are distinct from them. But the idea of infinity is exceptional in that its *ideatum* surpasses its idea, whereas for the things the total coincidence of their 'objective' and 'formal' realities is not precluded; we could conceivably have accounted for all the ideas, other than that of Infinity by ourselves... To think the infinite, the transcendent, the Stranger, is hence not to think an object. But to think what does not have the lineaments of an object is in reality to do more or better than think.[30]

What is 'aimed at' here is beyond the embrace, or grasp, of any *cogito*: in this case, there can be no thorough-going correlation of consciousness and its object. The Other's face is an exit point, or at least an exception, to the Husserlian conviction that consciousness is intentional through-and-through; the noetic-moematic 'totality' is, apparently, shattered. Both the idea of the infinite and the face of the Other necessarily over-flow my own finite, thinking. In this sense, then, alterity transcends finitude.

In another (but related) respect, Levinas also suggests that Infinity has a 'dimension' to it that is not just do with the immediate overflow of the Other's face.[31] (Infinity, that is to say, is not solely about the structural measurelessness of immediate, face-to-face encounter.) For, as well the *ideatum* of the face, Infinity *qua* infinition is also how we must understand the *generation* that the I's specifically erotic relation with the Other both presupposes and provides for. This generation, this fecundity, means that, despite the 'definitiveness of an inevitable death',[32] the 'I' still 'prolongs itself in the other'.[33] Our children, even those who not yet 'are', refute Heideggerian finitude. Fecundity denies the 'terrors' of finite *ek-stasis* and nothingness:[34] death is overcome, inasmuch as a part of 'me' now is always 'not yet born',[35] is beyond both Being and death. The future is other than my future; '[t]he meaningful continues beyond my death'[36] and beyond what might be present to me. Death, then, is not my limit, my end-point: 'the I, across the definitiveness of an inevitable death, prolongs itself in the other'.[37] Fecundity refers beyond finitude.[38]

This in itself is obviously a profound challenge to Heideggerian *Sein zum Tode*. But what is perhaps an even greater challenge to Heidegger is the related claim that this 'trans-substantiation', this infinite, 'ever recommencing being',[39] defines time itself. For the fundamental experience of temporality, Levinas suggests, is itself an 'aspect' of the more profound experience of alterity: it is only because of the Other as Infinite and the infinition which the Other allows that time flows and extends beyond me; it is only by encountering the 'non-simultaneous' Other, the Other who escapes my syntheses and self-presence, that reality is broken into past, present and future. (Time, that is to say, can only be taken to flow beyond my syntheses because I encounter Others whose time is not my time, who are not my total contemporaries; if every We were a matter of simultaneity, there could be nothing but my time.[41]) Time is, at base, 'a relationship with the Other',[40] a 'turning', 'disquieting', or even 'tearing' of the Same by the Other.[42] Thus: 'It is not the finitude of being that constitutes the essence of time, as Heidegger thinks, but its infinity'.[43] Ignoring the Other leaves Heidegger blind to the truth of temporality. Had he thought Other-wise, Heidegger might have glimpsed how 'time [is] not... the ontological horizon of the *being of a being* but [is]... a mode of the *beyond being*'.[44] And, once we give proper attention to the event of alterity, to 'this forgotten but effective sociality',[45] so any temporal narrative – even Heideggerian temporal narrative – is necessarily deformalised.[46] The result is that the Levinasian Other stretches Heideggerian *ek-stases* (the understanding of temporality as the overlapping of anticipation and retention) to a point where they become un-present-able, where they tumble over any lines of 'containment'. Alterity conjures up a past beyond recovery and a future beyond anticipation. It 'is' a dia-chronic non-coincidence.

As regards the first of these 'deformalized ek-stases', Levinas's point is, in one regard, supremely simple: any description of a 'how' or a 'what' must always presuppose a 'to whom' – a *to whom* the description is offered, the explanation given, the hypothesis proposed...[47] But, of course, this supremely simple point has the most profound implications (in part because it has been so overlooked). What it means is that rationality, judgement and knowledge have something like a *pre-original*, autochthonous basis, which is fundamentally anterior, prior to representation, objectivity, visibility.[48] As Levinas puts it, it is 'as if the intrigue of alterity were knotted prior to knowledge':[49] what is Said (or written) conceals the prior event of 'the word given to the neighbour',[50] the Saying-to-another that gives rise to what is Said (or written), but which lies outside of the gathering, the synthesis, the synchrony and representation which the Said allows.[51] Alterity, the *ontic* event of the Other, is always presupposed, always pluperfect, and always leaves its traces; all else is secondary. Thus, when it comes to the problematic of ontology, or the thematisation of Being, we are at the realm of what is, ultimately, a derivation, an 'already derived order'.[52] Alterity comes before Being. It is, literally, an-archic, 'before the beginning'.

Meanwhile, as regards the futural aspect of Levinas's deformalisation, a kind of mirror pattern applies. What is yet to come is not merely my projection – or, rather, does not stretch only as far as my projection allows. Beyond a protention established upon and in terms of the present, beyond the presence of the future making itself present (by flowing towards my grasp), Infinition opens up a '*pure*' future, 'a future that will never be my present'.[53] That is to say: the generations that are not-yet overflow enclosure within 'the immanence of the *Jemeinigkeit* of the *Dasein* that has to be'[54] – and yet my *responsibility* for these generations-to-come is no empty illusion or self-deceit. It is not just that fecundity 'defeats' death in terms of my re-generation *via* my child; it is also that those who are not-yet possess 'an authority that is significant after and despite my death', that they represent 'a meaningful order significant beyond this death'.[55] My obligation exceeds my finitude because the future exceeds my future. What is meaningful exceeds both being-towards-death and nothingness.

Overall, then, time is only manifest to us in and through the Other. As such, time is, ultimately, uncontainable, and unassimilable: *qua* alterity – and so *qua* Infinity – time always exceeds my intentional reach.[56] Heidegger has failed fully to think temporality, because he has failed fully to think alterity.

Conclusion

Certainly, Heidegger's ruminations on finitude and authenticity are some of the most profound in the history of Western thought. Yet, despite their status, they are not unchallengable. For, as Levinas shows us, they are based upon an ultimate denial of the fundamentality of the Other: Heideggerian death, it seems, is more significant the less it is 'social'. If, against this assumption, we reinstate the fundamentality of alterity, the fundamentality of the relationship with the Other, our overall conception changes radically, and necessarily. If self-constant, self-standing, 'virile' *Dasein* is not the centre of philosophical gravity, it even becomes possible to 'un-say' the supposed primacy of finitude, mortality, and 'my death'. For what the primacy of *alterity* suggests is that there can be meaning and significance for me that are real, and rational, and yet *not* limited to my finite existence. Indeed, it would seem that perhaps the most significant and meaningful of all human phenomena – love of the Other, responsibility for the Other, the possibility of sacrifice on behalf of the Other – are, in themselves, refutations of Heidegger (and so refutations of any assumed primacy of finitude). For these Other-directed phenomena are greater than my being, but not beyond my concern. They overflow my existence, but not 'meaning and significance' as such; they can concern a future which will never be 'present' to me, but which matters to me, nonetheless. In love, responsibility, or sacrifice, I have the possibility 'giving meaning to the other and to the world which, though without me, still counts for me, and for which I am answerable (the great dissolution, in dying, of relationships with everyone else, as stated by Heidegger in Section 50 of *Sein und Zeit* notwithstanding)'.[57] Beyond my finitude there is 'a future which *counts* for the I and to which it is answerable: but [it is] a future *without-me* (both meaningful and future) which is no longer the to-come of a protended present'.[58] In short, the primacy of alterity can demonstrate that finitude is not the final horizon. The ultimacy of death is overcome – by the ultimacy of the Other.

Notes

1. *Being and Time*, trans. John Macquarrie & Edward Robinson (Oxford: Blackwell, 1962) Hereafter BT.
2. BT, 125.
3. BT, 127.
4. BT, 128.
5. BT, 129.
6. See also BT, 232: 'We have defined the idea of existence as a potentiality-for-Being – a potentiality which understands, and for which its own Being is an issue. But this <u>potentiality-for-Being</u>, as one which is in each case <u>mine</u>, is free either for authenticity or for inauthenticity...'
7. BT, 236.
8. BT, 240.
9. Ibid.
10. BT, 244.
11. BT, 251.
12. BT, 253.
13. See BT, 253: 'Dying is levelled off to an occurrence which reaches <u>Dasein</u>, to be sure, but belongs to nobody in particular. If idle talk is always ambiguous, so is this manner of talking about death. Dying, which is essentially mine in such a way that no one can be my representative, is perverted into an event of public occurrence which the 'they' encounters... By such ambiguity, <u>Dasein</u> puts itself in the position of losing itself in the 'they'.'
14. BT, 254.
15. BT, 261.
16. BT, 263.
17. BT, 266.
18. Levinas, E., *Time and the Other*, trans. Richard A. Cohen, (Pittsburgh, Pennsylvania: Duquesne University Press, 1987) p.70. Hereafter TO.
19. TO, 72.
20. TO, 74.
21. Ibid.
22. See Wyshogrod, E., *Emmanuel Levinas: The Problem of Ethical Metaphysics* (The Hague: Nijhoff, 1974) p.110, n.25.
23. See, for example, Levinas, E., *God, Death, and Time*, trans. Bettina Bergo (Palo Alto, California: Stanford UP, 2000) p.72: '[E]very death is a murder, is premature'; and p.90: 'Each death is a **first** death.' Hereafter GDT.
24. Levinas, E., *Totality and Infinity. An Essay on Exteriority*, trans. Alphonso Lingis (Pittsburgh, Pennsylvania: Duquesne University Press, 1969) p.234.
25. Ibid.
26. See, for example, GDT, 8-9.
27. TI, 179.
28. GDT, 105.
29. See, for example, GDT, 36.
30. TI, 48-49.
31. For Levinas, the Other's face is always greater than any idea I can form of it: it is as one, it seems, with Descartes' description of Infinity, where the *ideatum* will always surpass its idea.

32. TI, 282.
33. Ibid.
34. See TI, 269.
35. TI, 209.
36. Levinas, 'Diachrony and Representation', in TO, pp.97-120, p.116.
37. TI, 282.
38. See TI, 301: 'Fecundity opens up an infinite and discontinuous time. It liberates the subject from his facticity... It lifts from the subject the last trace of fatality.'
39. TI, 268.
40. See TO, 39.
41. GDT, 106.
42. See GDT, 109-111.
43. TI, 284.
44. TO, 30.
45. DR, 102.
46. Towards the end of his life, Levinas went as far as declaring that 'the essential theme' of his research was 'the deformalization of the notion of time'. See 'The Other, Utopia, and Justice', in *Entre Nous. On Thinking-of-the-Other*, trans. Michael Smith & Barbara Harshav, London: Athlone, 1998, pp.223-233, p.233. Hereafter OUJ.
47. See, for example, *Otherwise than Being or Beyond Essence*, trans. Alphonso Lingis (The Hague: Nijhoff, 1981) p.28. Hereafter OB.
48. See, for example: TI,209; OB,160.
49. DR, 106.
50. GDT, 156
51. The Said [le dit] is 'the great presence of synopsia, where being shines in all its brilliance' [GDT, 150]. But, for Levinas, 'the said does not count as much as the saying [le dire] itself. The latter is important... less through its informational contents than by the fact it is addressed to an interlocutor' [EI,42].
52. DR, 104.
53. OUJ, 233.
54. DR, 115.
55. DR, 114.
56. See, for example, TO, 32: '[Time is] not... a degradation of eternity, but... the relationship to that which – of itself unassimilable, absolutely other – would not allow itself to be assimilated by experience; or to that which – of itself infinite – would not allow itself to be comprehended... It is a relationship with the In-visible, where invisibility results not from some incapacity of human knowledge, but from the inaptitude of knowledge as such...'
57. OUJ, 128.
58. Ibid. See, also, MS, 92: 'To be for a time that would be without me, for a time after my time, over and beyond the celebrated 'being for death', is not an ordinary thought which is extrapolating from my own duration; it is the passage to the time of the other. Should what makes such a passage possible be called eternity? In any case, the possibility of sacrifice which goes to the limit of this passage discovers the non-inoffensive nature of this extrapolation: to be for death in order to be for that which is after me.'

Disadvantaged Youth and Faith

A Sign of Hope for the Future

Eilis Monaghan

Introduction

There is a lot of study in the area of young people and faith and also in the area of educational disadvantage, but very little about the relationship of one to the other. As a chaplain working in a school and an area that are designated as disadvantaged, there is a lot to be learnt from how pupils in a disadvantaged school operate in a faith context.

Many people are concerned about the future of the Catholic faith in Ireland, and rightly so. Those who work with young people and those who work in the wider faith community tell us that young people are turning away from the traditional forms of faith and we are often at a loss to know how to redress that movement. Having worked with disadvantaged young people and adults in Dublin for many years, I have seen the trend of dissociation from the Churches and religion growing among the poorer sectors of our society, and especially among the younger age groups. I think that those who work in this area are struggling, sometimes successfully, to find ways of reaching those on the margins of society and of the Churches. They have identified the issues and trends that are becoming more widespread in all areas of Church in Ireland, particularly in the area of youth faith development. The lessons they have learnt will be invaluable to those working with young people in more affluent areas. In looking at faith and disadvantaged youth, we have a forerunner of what may be, and some hint as to the strategies to be used with young people in the future.

This chapter will review the context in which school chaplains are working with young people and faith development and it will draw on my own research among pupils in a school in an area of social disadvantage.

Disadvantage

There is a need first of all to define what is understood by disadvantage. The term 'disadvantage' is used to imply unfavourable conditions or circumstances, detriment or prejudice.[1] This is obviously a very broad definition and in a school context it needs to be defined more. In the Education Act, 1998, educational disadvantage is defined as 'the impediments to education arising from social or economic disadvantage which prevent pupils from deriving appropriate benefit from education in schools.'[2] Conaty gives the criteria that are used in the Irish situation to designate a school as disadvantaged.

> In Ireland, the indicators of disadvantage in designated areas are related to the type of housing the pupils live in, the number of pupils whose family hold medical cards and are in receipt of unemployment benefit. In addition, the level of education of the mother, followed by that of the father, is taken into consideration.[3]

When we look at disadvantage in school, it is so often the case that pupils have many of these factors at work in their lives, and so the problems are increased.

The Education Bill gives as an aim 'to promote equality of access to and participation in education and to promote the means whereby pupils may benefit from education'.[4] There are obviously difficulties and challenges in bringing this to a reality in a disadvantaged school, but it remains the aspiration and goal of all who work in these schools.

Disadvantaged Youth and Faith

A lot of research is currently being done on the issue of faith and young people. A lot of research, much of it government funded, has been done on disadvantage. There is an absence however of any serious research on faith and disadvantaged youth. A large section of our population fall into the category of disadvantaged youth and so they cannot be understood as part of the youth culture alone. Research on faith does not normally distinguish between the socio-economic status of respondents.

We must acknowledge the differences that arise as a result of class and culture and circumstances. Boran puts it well:

> We talk about youth as if everything that is true for the young people who have a more stable lifestyle is also true for the disadvantaged youth. The needs, challenges and signs of life and death are not the same for all classes.[5]

Socio-economic background has a huge influence on the experience of people. Young people in disadvantaged settings have a different experience of life and therefore a different voice. Young disadvantaged people deserve to have their situation closely examined so that we can find better ways of serving them, particularly in a faith context. These are the young people on the margins, those to whom Jesus would have reached out. Teachers and school chaplains, who perceive themselves as representing the good news of the Gospel, must find ways that make a difference in reaching out to these young people.

Disadvantaged Youth – A Sign of the Future?

There is general agreement among those who work in the area of faith in Ireland that the greatest challenge or the greatest problem facing the Churches is in the area of youth faith development. We now see high levels of young people and young adults moving away from any active role or participation in the Churches or organised religion. This seems to be escalating in recent years in every part of the country. Boran says that 'Youth are a warning system of what is to come.'[6] Many people see the foundations of the Churches in Ireland in future years being laid and developed in what is now happening with our young people. And for many that poses a grim picture.

In disadvantaged areas, particularly in the cities, this has been the trend for many years, and those who are working with young people in these areas are already struggling with the problem. Thurston speaks about this growing alienation: 'For the word on the ground is that it is in sprawling suburbs where the lowest socio-economic groups live, that there is the greatest alienation from Church practice.'[7] Brennan identifies it as follows: 'This alienation of young urban, unemployed and low-wage earners is clearly illustrated in the interviews, and is one of the greatest challenges facing the Catholic Church in Ireland at the present time.'[8]

The lessons already learned and the strategies that are being used in socio-economically disadvantaged areas and schools that are designated as disadvantaged point to ways forward for all of those involved with young people in the Churches. If we succeed with youth in a disadvantaged setting we have done a service not just there, but also for all young people and the Churches, because disadvantaged youth are just ahead of others in terms of their disaffection and distance from the Churches. Boran says there is a need for 'strategies that can reverse a situation of approaching tragedy.'[9] To the outsider, the disadvantaged youth culture can seem a barren place in terms of religious faith and practice. But those who work there are convinced of the future because they can see what is possible. There is a lot to be gleaned from such a barren landscape. For those who work with young people in any setting, but especially with the disadvantaged, there is a need for confidence. Confidence in our young people, confidence in the message we preach, confidence in our role and confidence in the power and the strength of the Holy Spirit. With that confidence comes new ways of working with young people, which can make a difference in the lives and faith of all involved.

Indifference and Apathy Among Young People

One of the biggest challenges facing those who work in the area of faith in Ireland is the growing sense of indifference to matters of faith and religion. A recent report on lifestyle and attitudes *Irish Lifestyles: The Rise of the Immoral Majority*, was quoted in the national newspapers and was summarised by Fintan O'Toole, in the *Irish Times* of 19 March 2002, when he said 'For the first time, the perennial Irish question – where are we now? – finally has a clear answer: on the mobile phone in the car, heading from the gym to the pub, without stopping at the church.' Among the general population there is a movement to place faith on the sidelines rather than at the centre of life. Some commentators see this as a reaction to the strong influence that the Catholic Church had in every aspect of Irish life over the last century. Whatever the reasons, this poses difficulties for the school chaplain.

Brennan says that the 'attitude of young Irish men and women towards the Church can be characterized as 'indifference' not 'enmity'.'[10] Gallagher describes the unbelief of these young people:

> In short, this kind of unbelief is more passive than chosen, more drifting than militant and the unbeliever is more a victim of an impoverished or confusing culture than a deliberate rejecter of anything.[11]

To motivate pupils who are indifferent and uninterested is much harder than arguing against an anti-Church bias and yet this is part of the challenge. Brennan also points out: 'Disaffiliation from the Church tends to accelerate in late adolescence, particularly among those who move away from home.'[12] Thus there is a dual-edged sword that is facing all who work with young people in the context of faith in Ireland. We have the growing indifference of the general population combined with the stage of moving away from all that is seen as 'institutional'. As one of the pupils told me about his peer group and their values in life: 'All they are interested in is breaking the rules and getting a buzz out of it.'

Indifference and Apathy to Religion in School
Research suggests that young people today have a very consumerist approach to education, particularly as they progress through second-level. Lynch identifies it in her research within Irish schools:

> Research on second-level pupils in Ireland has shown that they have a highly instrumental approach to learning and are resistant to methodologies and curricula that are not perceived to be of immediate relevance.[13]

In other words, young people in school want to know what they will personally gain from every experience. They need to have a sense of relevance and authenticity about anything that is presented to them, especially in the area of faith and belief. If it is not seen as real and relevant, then it is ignored and apathy and indifference set in.

Many young people have, if not a negative, then a neutral experience of faith in school. Pupils, particularly in relation to their later years in school, recount this. Some of this is related to the stage of development that pupils are at and some is related to the individual experience of pupils in different schools:

> This lack of enthusiasm for religion classes mirrored a growing lack of interest in religion for large numbers of young people as they moved through adolescence into young adulthood. Cynicism and lack of interest appears (sic) to have been the norm and core.[14]

It is unfair to blame the teacher for the lack of enthusiasm for religion class. Each teacher will have to deal with 250 to 300 pupils per week. In the context of these demands on the religion teacher, the school chaplain can play an important support role. The chaplain can offer *moments* to otherwise apathetic pupils. The teacher who is faced with twenty-five pupils may find it difficult to address the needs of each individual pupil. The chaplain can work with the class teacher to identify areas that are outside of the curriculum, but might interest those who have already dissociated themselves from Religious Education in the classroom.

The chaplain has to present faith development to the pupils in an attractive and relevant way. When young people experience faith development in school that is life-giving and related to their everyday experience, they are keen for more, even in the face of growing demands on their time and energy within the examination system. Paul King deals with the role of the chaplain in relation to the new Religious Education syllabus in his chapter so there is no need for me to repeat what he has done so well elsewhere in this book.

Indifference and Apathy Among Disadvantaged Young People

In disadvantaged areas there is a sense of alienation from all structures in society, the Church being just one. Brennan says 'It is important to acknowledge that many who are caught in a low-income cycle of poverty feel alienated from all institutions in society.'[15] The pupils that I work with don't, in general, have any sense of power or association with the organisations or institutions that operate in their area. The Church is seen as another part of the system and a very irrelevant part for most. The chaplain has to try to counteract this in some way by presenting a vibrant and relevant Christian message that speaks to the lives of the pupils. Only then can links be made with those others in the wider community who share that message and with the structures in the area, namely the parish, that support the living out of Gospel commitment.

In a disadvantaged school, one of the daily struggles is with the motivation of the pupils. Many come from homes where survival is the focus and where parents and family have been downtrodden by life. This can create an acceptance and a passivity that become the pattern of behaviour for the young person. Teachers in disadvantaged schools battle daily with trying to motivate students to engage in the learning process. The chaplain has to try to motivate pupils to engage with the Christian message. This is all the more important when our pupils are surrounded by a culture that presents a totally different message.

Disadvantaged pupils find it hard, in general, to motivate themselves even when they see the outcome as desirable. How much more difficult is it for them to be motivated about faith and a message that is challenging and not widely held in their culture? Once again the person of the chaplain becomes central. When pupils feel that the chaplain is someone who listens to them and who accepts what they are saying, they will be more likely to take notice of what the chaplain stands for. Once there is an openness to listen and explore, the first step has been taken.

Faith as Counter-Cultural

One of the factors affecting everyone who works in the area of youth faith development is the struggle to work with the culture of young people. In many ways today, the Christian message comes as a message that is counter-cultural to young people. While many come from homes which inculcate Christian values even in an unnamed way, the fact remains that a more secular youth culture is the primary force in their lives. Those of us who are engaged in faith development must engage with that culture, but also challenge it.

In a disadvantaged area the Christian message is often viewed as an irrelevance or even as an antithesis of the culture. The school chaplain working with disadvantaged young people has to tread carefully and sensitively to challenge some of the cultural values while affirming the lives and the homes of the pupils. One example of this is that many pupils come from families where many children born within the past ten years have been outside of marriage. They live with siblings and parents who are in second and third relationships. The chaplain has to try to present the Christian value of marriage and commitment in such a way that it is seen as challenging, yet relevant and affirming to the pupils' situations.

Furthermore, teachers and chaplains need to challenge cultural values that are not Christian. And yet we must also show the Gospel value of love and acceptance. One way to address this is to work at challenging the cultural context rather than the personal lives of the students. Once the young person feels accepted and cared for by the adult, then there are possibilities of engagement in looking at difficult issues. The chaplain must handle that tension creatively and help pupils to see the cultural values they are living out of, while pointing to a better way of living by the Gospel.

For young people, the family and local culture are very strong. There is also the added voice of youth culture, which proclaims itself daily through the media. Very often this is the voice that can be most secular or even anti-Christian in that many of the messages that are sold to young people today by the media are counter to the Gospel message.

Pupils often take any criticism of their culture and what they follow as personal criticism and become defensive and even more allied to the other side. The chaplain has to find ways of challenging the values of their youth culture without pushing them further away from the Christian message. This is possible because of the unique and personal relationship that the chaplain develops with pupils. Being seen as one who cares about the pupils and their lives makes it easier to raise questions about things they value in their daily lives.

Disadvantaged Young People and the Church and Parish

One of the concerns articulated by all involved in the Churches both at local level and at diocesan level is that of the lack of involvement and absence of youth in our parishes. This is seen particularly in urban areas of disadvantage where less than 7 per cent of young people have any real attachment to the Church.[16] Though it is not defined, I assume that attachment to Church is indicated in some way by regular contact and Mass attendance.

The school I work in straddles two parishes, which comprise mostly low-income households in local authority housing. The picture in both parishes is similar. While both have a large number of nominal Roman Catholics, both suffer from poor Mass attendance and poor involvement across the generations. Figures for attachment to Church seem to fall even below the MRBI poll. Sunday Mass attendance would average between 4 and 6 per cent across all age groups. The young people of the area and of the school are, in general, noticeable by their absence.

This lack of attachment or disaffection with Church is not just confined to this geographical area, but is the norm in many inner city and disadvantaged parishes. Brennan says:

> On the basis of these statistics, it becomes clear that the young people living in socially deprived urban areas no longer have any practical attachment to the Church and have virtually abandoned the weekly celebration of the Eucharist.[17]

The school chaplain and the Religious Education teachers and the school are often the main or only connection between the student and church or parish. Is there a need for the pupils to be more connected with their parish? In order for faith to be living and relevant outside of school, the pupils must see it in action in some way in their own locality and dealing with the reality of their area and lives. They can see this in the parish and in those who go to make up the parish if there is a connection of some sort.

In his research Dowling interviewed young adults from all over Ireland and categorised the interviewees in terms of their involvement and commitment to the Catholic Church. She highlighted this lack of attachment and found it was identified with a particular cohort of interviewees:

> In the category of least active Intermediate Catholics – all the 'indifferent' women are drawn from the most deprived sectors of Irish society. Few ever attend organised religious services apart from weddings, baptisms and funerals.[18]

This fits into the profile of my pupils and their families. Key moments of their lives are linked with faith and public celebration of that faith. Every child is baptised and every person who dies is given a Catholic funeral. Every child is brought to the church to make First Communion and Confirmation.

There are many explanations why parents who are non-practising bring their children to receive the sacraments. In many instances it is seen as a social occasion or as a rite of passage rather than having a religious significance. Whilst acknowledging the theological difficulties that this presents, on a pastoral level it remains likely that, for many, these are the only meeting points with the parish and Church. They are moments when people are most open to and most in need of the love and care and support of the Christian community. Most parishes in disadvantaged areas recognise this and make every effort to welcome and support all those who come, especially those most marginalised. The result is that, in general, people see the parish in a positive light, even if there is no further engagement in terms of regular attendance.

For me, the fact that pupils attend church for these celebrations is a sign of hope and a window of opportunity. And the young people do attend, if sporadically. In interviewing pupils, they were all happy to engage with the local parish church for special occasions in their lives. They felt welcomed and accepted when they did visit the church for funerals, baptisms or at Christmas. They felt no antipathy or distance from the church at local level on the occasions when they did attend. Yet they felt no real connection with the parish or church either.

Cairns and Tuohy say of this task:

> The strategy here would be primarily to dispose them to listen. What blocks their listening is often not antagonism to the world of religion. Some young people have many other cares connected to survival. To them, religious commitment seems like an extra burden. Others do not have any personal experiences that relate to the world of religion. There may be no tradition or practice at home.[19]

If we can work with these key moments of contact between young people and the Churches and create positive experiences for them, we can leave them open in later life to connect or to reconnect with their Church communities. In an area of disadvantage, this is of great importance.

Prayer
Almost all of the pupils I interviewed said that they prayed, though many said they didn't pray on a regular basis.

> I pray in myself when I need help. For any reason – I wouldn't just pray for no reason. I'd pray for help or something like that, or for someone else to get help. When I pray I do it in my head, I just talk. Usually at night when I go to bed and when I need things.

They were quite at ease with praying to God and usually prayed prayers of petition, though one student did talk about going to Mass on special occasions to thank God for all the good things in his life.

Image of God
Most of the pupils talked about believing in God and were very definite in their belief in God's existence. When asked to describe their image of God they used phrases like 'soft and gentle', 'fair and forgiving', 'loving because he forgives you all the time', 'generous and holy', 'caring and loving' and 'someone there always to talk to'.

Overall, the pupils had a very positive image of God. They didn't see that faith in God was in any way dependent on Mass-going and many who were non-attendees had a strong sense of God and prayed regularly.

Family and the Transmission of Faith and Values

In his research Brennan found that 'Each would acknowledge, in varying degrees, that the values that were inherited from parents have made a lasting impression.'[20] The values that the pupils inherit from home are the key values that they have and work out of. This is a particular challenge for the chaplain working in a disadvantaged school where most pupils are coming from homes without any visible Church affiliation. Although most of the pupils are nominally Christian and have received all of the sacraments of initiation, few come from homes where practice of faith plays any real or important role.

What messages about the Church and faith have the pupils received from home? For most it is not an antagonistic message, but in the absence of some positive message, it becomes negative. The greatest message that many pupils in disadvantaged areas get from home about faith is that it is irrelevant and unnecessary and not related to the struggles of daily living. The pupils that I interviewed tended to take their cue as to religious practice from their parents, although in some cases there was practice by the mother, which was not followed by the children. Pupils talked about the person who most influenced them in their family as they were growing up and a pattern emerged that the religious practice of the student mirrored that of the influential adult. This study confirms the research of Cairns and Tuohy that young people tend to follow the example of their parents and base their values on those learnt at home.

What is done by the parents is done by the children. For my pupils, faith and practice are not a relevant or important part of daily home life. Prayer is not part of daily life at home and going to Mass or sacraments is usually only done on special occasions. This is reflected in the poor rate of Mass attendance among my pupils. It is very difficult for young people to practise values that are not those of their home. Cairns and Touhy say 'Not only did parents act as role models, as we saw earlier, but also, their affirmation and support was a vital part in the transmission of values.'[21] Several pupils spoke to me of not going to Mass more often because of lack of family support. As one student put it 'I don't go to Mass because I would be going on my own. I prefer to stay in bed on Sunday morning like everyone else.' In such cases the challenge falls to the chaplain to create some alternative form of support for those pupils who are open to exploring and practising their faith in a more active way.

One of the worrying implications of this reality of lack of formal practice of faith from homes is the growing recognition that there is a cumulative effect of non-practice. Boran says:

> Two generations are sufficient for people to lose any sense of real contact with Christianity. When the first generation decides not to practise or educate its children in the faith, the second generation has no faith reference.[22]

At present, most of our children are being educated in the faith through our schools and sacramental programmes. But the lack of a lived experience at home to back this up poses serious challenges to the development of a mature and lived faith in our young people. Boran points out that the option not to go to Mass is usually followed by an abandonment of other visible aspects of faith.[23] While on one level most people would acknowledge that regular Mass attendance cannot be the main criterion for faith and practice, it remains one of the key points of contact with a lived and living faith community and thus is important for young people in every situation.

In some cases the role of transmission of faith and Christian values falls to the grandparents. Dowling says 'Even if parents were somewhat lax, grandparents often kept an eye on the children.'[24] One student I interviewed identified her grandmother as the person who most influenced her in her faith and another spoke about her grandmother as being the person she thought a good role model of a person who lived their faith. She said:

> My granny is the person that I think of. I don't know why. It's just the way she is. She is a holy religious person. She does God's work and that is what I see in her.

Many of my pupils see religious practice in their family only in the lives of their grandparents. What message does this give to them about who practises and who faith is relevant for? I think for many it reinforces the message that religion is for children and old people. This is yet another challenge for the chaplain and all those involved in faith development within the school. Many pupils look for traditional structures and symbols of faith. This I think reflects their experience of faith formation under the guidance of a grandparent from an older generation.

One of the challenges for the school chaplain in working with young people in disadvantaged areas is to try somehow to use the symbols and *sacramentals* that pupils have received from the previous generation and have assimilated and given a value to. The pupils see these as important and they carry a value often unexplainable to them. Yet on the other hand they don't know how to relate them to their life today. The chaplain has to take these more traditional and often superstitious rituals and symbols and bring new meaning and life to them for the pupils. We have to enlarge these symbols by using them to the full, so that the pupils, who see them as important, can fully appreciate their meaning and depth. It would be a mistake to overlook or take a minimalist approach to these traditional symbols. They are a source of meaning for the pupils. Other symbols must also be offered that carry the same meaning but are more related to their lives and experience in a post-modern world.

Handing on the Faith

In terms of practice it is interesting that the perception of most of the pupils I interviewed was that they would choose to celebrate the key moments in their future in the church and would attend Mass for special occasions and at Christmas.

Several pupils spoke about having children and bringing them up as Catholics. They were very strongly in favour of this, mostly due to it being the way that they had been brought up. They were very positive about the effect of the sacraments on children and felt that it had made a difference to them and they wanted that for their children, even if they were not practising themselves.

School as the Main Community of Faith

The Christian life can never be a life lived alone. The Christian message is one of sharing the Gospel with others in a real way. This poses difficulties for pupils who find themselves in a vacuum of Christian experience in their local community, among their friends and in their own homes and families. For many disadvantaged young people this is the reality and it falls to the school to be the faith community to which they actively belong. Boran says:

> A young person on his/her own finds it difficult to maintain an alternative lifestyle – to swim against the current of a cultural environment that is drawing people in the opposite direction ... So leaders need to create permanent spaces where young people can cultivate alternative values and experience the support of others.[25]

The school may be the only place for many young people where they can share that faith with others in a supportive and nurturing way. And they both need and want that sense of community. One of the greatest needs of young people is to belong and to be accepted. They want to make a difference and to count as important. Brennan says: 'One of the characteristics of post-modern youth is they desire to belong to a faith community that is open to diversity and that they can influence to a significant degree.'[26] The school chaplain and the Religious Education teachers in the school have to try to provide that support and space for the pupils and to give them an experience of sharing the Christian message with others.

Several pupils I interviewed spoke about an adult in their school experience who acted as a role model for them in terms of religious faith and practice. Pupils talked about being influenced in school more by people than by the subject or the topics covered in class. The people associated with religion in the school were, for many pupils, the face of faith and the face of the church. The pupils saw faith in the people who represented religion in the school and their experience was positive because of some positive interaction with either a religion teacher or the chaplain.

General Trends

The overall attitude of the pupils that I interviewed was very positive towards the notion of faith and religion. The pupils were very open to religion and religious ideas, though few felt a need to put those ideas into practice by way of church involvement and attendance. They have a strong belief in God and a strong sense of having been given a faith, which they want to pass on to their children in the future. This seems to back the results found by Greeley and

Ward in their work on the International Social Survey Programme in 1998. They reported:

> The data reported thus far in this paper seems to confirm the popular impression that Irish young people tend to be disaffected from the Churches. While they continue to believe in God and identify themselves as religious, they have little confidence in the ecclesiastical institution, attend church services infrequently and ignore the traditional sexual ethics.[27]

Conclusion

The area of youth faith development is a very important issue for all who are committed to the future of the Churches in Ireland. The need to look forward with hope and confidence is paramount. But it has to be a hope and confidence based firmly in a strategy or plan of action. Where do we start? I think that those who work in the area of faith development with disadvantaged young people have a lot to offer in terms of a solution. What these young people express as the reality of their faith is a foretaste of the future of the Churches in Ireland. While there is cause to be concerned, there is also a lot to be hopeful and confident about.

In studying this topic and in talking with these young people, I found that their faith was strong, if not vibrant. Many talk about pre-evangelisation being the first step with young people nowadays. But I found that these young people had strong faith in God. They prayed regularly. They were open to, and very positive towards, those who represented the Churches and those who proclaimed the Gospel message. They had a strong sense of right and wrong with many of them living by the words of Jesus 'Do unto others as you would have them do unto you'. In the midst of the chaos that often surrounds them, they know God as loving and kind and caring. So what has gone wrong in terms of their association with the Churches? And more importantly, what lessons can be learnt and what can we do better in the future?

I think our young people are a very rich resource for the Churches, even if they are absent from the traditional structures and practices. We have to reach out in new ways to those who are at the margins. These young people are there, waiting to explore and to celebrate their faith in a way that is real and relevant for them. We must take all that is positive, especially the goodwill that is evident among many of these disadvantaged young people, and provide opportunities and invitations for engagement with the faith community, both at a local and a wider level. We must search for new ways to make the Gospel of Jesus a Gospel of Good News for these young people. We may need to reconsider our understanding of what it actually means in real terms to *practice* faith. These young people do not measure things in terms of constant attendance or total commitment. Can we offer them another way into communion with their Church? We cannot sit and wait in the hope that they will eventually join us. We must be proactive in reaching out to them. We will all be the richer for their participation and vitality.

We must also have patience. Some of these young people are not ready to be part of a Church, or maybe the Churches are not ready to make room for them at times. The time will come, hopefully, when these young people will feel welcomed and important to the rest of the faith community. In the meantime, all of us who make up Church must reach out in whatever way we can to give them a positive and life-giving experience of being Christian. The agents of the Churches that these young people come in contact with have left them open and positive to the Churches, if not ready to engage fully. We have to continue that mission to reach out in love and friendship and acceptance to these young people. Only then will they come to associate Church with that loving God they already know.

Those of us who work with these disadvantaged young people in the area of faith struggle at times to find our role and to see the way forward. What keeps us going is the conviction that there is reason to hope. God is at work already. We keep sowing the seeds of faith and wait with patience and hope for the harvest

Notes

1. Mortimore, J. and Blackstone, T., *Disadvantage and Education* (London: Heinemann Educational Books, 1982), p. 3.

2. Department of Education, *Education Act, 1998*, Section 32 (9)

3. Conaty, C., *Including All: Home, School and Community United in Education* (Dublin: Veritas, 2001), p. 21.

4. Department of Education, *Education Bill (No. 2)*, Section 6 (g).

5. Boran, G. *The Pastoral Challenges of a New* Age (Dublin: Veritas, 1999), p. 115.

6. *Ibid.*, p. 12.

7. Thurston, A. 'A Not So Secular City', in *Doctrine and Life* 50 (2000), p. 630.

8. Brennan, O., *Cultures Apart? The Catholic Church and Contemporary Irish Youth* (Dublin: Veritas, 2001), p. 174.

9. Boran, G., *The Pastoral Challenges of a New Age* (Dublin: Veritas, 1999), p. 13.

10. Brennan, O., *Cultures Apart? The Catholic Church and Contemporary Irish* Youth (Dublin: Veritas, 2001), p. 39.

11. Gallagher, M.P., 'New Forms of Cultural Unbelief', in Hogan, P. and Williams, K. (eds) *The Future of Religion in Irish Education* (Dublin: Veritas, 1997), p. 21.

12. Brennan, O., *Cultures Apart? The Catholic Church and Contemporary Irish Youth* (Dublin: Veritas, 2001), p. 108.

13. Lynch, K., *Equality in Education* (Dublin: Gill and Macmillan, 1999), p. 50.

14. Dowling, T., 'Young Catholics in Ireland', Fulton et al. (eds) *Young Catholics at the New Millennium* (Dublin: UCD Press, 2000), p. 59.

15. Brennan, O., *Cultures Apart? The Catholic Church and Contemporary Irish Youth* (Dublin: Veritas, 2001), p. 83.

16. MRBI Poll (Dublin: Irish Times January 1998).

17. Brennan, O., *Cultures Apart? The Catholic Church and Contemporary Irish Youth* (Dublin: Veritas, 2001), p. 83.

18. Dowling, T., 'Young Catholic Adults in Ireland', Fulton et al (eds) *Young Catholics at the New*

Millennium (Dublin: UCD Press, 2000), p. 64.

19. Cairns, P., Tuohy, D., *Youth 2K: Threat or Promise to a Religious Culture?* (Dublin: Marino, 2000), p. 199.

20. Brennan, O., *Cultures Apart? The Catholic Church and Contemporary Irish Youth* (Dublin: Veritas, 2001), p. 122.

21. Cairns, P., Tuohy, D., *Youth 2K: Threat or Promise to a Religious Culture?* (Dublin: Marino, 2000), p. 66

22. Boran,G., *The Pastoral Challenges of a New Age* (Dublin: Veritas, 1999), p. 18

23. *Ibid.*

24. Dowling, T., 'Young Catholic Adults in Ireland'. Fulton et al. (eds.) *Young Catholics at the New Millennium* (Dublin: UCD Press, 2000), p. 56.

25. Boran, G., *The Pastoral Challenges of a New Age* (Dublin: Veritas, 1999), p. 149.

26. Brennan, O., *Cultures Apart? The Catholic Church and Contemporary Irish Youth* (Dublin: Veritas, 2001), p. 179.

27. Greeley A., Ward, C., 'How Secularised is the Ireland We Live In?' in *Doctrine and Life* 50 (2000), p. 590.

Appendix One

Questionnaire

Survey into the Pastoral Competence of Irish Post-Primary Schools

Thank you for taking the time to complete this survey. The data will be made available in a paper presented to the ESAI Conference in September 2001. Please return the survey to: The Secretary, Mater Dei Institute of Education, Dublin City University, Clonliffe Road, Dublin 3.

Please indicate the college from which you received your teaching qualification.

☐ 1. UCC   ☐ 2. TCD   ☐ 3. MI/UL
☐ 4. UCD   ☐ 5 NUIG   ☐ 6. SPCD/DCU
☐ 7. NUIM   ☐ 8. MDIE/DCU   ☐ 9.Thomond College/UL

Please indicate the total length of service you have since qualifying.

☐ 1. 1-5 Years   ☐ 2. 5-10 Years   ☐ 3. 10-15 Years
☐ 4. Over 15 Years

Apart from your basic teaching qualification (B.Ed., B.Rel.Ed. etc.) please indicate any further post-graduate qualification you have obtained since you qualified as a teacher.

Indicate the response by selecting one or more value labels

☐ 1. MA   ☐ 2. M.Ed.   ☐ 3. M.Ed.S.L.
☐ 4. H.Dip.Ed.Man   ☐ 5. H.Dip School Guidance   ☐ 6. MA School Chaplaincy
☐ 7. Ph.D.,Ed.D.   ☐ 8. Other

4. If you have had a break in service please indicate how long it is since you returned to teaching.

5. Please indicate your most recent in-service programmes (if any).

6. Do you hold a position of responsibility in your school?

☐ 1. Yes   ☐ 2. No

7. If yes, please describe this post.

8. Does your school have a:

☐ 1. Guidance Counsellor   ☐ 2. Full-time Chaplain   ☐ 3. Part-time Chaplain
☐ 4. Home/School/
      Community Liason

Indicate the response by selecting one or more value labels.

9. Does the area in which your school is located have disadvantaged area status?

☐ 1. Yes   ☐ 2. No

10. In your work as a subject teacher, how often do students' personal problems affect your teaching?

☐ 1. Daily   ☐ 2. Weekly   ☐ 3. Monthly
☐ 4. Hardly ever   5. Never

11. Do you consider pastoral care as one of your duties as a teacher?

☐ 1. Yes   ☐ 2. No

12-23. Which of the following problems have you encountered among your students over the past 12 months and how often?

	Frequently	Occasionally	Hardly ever	Never
Bereavement	☐	☐	☐	☐
Suicide	☐	☐	☐	☐
Separation/Divorce	☐	☐	☐	☐
Substance Abuse	☐	☐	☐	☐

Teenage Pregnancy	☐	☐	☐	☐
Sexual Abuse	☐	☐	☐	☐
Homosexuality	☐	☐	☐	☐
Illness	☐	☐	☐	☐
Financial Disadvantage	☐	☐	☐	☐
Domestic Violence	☐	☐	☐	☐
Chronic Low Self-esteem	☐	☐	☐	☐
Depression	☐	☐	☐	☐

24-28. Which of the following issues have you encountered among your students over the past 12 months and how often?

	Frequently	Occasionally	Hardly ever	Never
Eating Disorders	☐	☐	☐	☐
Bullying	☐	☐	☐	☐
Chronic Exam Stress	☐	☐	☐	☐
Social Exclusion	☐	☐	☐	☐
Serious Aggression in the Classroom	☐	☐	☐	☐

29. Was the area of pastoral care specifically included as part of the curriculum in your teacher training college?

☐ 1. Yes   ☐ 2. No

30. Overall, do you consider your teacher training in the area of pastoral care:

☐ 1. Excellent   ☐ 2. Very Good   ☐ 3. Adequate
☐ 4. Inadequate

31. Overall, would you say that your teacher training adequately prepared you to deal with students' personal issues?

☐ 1. Yes   ☐ 2. No

32-37. Please indicate the manner in which the above issues affect your job as a classroom teacher.

	Frequently	Occasionally	Hardly ever	Never
Student Absenteeism	☐	☐	☐	☐
Disruptive Behaviour In Class	☐	☐	☐	☐
Lack of Concentration	☐	☐	☐	☐
Student Attainment Levels	☐	☐	☐	☐
Communication Problems	☐	☐	☐	☐
Forced to Exclude Student from Class	☐	☐	☐	☐

38. If your school has a guidance counsellor, how often would you refer students to him/her?

☐ 1. Frequently   ☐ 2. Occasionally   ☐ 3. Hardly ever
☐ 4. Never

39. If your school has a full-time School Chaplain, how often would you refer students to him/her?

☐ 1. Frequently   ☐ 2. Occasionally   ☐ 3. Hardly ever
☐ 4. Never

40. If your school does not have a full-time school chaplain, do you think it would be beneficial to your students to have one?

☐ 1. Yes   ☐ 2. No

Appendix Two

Questionnaire

Texas Revised Inventory of Grief

Inventory Description:
The following inventory can be used to assess grief associated with death of a loved one (Faschingbauer et al., 1987).

Inventory items:

Name or #_____ Age:_____ Sex:_____

The person who died was my (check only one):

☐ Father   ☐ Wife

☐ Mother   ☐ Son

☐ Brother   ☐ Daughter

☐ Sister   ☐ Friend

☐ Husband   ☐ Other (Specify) _____

> Looking back, I would guess that my relationship with this person was: (check only one)

☐ Closer than any relationship I've ever had before or since.

☐ Closer than most relationships I've had with other people.

☐ About as close as most of my relationships with others.

☐ Not as close as most of my relationships.

☐ Not very close at all.

How old was this person when they died? _____

This person died (check only one box):

☐ within the past 3 months   ☐ 9–12 months ago   ☐ 5–10 years ago

☐ 3–6 months ago   ☐ 1–2 years ago   ☐ 10–20 years ago

☐ 6–9 months ago   ☐ 2–5 years ago   ☐ more than 20 years ago

This person's death was:

☐ Expected   ☐ Unexpected   ☐ Slow   ☐ Sudden

Part 1: Past Behaviour

Think back to the time this person died and answer all of these items about your feelings and actions at that time by indicating whether each item is Completely True, Mostly True, Both True and False, Mostly False, or Completely False as it applied to you after this person died.
Check the best answer.

Use the following response categories for scales

a.   Completely true
b.   Mostly true
c.   Neutral
d.   Mostly false
e.   Completely false

☐ After this person died I found it hard to get along with certain people

☐ I found it hard to work well after this person died

☐ After this person's death I lost interest in my family, friends, and outside activities

☐ I felt a need to do things that the deceased had wanted to do

☐ I was unusually irritable after this person died

☐ I couldn't keep up with my normal activities for the first 3 months after this person died

☐ I was angry that the person who died had left me

☐ I found it hard to sleep after this person died

Part II: Present Feelings

Now answer all of the following items by checking how you presently feel about this person's death.
Do not look back at Part I.

☐ 1. I still cry when I think of the person who died

☐ 2. I still get upset when I think about the person who died

☐ 3. I cannot accept this person's death

☐ 4. Sometimes I very much miss the person who died

☐ 5. Even now it's painful to recall memories of the person who died

☐ 6. I am preoccupied with thoughts (often think) about the person who died

☐ 7. I hide my tears when I think about the person who died

☐ 8. No one will ever take the place in my life of the person who died

☐ 9. I can't avoid thinking about the person who died

☐ 10. I feel it's unfair that this person died

☐ 11. Things and people around me still remind me of the person who died

☐ 12. I am unable to accept the death of the person who died

☐ 13. At times I still feel the need to cry for the person who died

Part III: Related facts

Now please answer the following items by circling either True or False.

1. I attended the funeral of the person who died

        ☐ True   ☐ False

2. I feel that I have really grieved for the person who died

        ☐ True   ☐ False

3. I feel that I am now functioning about as well as I was before the death

        ☐ True   ☐ False

4. I seem to get upset each year at about the same time as the person died

        ☐ True   ☐ False

5. Sometimes I feel that I have the same illness as the person who died

        ☐ True   ☐ False

Thank you for answering all of these questions. I am also very interested in your special thoughts and comments. Please use the rest of this side to tell me about any thoughts and feelings you have.

Appendix Three

Critical Incident Plan:
Sample Statement for Media

It is with profound sadness that the Management, staff and pupils of ----- School, have learned of the tragic death of ----- N.

Our sincerest sympathy is extended to the family of N.

On hearing the tragic news the College Critical Incident Response Plan was put into immediate operation. The Critical Incident Team convened a meeting to ensure that pupils affected by this loss are cared for adequately. Procedures are in place to ensure that all in the college community affected by this loss are given all the help they need to cope at this time.

The college is offering counselling and support for pupils and parents affected by this tragedy. The chaplain has held prayer services and will be there to offer on going support to the pupils. Pupils will attend and participate in the funeral service, in accordance with the wishes of the family.

Our prayers and support are with everyone affected by this tragedy.

Bibliography

Adams, G.R. and Marshall, S.K., 'A developmental Social Psychology of Identity: Understanding the Person-in-Context' in *Journal of Adolescence*, 19 (1996) 429-42.

Albright, C.R. & Ashbrook, J.B., *Where God Lives in the Human Brain*, (Naperville, Illinois: Sourcebooks Inc., 2001).

American Psychiatric Association, *Diagnostic and Statistical Manual of Mental Disorders*, 4th Ed. (American Psychiatric Association, Washington, 1994).

Archard, D., *Impact No.7: Sex Education Britain*: (Oxford: Blackwell, The Philosophy of Education Society of Great Britain).

Barrington, J., Keane J. 'Campaign To Separate Church and State Ltd. v. Minister of Education, Attorney General, and Others: Supreme Court Decision' in *Irish Reports 3* (1998), pp. 321-367.

Begley Michael et al (1999) 'Asylum in Ireland – A Public Health Perspective' (Department of Public Health UCD & Congregation of the Holy Ghost Dublin).

Bergin, A. E., 'Values and Religious Issues in Psychotherapy and Mental Health' in *American Psychologist*, 46:4 (1991) 393-403.

Boyle, P.J. (2003) 'Engaging with Ethnic Minorities' in *Reimagining the Catholic School*, eds Prendergast, Ned & Monahan, Luke (Veritas, Dublin).

Burge, D., Hammen, C., Davila, J. and Daley, S., 'Attachment cognitions and college and work functioning two years later in late adolescent women' in *Journal of Youth and Adolescence* 26 (1997) 285-301.

Commission on Children at Risk, US, 2003, *Hardwired to Connect: The scientific case for authoritative communities*, http://www.americanvalues.org/html/hardwired_-_ex_summary.html, downloaded 3rd November 2003.

Corey, G., *Theory and Practice of Counselling and Psychotherapy* 6th Ed. (Pacific Grove, CA: Brook–Cole/Wadsworth, 2001).

Costello, J. 'Campaign To Separate Church and State Ltd. v. Minister of Education, Attorney General and Others: High Court Decision 1996' in *Irish Reports 3* (1998), pp.321-367.

Crotty, M., *The Foundations of Social Research: Meaning and Perspective in the Research Process* (London: Sage, 1998).

Cullen, Paul (2000) *Refugees and Asylum Seekers in Ireland* (Cork: Cork University Press).

De Souza, M., Cartwright, P. & McGilp, E.J., *An Investigation into the Perceptions of the Spiritual Wellbeing of 16-20 year-old Young People in a Regional Centre in Victoria*, unpublished report (Ballarat, Australian Catholic University, 2002).

Deenihan, T. 'Religious Education and Religious Instruction' in *The Furrow 53* (2002), pp. 75-83.

Department of Education and Science *Resource Material for R.S.E Post-Primary: Senior Cycle* (Dublin: Brunswick Press, 1999).

Department of Education and Science *Information Booklet for Schools on Asylum Seekers* (Dublin: Government Stationery Office, 2001).

Department of Education and Science, *Charting our Education Future: White Paper on Education* (Dublin: The Stationery Office, 1995).

Department of Education and Science, *Implementing The Agenda for Change* (Dublin: Brunswick Press, 1998).

Department of Education and Science, *Junior Certificate Religious Education Syllabus* (Dublin: The Stationery Office, 2000).

Department of Education and Science, *Official Guidelines For The Chaplain In A Community School (Agreed by the Department Of Education with Archdiocese of Dublin, 2nd June 1976).*

Department of Education and Science, *Religious Education, Junior Certificate: Guidelines for Teachers* (Dublin: The Stationery Office, 2001).

Department of Education and Science, *School Development Planning: An Introduction for Second Level Schools* (Dublin: Brunswick Press 1998).

Department of Education and Science, *Whole School Evaluation: Report on the 1998/1999 Pilot Project* (Dublin: Stationery Office, 1999).

Department of Education, Department of Health and Children and Mater Dei Counselling Centre, *On My Own Two Feet: Substance Abuse Prevention Programme* (Dublin: Department of Education, 1994).

Department of Health *The National Children's Strategy: Our Children, Their Lives* (Dublin: Government Publications, 2000).

Department of Health, *The National Task Force on Suicide* (Dublin: 1998).

Devitt, P.M. *Willingly to School: Religious Education as an Examination Subject* (Dublin: Veritas, 2000).

Dewey, J., 'John Dewey's Philosophy of Education' in R.S. Robert (ed) *Essays on Educators* (London: George Allen & Unwin Publishers, 1981) pp.72-87.

Dewey, J., *Democracy and Education* (London: Collier MacMillian, 1916).

Dewey, J., *Experience and Education, The Kappa Delta PI Lecture Series* London: Collier Books, 1963).

Dolan, Rose, *Student Leadership Programmes*, an Unpublished Master's Thesis (National University of Ireland, Maynooth, 2001).

Doyle, R., *A Star Called Henry* (Jonathan Cape: London, 1999).

Dunne, J., 'What's Good in Education' in P. Hogan (ed) *Partnership and the Beliefs of Learning* (Maynooth: Educational Studies Association of Ireland, 1995) pp. 60-82.

Education Act 1998, (Dublin: The Stationery Office, 1998).

Education (Welfare) Act 2000 (Dublin: The Stationery Office, 2000).

Education and Life Long Learning (Washington D.C: U.S.C.C.).

Egan, G., *The Skilled Helper* 7th Ed. (Pacific Grove, CA: Brooks-Cole/Wadsworth, 2002).

Everly, G., Mitchell, S., Jeffrey T., *Critical Incident Stress Management: Advanced Group Crisis Interventions* (Baltimore, Maryland: International Critical Incident Stress Foundation, 2000).

Everly, G., Mitchell, S., Jeffrey T., *Critical Incident Stress Management: The Basic Course Workbook* (Baltimore, Maryland: International Critical Incident Stress Foundation, 1998).

Face Up, November, *Vol. 3:9* (Dublin: Redemptorist Publications, 2003).

Fanning B., Veale A., O'Connor D., *Beyond The Pale: Asylum-Seeking Children and Social Exclusion in Ireland* (Dublin: Irish Refugee Council, 2001).

Farrell, F., Watt, P., *Responding to Racism in Ireland* (Dublin: Veritas, 2001).

Faschinbauer, T., Zisook, S., De Vaul, R., 'The Texas Revised Inventory of Grief' in Ziscook, S. (ed) *Biopsycholosocial Aspects of Bereavement* (Washington, DC: American Psychiatric Press, 1987).

Fontana, D. *Psychology, Religion and Spirituality* (Malden, USA, BPS Blackwell, 2003).

Fowler, J., *Stages of Faith* (Melbourne: Dove, 1981).

Fullen, M., Hargreaves, A., *What's Worth Fighting for in Your School?* (London: Open University Press, 1992).

Fuller, A., Johnson, G., Bellhouse, B. & McGraw, K., *START: School Transition and Resilience Training* (Victoria, Australia, Department of Education and Training, 2003).

Gannon, M., *Changing Perspectives – Cultural Values, Diversity and Equality in Ireland and the Wider World – A Recourse for Civic Social and Political Education* (Dublin: CDVEC/NCCRI, 2001).

Gardner, H., *Frames of Mind* (New York, Basic Books, 1983).

Geldard, K., Geldard, D., *Counselling Adolescents* (London : Sage, 1999).

Gerevich, J., Bacskai, E., 'Protective and Risk Predictors in the Development of Drug Abuse' in *Journal of Drug Education* 26 (1996) 25-38.

Gibbon, M., *The Pupil* (Dublin: Wolfhound Press, 1980).

Glod, C. and Teicher, M., 'Relationship between Early Abuse, Post-traumatic Stress Disorder and Activity Levels in Pre-pubertal Children' in *American Academy of Child and Adolescent Psychiatry* 34 (1996) 1384 –93.

Goleman, D., *Emotional Intelligence: Why It Can Matter More Than IQ* (London, Bloomsbury Publisher Inc., 1995).

Government of Ireland, *Green Paper on Abortion* (Dublin: The Stationery Office, 1999).

Government of Ireland, *National Development Plan* (Dublin: Government Publications, 2000).

Government of Ireland, *Report of the Expert Advisory Group on Relationships and Sexuality Education* (Dublin: The Stationery Office, 1995).

Government of Ireland. *Report on the Survey of Child Abuse Prevention Programme (Stay Safe)* (Dublin: The Stationery Office, 1995).

Grace, G. *Catholic Schools: Mission, Markets and Morality* (London: Routledge Falmer, 2002).

Grant, R., *Oakeshott* (London: Claridge Press, 1990).

Groome, T. H., *Educating for life* (Texas: Thomas Moore, 1998).

Guidelines on Anti-Racism and Intercultural Training 2001 (Dublin: NCCRI).

Handy, C., Aitken, R., *Understanding Schools as Organisations* (London: Pelican Books, 1986).

Hanegraaff, W.J., 'New Age Spiritualities As Secular Religion: A Historian's Perspective' in *Social Compass 46:2* (London: Sage, 1999) pp. 145-160.

Hargeaves, A., *Changing Teachers, Changing Times: Teachers' Work and Culture in the Post-Modern Age* (London: Cassell, 1994).

Harris, M., Moran, G., *Reshaping Religious Education* (Louiseville, Kentucky, Westminster John Knox Press, 1998).

Hay, D., Nye, R., *The Spirit of the Child*, London, Fount Paperbacks, 1998).

Head,J., *Working with Adolescents Constructing Identity* (London: The Falmer Press, 1997).

Hogan, P., 'Power, Partiality and the Purposes of Learning' in *Partnership and the Benefits of Learning* (Dublin:Educational Studies Association of Ireland, 1995). pp. 107-120.

Hogan, P., *The Custody and Courtship of Experience: Western Education in Philosophical Perspective* (Dublin: Columba Press, 1995).

Inskipp, F., Proctor, B., Making the Most of Supervision, Part 1 (Twickenham, Middlesex: Casade Publications, 1993).

International Organisation for Migration, International Comparative Study of Migration Legislation and Practice (Dublin: The Stationery Office, 2002).

Kelly, T., A New Imagining: Towards and Australian Spirituality (Melbourne, Australia, Collins Dove, 1990).

Kerrigan, G, Another Country: Growing Up in 1950s Ireland (Dublin: Gill and Macmillan, 1998).

Kessler, R., The Soul of Education: Helping Students Find Connection, Compassion and Character at School (Alexandria: Association for Supervision and Curriculum Development, 2000).

Law, S., Glover, D., Educational Leadership and Learning Practice, Policy and Research (Buckingham: Open University Press, 2000).

Lindsay, R., Recognizing Spirituality. The Interface Between Faith and Social Work, (Western Australia: University of Western Australia Press, 2002).

Looney, A. 'Teaching Religion to Young People Today' in J.M. Feheney (ed.) From Ideal To Action: The Inner Nature of a Catholic Today (Dublin: Veritas, 1998), pp. 72-81.

Lynch, Margaret (2001) 'Providing Healthcare for Refugee Children and Unaccompanied Minors' in Medicine, Conflict and Survival Vol. 17 No.2 April – June 2001.

Mabey, J., Sorensen, B., Counselling for Young People (Buckingham and Philadelphia: Open University Press, 1995).

MacLachlan, M., O'Connell, M. ed. Cultivating Pluralism: Psychological, Social and Cultural Perspectives on a Changing Ireland (Dublin: Oak Tree Press, 2000).

Vincentian Refugee Services, Making the Links, Breaking Barriers: Annual Report (Dublin: Vincentian Refugee Centre, 2001).

Martin, M., Discipline in Schools, A Report to the Minister for Education, Niamh Breathnach (Dublin: Government Publications, 1997).

Meshot, C., Leityner, L., 'Adolescent Mourning and Parental Death' in Amiga Journal of Death and Dying 26 (1993) pp. 287-99.

Miller, J., *Education and Soul* (Albany, NY: State University of New York Press, 2000).

Mission Australia, 2002, *Mission Australia Youth Survey Results*, http://www.mission.com.au/uploadedFiles/Youth%20Survey%20-%20national.pdf, downloaded 7th November 2003.

Moffett, J., *The Universal Schoolhouse* (San Francisco: Jossey-Bass, 1994).

Monahan, L. (ed) *Suicide, Bereavement and Loss – Perspectives and Responses* (Dublin: Irish Association for Pastoral Care in Education, Marino Institute of Education, 1999).

Monahan, L., Foster-Ryan, S., (Eds.) *Echoes of Suicide* (Dublin: Veritas, 2001).

Monahan, L., *Moving Forward with Students* (Dublin: Irish Association for Pastoral Care in Education, Marino Institute of Education, 1999).

Moran, G. 'Understanding Religion and Being Religious', *PACE* 21 (1992) pp. 249-252.

Morgan, M., *Relationship and Sexuality Education: An Evaluation and Review of Implementation: Summary of Main Findings* (Dublin: Government of Ireland, 2002).

National Curriculum Council, UK, *Spiritual and Moral Development: A Discussion Paper* (York, NCC, 1993).

NCCA, *Relationships and Sexuality Education: An Aspect of Social, Personal and Health Education: Interim curriculum* (Dublin: Department of Education, 1996).

Newberg, A., D'Aquili, E., Rause, V., *Why God Won't Go Away: Brain Science and the Biology of Belief* (New York: The Ballantine Publishing Group, 2001).

Norman, J. *Pastoral Care in Second-Level Schools: The Role of the Teacher, A Research Report* (Dublin: Mater Dei Institute of Education, Dublin City University, 2003).

Norman, J., 'Educational Underachievement: The Contribution of Pastoral Care and School Chaplaincy' in *Irish Educational Studies* (Dublin: Educational Studies Association of Ireland, 2002) pp. 33-46.

Norman, J., 'Teacher Professionalism: The Pastoral Dimension' in *Oideas 50, Journal of the Department of Education and Science* (Dublin: Government Publications, 2003) pp. 66-78.

Norman, J., *Ethos and Education in Ireland* (New York: Peter Lang, 2003).

Norman, J., *Pastoral Care in Second-Level Schools: The Chaplain, A Research Report* (Dublin: Mater Dei Institute of Education, Dublin City University, 2002).

O'Koon, J., 'Attachment to Parents and Peers in Adolescence and their Relationship with Self Image' in *Journal of Adolescence 32 (1997)* 471-82.

O'Cuanacháin C., 'Intercultural Education in Irish Primary Schools' in *Intouch INTO Journal 52* (Dublin: INTO, October 2003).

O'Regan C., 'A Report of a survey of the Vietnamese and Bosnian Refugee Communities in Ireland' (Dublin: Irish Refugee Agency,1998).

O'Connell Consultancy, *Evaluation of the Community Response to Six Incidents of Youth Suicide in Hume Region, June – September 1999: Community Document* (Victoria: Human Services, 1999).

O'Farrell, U., *First Steps in Counselling* (Dublin: Veritas, 1993).

Office for Standards in Education, *Handbook for the inspection of schools* (UK: Ofsted,1994).

Office of Refugee Applications Commissioner (ORAC) Annual Report (Dublin: 2002).

Palmer, P., *The Active Life: A Spirituality of Work, Creativity and Caring* (San Francisco: Jossey-Bass Publisher, 1990).

Palmer, P., *The Courage to Teach: Exploring the Inner Landscape of a Teacher's Life* (San Francisco: Jossey-Bass Publisher, 1998).

Pearce, J.C., *The Biology of Transcendence: A Blueprint of the Human Spirit*, (Vermont: Park Street Press, 2002).

Persinger, M.A., 'Feelings of Past Lives As Expected Perturbations Within Neurocognitive Processes that Generate the Sense of Self: Contributions from Limbic Liability and Vectorial Hemisphericity' in *Perceptual and Motor Skills, 83:Part 2* (1996) pp. 1107-21.

Phinn, G., *Over Hill and Dale* (London: Penguin, 2000).

Quinlan, J. *Pastoral Relatedness: The Essence of Pastoral Care* (University Press of America, 2002).

Raising Awareness of Diversity and Racism, An Activity Pack for Schools and Youth Workers (Dublin: NCCRI, 2002).

Ramachandran, V.S., Blakeslee, S., *Phantoms in the Brain* (London, Fourth Estate, 1998).

Refugee Information Service, *Progress Report 1999-2000* (Dublin: RIS, 2000).

Rice, P.F., Dolgin, K., *The Adolescent: Development Relationships and Culture* (Boston: Allyn & Bacon, 2002).

Robson, C., *Real World Research* (Oxford: Blackwell, 1993).

Roe, P., 'Asylum Seekers and Refugees in Ireland Today' in *Intercom* (Dublin: Veritas, October 2000) pp. 8-9.

Rogers, C.R., 'Rogers, Kohut and Ericson,: A Personal Perspective on Some Similarities and Differences' in *Person Centred Review* , 1 (1986) pp. 125-140.

Rogers, C.R., *Client Centered Therapy: Its Current Practice, Implications and Theory* (Boston: Houghton-Mifflin, 1965).

Rossiter, G. 'The Need for a "Creative Divorce" between Catechesis and Religious Education in Catholic Schools' in *Religious Education* 77 (1982), p. 21-40.

Sacred Congregation for Catholic Education, *The Religious Dimension of Education in a Catholic School* (Rome: 1988).

Salovey, P., Mayer, J.D., 'Emotional Intelligence' in *Imagination, Cognition and Personality*, 9 (1990) pp.185 – 211.

Salzman, J., 'Ambivalent Attachment in Female Adolescents: Association with Affective Instability and Eating Disorders' in *International Journal of Eating Disorders* 21 (1997) 251-9.

School Curriculum and Assessment Authority, (SCAA) *Discussion Paper on Spiritual and Moral Development* (UK, SCAA, 1995).

Shade, B., Kelly, C., Oberg, M., *Creating Culturally Responsive Classrooms* (Washington DC: American Psychological Association, 1997).

Smith, C., 'Factors Associated with Early Sexual Activity Among Urban Adolescents' in *Social Work Journal* 42 (1997) pp. 334-46.

Smith, D. 'Spirituality and Teaching Methods: Uneasy Bedfellows?' in R. Best (ed.) *Education for Spiritual, Moral, Social and Cultural Development* (London and New York: Continuum, 2000), pp. 52-65.

Smith, S., *Tools For Change* (Dublin: National Committee for Development Education, 1999).

The Irish Catholic Bishops Conference, *Guidelines for the Faith Formation and Development of Catholic Students: Junior Certificate Religious Education Syllabus* (Dublin: Veritas, 1999).

Toner, B., 'Wanted: An Immigration Policy' in *Working Notes December, Issue 33* (Dublin: Jesuit Centre for Faith and Justice, December 1998).

Torode, R., Walsh, T., Woods, M., 'Working with Refugees and Asylum Seekers: A social work resource book' (Dublin: Trinity College, 2001).

Tuffy, G., 'Embracing Interculturalism' in *ASTIR* (Dublin: ASTI, 2002) pp. 19-20.

Tuohy, D., Cairns, P., *Youth 2K: Threat or Promise to a Religious Culture?* (Dublin: Marino Institute of Education, 2000).

Tuohy, D., *School Leadership and Strategic Planning* Ireland (Dublin: Association of Secondary School Teachers, 1997).

Vekic, K., *Unsettled Hope: Unaccompanied Minors in Ireland, From Understanding to Response* (Dublin: Marino, 2003).

Walford, G., 'Redefining School Effectiveness' in *Westminster Studies in Education*, 25 (2002), pp. 47-58.

Walter, J., Peller,J. *Becoming Solution-focused in Brief Therapy* (New York: Brunner/Mazel, 1992).

Ward, B et al. *Good Grief: Exploring Feelings, Loss and Death with Over 11's and Adults* (Barbara Ward: UK 1992).

Warren, S., Huston, L. Edgeland, B., Sroufe, L., 'Child and Adolescent Anxiety Disorders and Early Attachment' in *Journal of the American Academy of Child and Adolescence Psychiatry 36* (1997) 637-44.

Watt, P., 'The Challenge to Build an Anti-Racist and Intercultural Society in Ireland' in *Focus Issue 64* (Dublin: Comhlámh, 2001) pp. 34-35.

Williams, K., 'Student Teachers Remember Good Teaching in their Schooldays' in *Prospero 4* (1998), pp. 31-34.

Winch, C., 'The Economic Ends of Education' in *The Journal of Philosophy of Education*, 36, (Oxford: Blackwell, 2002) pp. 101-118.